METATHEOLOGY

Oliver Crisp

METATHEOLOGY

THE FOUNDATIONS OF DIVINITY

Oliver Crisp

LONDON • NEW YORK • OXFORD • NEW DELHI • SYDNEY

T&T CLARK

Bloomsbury Publishing Plc, 50 Bedford Square, London, WC1B 3DP, UK
Bloomsbury Publishing Inc, 1359 Broadway, New York, NY 10018, USA
Bloomsbury Publishing Ireland, 29 Earlsfort Terrace, Dublin 2, D02 AY28, Ireland

BLOOMSBURY, T&T CLARK and the T&T Clark logo are trademarks of Bloomsbury Publishing Plc

First published in Great Britain 2026

Copyright © Oliver Crisp, 2026

Oliver Crisp has asserted his right under the Copyright, Designs and Patents Act, 1988, to be identified as Author of this work.

For legal purposes the Acknowledgements on pp. viii-ix constitute an extension of this copyright page.

Cover design: Lara Himpelmann
Cover Image "West Sands, St Andrews" courtesy of Dr Danielle W. Jansen. Used with permission.

All rights reserved. No part of this publication may be: i) reproduced or transmitted in any form, electronic or mechanical, including photocopying, recording or by means of any information storage or retrieval system without prior permission in writing from the publishers; or ii) used or reproduced in any way for the training, development or operation of artificial intelligence (AI) technologies, including generative AI technologies. The rights holders expressly reserve this publication from the text and data mining exception as per Article 4(3) of the Digital Single Market Directive (EU) 2019/790.

Bloomsbury Publishing Plc does not have any control over, or responsibility for, any third-party websites referred to or in this book. All internet addresses given in this book were correct at the time of going to press. The author and publisher regret any inconvenience caused if addresses have changed or sites have ceased to exist, but can accept no responsibility for any such changes.

Library of Congress Cataloging-in-Publication Data
Names: Crisp, Oliver author
Title: Metatheology : the foundations of divinity / Oliver Crisp.
Description: London ; New York : T&T Clark, 2026. | Includes bibliographical references and index. | Summary: "Systematic theology has become balkanised. Today there are multiple approaches to theology, and each tells a very different story about the shape and function of Christian doctrine. There has been a renewed interest in the writing of systems of doctrine, with a number having been written in the last two decades and more underway or promised. For these reasons, this seems an opportune time to have a study that weighs up different approaches to theology and sketches a way forward for systematic theology. Crisp builds on his previous work in this area in both theological method, historical theology, and Christian doctrine, to diagnose some pressing problems in theology and set out the framework for a constructive approach to the discipline"– Provided by publisher.
Identifiers: LCCN 2025034381 | ISBN 9780567721785 hardback | ISBN 9780567721778 paperback | ISBN 9780567721808 pdf | ISBN 9780567721792 epub
Subjects: LCSH: Theology, Doctrinal
Classification: LCC BT75.3 .C75 2026
LC record available at https://lccn.loc.gov/2025034381

ISBN: HB: 978-0-5677-2178-5
PB: 978-0-5677-2177-8
ePDF: 978-0-5677-2180-8
eBook: 978-0-5677-2179-2

Typeset by Deanta Global Publishing Services, Chennai, India
Printed and bound in Great Britain

For product safety related questions contact productsafety@bloomsbury.com.

To find out more about our authors and books visit www.bloomsbury.com and sign up for our newsletters.

To Professor Andrew B. Torrance:

'To dare is to lose one's footing momentarily.
Not to dare is to lose oneself.'

– Søren Kierkegaard

CONTENTS

Acknowledgements	viii
Introduction	1
1 **On metatheology**	11
2 **Using models**	27
3 **Theological ambition**	39
4 **Divine ideas**	53
5 **Scriptural insufficiency**	73
6 **Whence Trinitarianism?**	89
7 **Trinitarian minimalism**	107
8 **God's bodies**	125
9 **Christ's maleness**	141
10 **Realized eschatology**	153
11 **Creation fulfilled**	167
Bibliography	183
Index	190

ACKNOWLEDGEMENTS

I thank my friends, colleagues and students in the Logos Institute, and in the School of Divinity in the University of St Andrews more broadly, for their help, support and friendly criticism of earlier iterations of the chapters contained within the covers of this volume. Special thanks go to Professor Andrew Torrance, as my colleague in the Logos Institute who has been a fast friend over the past few years in what have often been challenging times. Thanks also go to Dr Andrew Everhart, Emily Hammer, Dr Parker Haratine, Tessa Hayashida, Dr Mark Hertenstein, Christian Kalmbach, Dr Jon Kelly, Benjamin Keogh, Tiago Martins, Sam Norman, Dr Jason Stigall, Dr David Stuart, Cody Warta, Tammy Wiese, Dr Chris Whyte and Nok Yeung. I am very grateful to Dr Aaron Davis and Dr Danielle Jansen who commented on several chapter drafts to my considerable benefit and to Dr Harvey Cawdron and Rev Dr Jared Michelson who read through an earlier iteration of the manuscript and offered very helpful feedback. I am also grateful to an anonymous reader for the publisher, whose report saved me from several potentially egregious mistakes and helped bring the book to its final form. The work is certainly much better because of the feedback of these individuals.

Several chapters were first given as papers in seminars and conferences. The first chapter was originally given online in the Historical and Systematic Theology Seminar in St Andrews, and at the 'Winter Seminar on the Future of Theology' held under the auspices of the Abraham Kuyper Centre at the Free University of Amsterdam in January 2022. My thanks to Rev Professor Gijsbert van den Brink and Dr Rik Peels for that invitation. An earlier version of the second chapter appeared in the *T&T Clark Handbook of Analytic Theology*, edited by Rev Dr James Arcadi and Dr J. T. Turner, Jr. It is used, with permission of the publisher. The third, fifth, and sixth chapters all first saw the light of day as papers given to the Logos Institute Research Seminar. Chapter 8 was presented at the 'Seek This Jesus' Seminar hosted by the Maxwell Institute in Pembroke College, Oxford, in April 2024. The ninth chapter was given to the Logos Institute Writing Salon to read. Chapter 10 was originally given at a conference for the 'New Visions in Theological Anthropology' (NViTA) Templeton-funded major research project on science-engaged theology in St Mary's College, University of St Andrews, under the leadership of Dr John Perry, Dr Joanna Leidenhag and Dr Sarah Lane Ritchie in September 2019. My thanks to all three for their encouragement, friendship and help over the years. A revised version of the chapter was given at the Helsinki Analytic Theology (HEAT) Workshop in February of 2024 at the University of Helsinki. My thanks to Rev Professor Olli-Pekka Vainio and Dr Aku Visala for ten years of this wonderful workshop and their warm Finnish hospitality in the chilly Scandinavian winter! The eleventh chapter was originally given as a talk at the 'Creation, Nature and Grace: Catholics and Reformed in Dialogue' Conference held at the Pontifical University of St Thomas Aquinas in Rome in the Spring of 2023, led by the Rector of the University, Fr Thomas Joseph White OP, and Rev Professor Bruce McCormack of Princeton Theological Seminary and the University of Aberdeen. It was an occasion of true ecumenical engagement that I will not quickly forget.

INTRODUCTION

> There is undoubtedly a place for the scientific study of religious people, of religious phenomena and of religious language, but none of these can be a substitute for the Philosophy of Theology in which we are concerned with the meta-science of our direct cognitive relation with God. Science and Meta-science are required not because God is a problem but because we are . . . It is because our relations with God have become problematic that we must have a scientific theology.
>
> —T. F. Torrance[1]

There is theology, the 'study of God and all things in relation to God' as Thomas Aquinas famously put it. Then there is the study of issues at the foundations of theology or what Thomas Torrance calls the 'meta-science of our direct cognitive relation with God'. This has to do with the philosophical and theological ideas that inform and shape our theology in fundamental ways. These days reflection on the conceptual foundations of philosophy, the philosophy of philosophy if you will, is called metaphilosophy. This is a book about *metatheology*. By metatheology, I mean the study of foundational issues in theology – its nature, aims, methods, scope and bounds.

In some important respects this book is a next step after my previous work, *Analyzing Doctrine*, which set out an overview of the main conceptual structures in Christian doctrine from the perspective of analytic theology.[2] The hope is that this research trajectory will eventually yield something more comprehensive – a systematic theology of some sort. But there is still much work to be done before that is feasible. One of the areas that needed to be addressed along the way towards such a larger work falls under the description of metatheology. For the divine must have some grip on the nature, aims, methods, scope and bounds of theology to make principled decisions about its shape and content – what goes where, what succeeds what theologically speaking and why. It is like the architect who, upon being presented with a brief for a new and magnificent building, sets about thinking not just about the shape it will take or the rooms and other structures it will contain, but also about the foundations upon which it will sit. Without adequate attention to the foundation and elevation of the building the structure is likely to be unstable, and perhaps unable to support its own weight. Thus, although we do not normally see the work that has gone into thinking about the foundations of a building

---

[1] Thomas F. Torrance, *Theological Science* (Edinburgh: T&T Clark, 1969), v.
[2] See Crisp, *Analyzing Doctrine: Toward a Systematic Theology* (Waco: Baylor University Press, 2019). As the reader will find, several of the chapters in this book take forward or build upon arguments set out in *Analyzing Doctrine*.

once it is erected, thorough preparation is a *sine qua non*. Just so, it seems to me, with the writing of systematic and constructive theology. We cannot avoid questions about its conceptual foundations.

There is a long history to metatheology, although it has not usually gone by that name in the past.[3] Older books of dogmatics usually have a section at the beginning that deals with matters of prolegomena. These are the first things that need to be said in preparation for the study of dogmatics proper. It is usually a kind of ground clearing exercise, as well as a place where the divine can demarcate the bounds of theology from other, related disciplines. Some historic theologians are more attuned to this than others. Friedrich Schleiermacher is a good example of a thinker who understood that prolegomena is not dogmatics, but rather reflection on what we might call metadogmatics – the theology or philosophy of dogmatics. This is immediately clear to the reader of Schleiermacher's constructive work, *The Christian Faith*, which begins by explaining this. He writes, 'since the preliminary process of defining a science cannot belong to the science itself, it follows that none of the propositions which will appear in this part [the Introductory section of *The Christian Faith*] can themselves have a dogmatic character'.[4] The same surely applies, *mutatis mutandis*, to theology more generally.

Overview of the chapters

I have indicated that metatheology is concerned with fundamental issues at the foundations of the study of theology itself. But is metatheology still theology, or is it philosophy? And how does our response to this question shape our view of the scope and nature of theology? For, surely, if the foundational issues that inform theology are in fact philosophical in nature, then it looks like it is philosophy that informs theology, whereas if the foundations of theology are still in some sense theological, then theology would appear to remain independent of philosophy. This is surely where a study of metatheology must begin, and for that reason it is the topic of the first chapter. In dialogue with Thomas Aquinas, I argue for the view that the foundational questions asked by metatheologians are philosophical in nature.

Having addressed the question of the nature, aims, methods, scope and bounds of metatheology, the second chapter considers an important conceptual tool that is

---

[3]In the recent literature there has been some work on metatheological themes that goes under that name. Jonathan L. Kvanvig's book *Depicting Deity: A Metatheological Approach* (Oxford: Oxford University Press, 2021) is a case in point. However, his project is rather different than this one. He is concerned with assessing three different programmes in conceiving the deity of theism, not with matters that are particular to the Christian Faith. Thus, his work falls under the description of philosophy of religion as I understand that term, whereas this book is concerned with metatheological questions that pertain to the Christian tradition. It is thus a work in what might be called the philosophy of Christian theology.
[4]Friedrich Schleiermacher, *The Christian Faith*, trans. H. R. MacIntosh and J. S. Stewart (Edinburgh: T&T Clark, 1999 [1830]), 2.

often deployed in theological discourse, particularly analytic theology, namely, the use of models. This seems like a natural second step since having thought about what metatheology is, it seems appropriate to turn to the question of the kinds of conceptual apparatus that theologians use that might be susceptible to examination by the metatheologian. The role of conceptual models plays an important part in subsequent chapters of the volume, so it seems appropriate to begin here. I argue that theological models, like scientific models, are simplified conceptual frameworks or descriptions by means of which complex sets of data, systems, and processes may be organized and understood. This, so it seems to me, makes modelling an important component of much theology, especially systematic and constructive theology.

Chapter 3 focuses on the ambitions of theology, or what we might call the teleology of theology. If metatheology is about the conceptual foundations of theology, and models provide an important tool with which to pursue this task, what do theologians think they are aiming at in setting out the arguments that they do? What are they motivated to achieve? I argue for a kind of intellectual humility on the part of theologians. If the aim of theology is realist in nature, providing truth-aimed arguments for conclusions concerning God as a creaturely mind-independent entity, what can the theologian or divine expect to be able to produce? Can theologians make progress in their theologizing? It seems to me that all theology this side of the grave is fragile and fallible. This is for several reasons. First, we have a limited data set that depends in important respects upon appeals to authority: Scripture and tradition. For much of the history of theology, it has been thought that God reveals Godself in Scripture and, for most Christians, in the post-biblical tradition as well.[5] But the relationship between these sources of authority, and what they yield as far as materials for the construction of theological arguments goes, is a contested matter. This, like the question of theological models, is a matter to which we shall return in later chapters in the book. The second, and closely related reason for the fallibility of theological statements is that the object of theology, God, is a mystery. In this context, a mystery is a truth that is intelligible in principle, but which may not be entirely intelligible to human beings in their current state of cognitive development. Applied to God, we can say (echoing many historic divines) that God is the creator of all that is not God and is intelligible in principle but is not entirely intelligible to humans as finite creatures of limited cognitive abilities. Thus, the ambitions of the theologian *qua* theologian should be calibrated to what the theologian can reasonably be expected to produce. I think that theology has an important place in the life of the Christian Church, but that the work of theologians must be understood to be fragile, fallible and incapable of fully apprehending the object of our study.

The fourth chapter considers a fundamental issue for the doctrine of God, having to do with the scope of divine sovereignty over all that is not God. In particular, this chapter

---

[5]This is the case given that the majority of Christians both past and present are Roman Catholic, Anglican or Eastern Orthodox. Protestants that dispute the fundamental role of tradition in making theological judgements represent a minority report, theologically speaking.

considers the question of God's relationship to what we conventionally think of as the realm of abstract objects, such as numbers or properties. Perhaps the best way to set up this problem is to point to its historic appearance in Plato's *Euthyphro*, in which Socrates frames the concern in the famous Euthyphro Dilemma. He puts it like this: 'is what is pious loved by the gods because it is pious, or is it pious because it is loved by them'?[6] We can transpose his wording to suit the present purpose so that the question becomes whether properties like 'being pious' or 'piety' are loved by God because it is pious, that is, because piety exists as an abstract object in the platonic horde of forms independent of the Deity, or whether it is that piety is pious because it is loved by God? For in the latter case, it seems that it is God who, in approving of piety, in some sense makes it the case that it is pious. So, the issue is whether there is some realm of abstract objects that are instantiated in creatures and by the divine nature or whether God makes truth in these matters, deciding the content and value of particular abstract objects.

The first horn of the dilemma makes God subject to something outside the divine nature, namely, abstract objects. For even God instantiates certain qualities that exist independent of God on this way of thinking. But that seems troublesome if God is sovereign over all that is not God and exists independently of all that is not God (i.e. is *a se*). However, what if God makes true the content and value of certain abstract objects? Then it seems that the content and value of such entities are the product of the divine will, which appears to be a version of theological voluntarism many will find unpalatable. (Can God assign content and value to such entities as God sees fit? Then the content and value of abstract objects seems entirely dependent on divine megrim.) But perhaps there is a middle way. One such *via media* is the doctrine of divine ideas, according to which the things that we think of as paradigm abstract objects are in fact ideas in the mind of God. Thus, there is nothing outside God upon which God is dependent and divine aseity is preserved. What is more, God ensures that creatures bear the properties they do based on the exemplar of these things in the divine mind.

In this chapter I develop an account of divine ideas that builds in important respects upon the position taken by Anselm of Canterbury in his *Monologion*.[7] His account is interesting because he ties the doctrine of divine ideas to the procession of the Second Person of the Trinity. Thus, his position is a profoundly Trinitarian iteration of the doctrine of divine ideas, and one that (so it seems to me), contemporary theologians would do well to consider with care. The implications of this debate are far-reaching, for they have to do with the scope of divine sovereignty. Thus, although the doctrine of divine ideas seems at first glance to be a rather arcane matter, it has enormous theological implications concerning both the doctrine of God and of creation that are properly metatheological concerns.

---

[6] Plato, *Euthyphro* 10a. in *The Last Days of Socrates*. Penguin Classics, trans. Christopher Rowe (Harmondsworth: Penguin, 2010).
[7] See *Monologion* in Anselm, *The Complete Treatises*, trans. Thomas Williams (Indianapolis: Hackett, 2022).

Introduction

Chapter 5 focuses on the metadogmatic dimension to the claim that Scripture is historically thought to be the norming norm that norms all other norms in Christian theology. The Bible's position as a source for theological judgements is an obvious topic for metatheological and metadogmatic analysis. In confessional Protestantism, Scripture is often said to be *sufficient* for salvation. This is the core claim of the doctrine of the sufficiency of Scripture. However, it seems to me to be a mistaken doctrine that has been the cause of some serious misunderstanding. I argue that Scripture is conditionally necessary but strictly insufficient for an understanding of salvation. Other conditions include the secret prevenient work of the Holy Spirit in regeneration, and an appropriate understanding of the nature of Scripture, which is to say, an appropriate hermeneutical framework for rightly understanding sources of theological authority. Scripture is also insufficient in the formation of core Christian doctrine such as the Trinity, incarnation, and atonement – all of which are inevitably shaped in important respects by non-biblical factors. For these reasons, I argue that the notion of the sufficiency of Scripture should be set aside as an unhelpful and obfuscating dogmatic accretion. Nevertheless, the question of biblical sufficiency is distinct from the question of biblical authority. The argument offered in this chapter does not seek to derogate from biblical authority in the formation of Christian doctrine. Rather, it seeks to reframe the scope of that authority in a way that reflects how Scripture is used in the forming of Christian doctrine.

Chapter 6 follows on from consideration of the sufficiency of Scripture. For in addition to questions about the scope of Scripture's status as a theological norm, there are issues about whether or to what extent we can source various key doctrinal claims in Scripture, a question that is metadogmatic. The dogma of the Trinity is surely one of the central and defining doctrines of Christian theology – perhaps *the* most distinctive Christian doctrine. It also has a rather complicated backstory. This chapter considers the conceptual development of Trinitarianism in Christian theology. The fact is the dogma of the Trinity was not promulgated until the Nicene-Constantinopolitan symbol of AD 381. That is a long time after the events recorded in the New Testament. It would be like setting out a definitive view in the twenty-first century of events that took place in the 1600s. The road towards the Trinitarian settlement of the fourth century was a hard-fought one. Often, theologians who acknowledge this nevertheless claim that the kernel of the dogma of the Trinity can be found in the New Testament, perhaps even in Scripture as a whole. When read through 'Easter eyes', so to speak, after the resurrection of Christ and alongside the community of the early Church, it seems obvious that there are intimations of the Trinity throughout Scripture. Some recent theologians have even begun with this assumption: the Trinity is a biblical doctrine, and it is on this basis that we begin our thinking about the Christian doctrine of God.[8]

With some reluctance, I have come to think that this is a mistake. There is no clear statement of the Trinity in Scripture, and (crucially) I do not think that there is sufficient

---

[8] See, e.g., Fred Sanders, *The Triune God*. New Studies in Dogmatics (Grand Rapids: Zondervan Academic, 2016).

warrant for thinking that there are embryonic versions of the Trinity in the biblical texts either. This is true even with respect to those passages that are usually taken to be paradigmatic of Trinitarian thought, such as the Great Commission of Mt. 28:19 or the canonical gospel stories of the baptism of Jesus.[9] How then should we think about the Trinity? To my mind, it is a doctrine that develops as the early Church came to a mature understanding of the divine nature through reading Scripture, reflecting on the teaching of the Apostles, the Rule of Faith, liturgies and other practices carried over from earlier times. Taken together, this produced a particular way of reading the biblical texts. Eventually, the leaders of the Church came to see that only a notion of triunity was sufficient to make sense of the various data they had. Thus, the dogma of the Trinity depends in crucial respects upon a kind of reading strategy adopted by the Fathers and other ecclesiastical leaders as they looked back to the teaching of Scripture. It is not that the early church anachronistically imposed a particular way of thinking about the divine nature on the biblical texts. Rather, the community of the Church came to see over time that this was the most appropriate way to understand the overarching themes of God's action in the world in creation, fall and redemption expressed in Scripture. Thus, the Trinity is not a doctrine found *in* Scripture, if by this is meant clearly taught or implied by the texts of Scripture. It is a doctrine developed by the early Church as it interacted with, and reflected upon, the shape of the biblical texts and on the wider deposit of Christian tradition. This, I think, is how several other core Christian doctrines developed as well, such as the doctrine of sin or the doctrine of the incarnation, though there is not space to explore these further claims here. Having said that, it would not be difficult to adapt the argument of this chapter to apply to these other doctrines with similar results.

Chapter 7 focuses on the dogma of the Trinity in more detail. It concerns a particular project in recent Trinitarian theology to which I have contributed, namely, Trinitarian mysterianism and its cautious approach to thinking about the divine nature, which (I think) is a mystery beyond our ken. The core claim of such mysterianism is what might be called *Trinitarian minimalism*. This is the idea that we should say as little as possible about the triune life of God given the dearth of data we have concerning the divine nature. In the recent literature Professor Sameer Yadav has criticised my attempt to articulate a version of Trinitarian minimalism in the mysterian approach to the dogma set out in *Analyzing Doctrine*.[10] In responding to him, I attempt to set this recent discussion

---

[9] In short, neither of these passages yields a *doctrine* of the Trinity (i.e. the claim that God is one in essence and subsists in three persons). The reader must bring the doctrine to these texts. To see this, compare a situation in which someone reads an ancient Sanskrit text proclaiming that 'Brahma is the Creator, Vishnu the Preserver, and Shiva the Destroyer'. These are the three historic *murti* or forms of Brahman, the source of Ultimate Reality and make up the *trimurti* or three key forms of Brahman in Hinduism. But the doctrine of trimurti is not found in the text; it is brought to the text as a way of understanding its claims about the three *devas* or gods in question.

[10] See Sameer Yadav, 'The Mystery of the Immanent Trinity and the Procession of the Spirit', in *The Third Person of the Trinity: Explorations in Constructive Dogmatics*, ed. Oliver D. Crisp and Fred Sanders (Grand Rapids: Zondervan Academic, 2020), 55–67.

into the broader context of contemporary Trinitarian theology and the metadogmatic issues it raises concerning our epistemic access to the divine nature and the prospects for theorising about the triunity of God. I argue for a three-tiered approach. There is the data of Scripture and tradition that together give us the dogmatic framework for the Trinity. Then there is theological reflection on that framework, which yields models of the Trinity. Trinitarian minimalism is one such model. By its very nature it is conceptually thin, attempting to provide a cautious approach to Trinitarian theorizing. Other historic models are often conceptually more expansive, such as Latin, social and constitutional models. These may be permissible as theologoumena or theological opinions, a kind of third tier of speculation about the divine nature that may be true for all we know. To this extent one can be both a mysterian and someone who is willing to hazard a metaphysical just-so story that 'fleshes out' the dogma of the Trinity to give some account of the 'essence' and 'persons' of the Trinity. However, we must be alert to the fact that such accounts are not the credal doctrine of the Trinity as such, but extrapolations of that doctrine in particular accounts and models of divine triunity.

Chapter 8 turns from the doctrine of God to the consideration of God's relation to creation. It is a staple of much historic creedal Christianity that God is said to be incorporeal, that is, without a body. For, so it is said, God is a spirit – based on biblical passages like Jn. 4:24. Yet, despite this, God is said to be incarnate in Christ. Not only that: for most Christians down through the ages Christ is thought to be corporeally present in the consecrated elements of the Eucharist. There is also a third sense in which God is said to be intimately related to the material creation. This has to do with the question of God's immensity or omnipresence in the cosmos. How is God present everywhere and at every place? And how is the created order related to its creator? Following the adage of the Apostle Paul that 'in him we live and move and have our being' (Acts 17), many Christian thinkers have argued for a version of panentheism. This is the idea that the world is somehow contained 'within' God, though God is greater than the world. Additionally, in the recent philosophical literature, there has been a resurgence of interest in the doctrine of divine omnipresence with some notable attempts to argue that God is *located* at every place in creation. Such views would appear to commit their advocates to the idea that the cosmos is God's body too. Trying to make some sense of these puzzling and paradoxical claims is an important matter for any prolegomena to the doctrine of creation. Thus, it is a fitting topic for metatheological exploration. I argue that God is indeed essentially incorporeal, and yet embodied in Christ, and in the Eucharist, though in rather different ways. However, I resist the idea that God is 'embodied' in the cosmos taken as a whole. Instead, I argue for a metaphorical or deflationary account of divine immensity that parcels out omnipresence to the conjunction of divine power and knowledge. If God is omniscient and omnipotent, then God is capable of being present 'everywhere' in virtue of his power and knowledge. This, it seems to me, is a more satisfying way of thinking about God's presence in creation as a whole, and sits better with traditional claims about God's relation to creation that try to hold in tension the essential incorporeality of God alongside the doctrine of the incarnation and real corporeal eucharistic presence.

Metatheology

In Chapter 9 we turn from general considerations about putative divine bodies to the consideration of methodological issues in Christology proper. In this connection, one set of issues has to do with the metaphysics of the incarnation, and which model of the incarnation we find most persuasive or attractive. I hold to a compositional account, according to which the incarnation involves the assumption by God the Son of a concrete particular, namely, the human nature of Jesus of Nazareth. Thus, Christ is composed of three 'parts': God the Son; and the human nature the Son assumes, which comprises his human body and rational soul or mind. A related methodological issue that has arisen in feminist theology has to do with whether a male Christ can be the saviour of all of humanity, women included. Feminist theologians have been critical of traditional Christology and of the way in which such Christology has been used to buttress patriarchal views about humanity, such as one can find in some of the literature on male representation of Christ in the priesthood. But should the defender of classical Christology with its two natures doctrine of the incarnation hold that the maleness of Christ is requisite for human salvation? In this chapter I argue in the negative. In fact, the person at the root of Christ, so to speak, is a divine person and divine persons lack gender and the biology necessary to be male, female or intersex. Jesus of Nazareth had a human body, and that would have had a particular biology including a given biological sex. In light of recent developments in our understanding of human biology, we cannot *conclusively* establish Christ's sex, despite the fact that the Christian tradition unwaveringly presumes Christ is male. Nevertheless, it is not impossible that Christ could have been, say, biologically intersex. But even if he was male as the tradition holds, this does not mean that maleness is somehow privileged in the divine order of things. For, although the person of Christ includes a human body with a particular sex, this does not mean that the *person* of Christ was male or even that Christ had a first-person perspective that was masculine (for, as I have already said, the person 'in' Christ, so to speak, is the Second Person of the Trinity). For these reasons, I argue that we should resist attempts to assimilate classical Christology to a particular way of thinking about the maleness of Christ and its supposed normative status in much traditional and historic theology.

Chapter 10 focuses on metadogmatic issues in eschatology. This usually comprises the study of the four last things: death, judgement, heaven and hell. All four of these items pertain to life beyond the grave. Christianity is eschatologically hardwired: it is teleologically focused on God's goals for creation and what they will look like. As Karl Barth opines, 'If Christianity be not altogether thoroughgoing eschatology, there remains in it no relationship whatever with Christ'.[11] But must Christian eschatology presume that this life is preparation for the hereafter? Is there a place for a view of the end or goal of God's work in creation that is fulfilled this side of the grave, so that there is no personal afterlife of which to speak? This is the project of *fully realized eschatology*. It

---

[11]Karl Barth, *The Epistle to the Romans*, 6th ed., trans. Edwyn C. Hoskins (Oxford: Oxford University Press, 1968 [1933]), 314.

has had its defenders in the work of various modern theologians.[12] I set out and criticize a version of this view, drawing on a thought experiment provided by Professor Kathryn Tanner to do so. I argue that there are serious shortcomings with this doctrine even though it has been entertained by important thinkers in modern theology. The Christian hope is, as Professor Christopher Insole puts it, a realist one[13] that requires the existence of a world to come that cannot be demythologized or reduced to some aspect of life this side of the grave.

The eleventh and final chapter considers the fulfilment of creation in and through the agency of Christ. It takes forward a constructive theological proposal regarding the conditional necessity of Christ for God's purposes in the fulfilment of creation, drawing on aspects of my earlier work in *Analyzing Doctrine* to do so. I begin by setting out four fundamental assumptions about creation. To this I add two christological conditioning principles that provide a dogmatic lens through which to consider God's goal or end in creation. The goal is unitive, having to do with creaturely participation in the divine life. These claims are then conjoined with an argument according to which Christ is the instrument by means of which God secures the eschatological goal of the reconciliation of *all things* to Godself, in keeping with the teaching of Colossians 1. On this way of thinking about the shape of Christian doctrine it is fundamentally a message of hope and restoration – an appropriately optimistic metadogmatic note on which to end this study.

---

[12]A helpful discussion of this wider context can be found in Veli-Matti Kärkkäinen, *Hope and Community. A Constructive Christian Theology for the Pluralist World, Vol. 5* (Grand Rapids: Eerdmans, 2016).
[13]Christopher J. Insole, *The Realist Hope: A Critique of Anti-Realist Approaches in Contemporary Philosophical Theology*. Heythrop Studies in Contemporary, Philosophy, Religion and Theology (Aldershot: Ashgate, 2006).

CHAPTER 1
ON METATHEOLOGY

Metatheology is the study of the foundations of theology – its nature, aims, methods, scope and bounds. More expansively, metatheology is concerned with the *nature of theology*, that is, what it is in distinction from other disciplines such as the social scientific study of religion. It is concerned with the *aims of theology*, that is, what the goals of theology are and how they are ordered. It is concerned with the *methods of theology*, that is, how the theologian goes about the task of theology and on what basis. It is concerned with the *scope of theology*, that is, the extent to which theology reaches. And it is concerned with the *bounds of theology*, that is, the boundaries that mark out where the domain of theology ends or gives way to other disciplines and approaches. These distinct aspects of metatheology are often conflated; indeed, metatheology itself is often misunderstood or mischaracterized where it is identified at all.

It is the task of this first chapter to give a brief account of metatheology to set the scene for what follows. Because this is an area of such misunderstanding, confusion and dispute, much of the chapter will be concerned with trying to clear the ground to provide a proper characterization of metatheology. The first section begins the task of clarification. Given the conceptual proximity of metatheology to analytic theology (with which I am usually concerned), it also seems appropriate to say something about the relationship between metatheology and analytic theology, and how they are different. In the second part of the chapter, I do just that. Then, applying this analysis to a perennial question for theology, the third section considers whether theology is a progressive discipline. I conclude with some reflection on the importance of this discussion for the study of theology as such, which will segue into the next two chapters on the use of models in theology and the ambitions of theology, respectively.

Clarifying 'metatheology'

Let us begin with some ground clearing.[1] Some might think that, as I have characterized it thus far, metatheology is the *philosophy of theology*, just as metametaphysics is the

---

[1] I will not entertain the objection that there are no foundations of theology. I do not think this view is a live theological option. But even if it were, it would be self-referentially incoherent since the claim that there is no foundation to theology is already a metatheological claim. It is akin to saying in metaphysics, 'there is no metaphysics', a claim that is patently metaphysical.

philosophy of metaphysics. That is indeed my view, but it is a view that is contested. Some divines will deny that there is a conceptual place outside the bounds of theology where we can contemplate and reflect on the nature, aims, methods, scope and bounds of theology. For, as they draw the boundaries, theology has to do with 'God and all things in relation to God' – a broad scope indeed![2] Let us call this the *theologically expansive sensibility*. On this way of thinking, there is no non-theological space from which we may regard the nature, aims, methods, scope and bounds of theology for any such putative space would already be within the purview of theology, so to speak. In a similar manner, philosophers these days speak of *meta*metaphysics. But if that is equivalent to the philosophy of first philosophy, then it is still philosophical reflection of a sort – just philosophical reflection on the foundations of philosophy itself. The 'meta' of metametaphysics does not place it in some putatively objective space outside philosophy from which the philosopher may assess the merits of metaphysics as a species of philosophy.

With this in mind, we could characterize the expansive sensibility like this:

EXPANSIVE SENSIBILITY: If theology is about God and all things in relation to God, then there is no field of human endeavour, no intellectual discipline or science that falls outside the scope of theology. To search for the foundations of theology, as if those foundations are something *distinct* from theology on which it stands like a great monument whose foundations lie deep in the earth, is to mischaracterize theology. For theology has no foundations in this sense – that is, no foundations that are *distinct from*, or lie *outside* the domain of theology, so to speak. In the case of theology, the 'space' that is given as the purview of theology is the created order. That is, all that is not God. So, there is God; and there is all that is not God, which God creates, and which depends on God for its continued existence thereafter. Theology concerns both things. It is concerned with God, and all that is not God – the creation – in relation to the one that creates all these things. There is nothing besides this that the theologian must consider for, on this conception of things, there can be nothing more than God and all that is in relation to God. Once we have accounted for God and all that exists in relation to God, we have accounted for all there is. But that is what theology concerns itself with, so there is no metatheological 'view from nowhere.' To speak of what you are calling metatheology is already to think from *within* the bounds of theology. It is to reflect on the foundations of theology from within the bounds of theology, rather like the cosmologist who, in pondering the singularity from which the universe sprang, thinks about the origins of the cosmos *from within* the cosmos, as one of the constituents of the cosmos. We cannot exit theology to ponder its foundations

---

[2] This is the traditional view of Thomas Aquinas in his *Summa Theologiae*. It is discussed in Judith Wolfe's recent survey essay, 'Christian Theology', *Saint Andrews Encyclopaedia of Theology* (2021), located at: https://www.saet.ac.uk/article/christian-theology.

in some philosophical antechamber. To think otherwise is to misunderstand the nature of theology.

Thus, according to the defender of the expansive sensibility, metatheology is a kind of category mistake writ large. Now, as I have expressed it here, the person who takes this sort of view thinks that theology concerns God and all things in relation to God. This expansive vision of theology is often ascribed to Thomas Aquinas and has recently been reiterated with approval by two St Andrews theologians, namely, the late Professor John Webster and Professor Judith Wolfe.[3] But in fact, this does not appear to be the view of Thomas Aquinas – or at least, not without qualifications that alters the picture before us in significant respects.

To see this, we will need to briefly consider what Aquinas says at the very beginning of his *Summa Theologiae* in Part 1. Q. 1, on 'The Nature and Extent of Sacred Doctrine'. Over the ten articles he tackles there, he makes several distinctions that are pertinent to our concern. In the first article, he distinguishes between theology that falls under the description of first philosophy or metaphysics, and theology that falls under the description of revealed theology. Aquinas thinks that *theology* is a term the description of which ranges over a very wide domain that is not discipline-specific. It includes the part of first philosophy, or metaphysics, that (according to Aristotle) has to do with matters pertaining to God.[4] In other words, the aspect of metaphysics that considers questions of God's nature and existence is, by Aquinas' lights, theology. It is properly described as theology as it is concerned with the being and nature of God. We might call this *the metaphysics of theism*.

Now, it is important to note at this juncture that Aquinas is not denying that the metaphysics of theism is philosophy. He concedes that point. Thus, in the resolution to *Summa Theologiae* 1.1.1, Aquinas says, '*I answer that*, It was necessary for man's salvation that there should be a knowledge revealed by God, *besides philosophical science built up by human reason*'. (Emphasis added.) And later, 'It was therefore necessary that, *besides philosophical science built up by reason* there should be a sacred science learned through revelation'. (*ST* 1.1.1, emphasis added.) But clearly, this presumes that there are two distinct intellectual domains in view: that of philosophy, which approaches matters of theology via mere ratiocination; and that of sacred doctrine, which approaches

---

[3] According to Webster, 'the object of Christian theology is twofold: God the Holy Trinity and all other things relative to God'. In 'What Makes Theology Theological', *God Without Measure: Working Papers in Christian Doctrine Vol. 1: God and the Works of God* (London: T&T Clark, 2016), 213. I have already noted Wolfe's endorsement of this sensibility in her SAET article, 'Christian Theology'.

[4] He writes, 'there is a part of philosophy called theology, or the divine science, as Aristotle has proved (*Metaphy*. vi).' *Summa Theologiae* 1.1.1. I am using the translation by the Fathers of the English Dominican Province of 1911, which is widely available. Hereinafter, it is cited parenthetically in the body of the text as *ST* followed by Part; Question; Article.

matters of theology via an appeal to the authority of divine revelation.[5] His concern is to show that the study of theology spans aspects of two distinct intellectual disciplines, including the aspect of first philosophy that has to do with the metaphysics of theism. Put differently, he thinks that the metaphysics of theism does indeed address itself to theological questions. So, there is an area of philosophy that is concerned with theology. However, in addition to this, there is the subject matter of revealed theology. Although Aquinas seems to think that human beings may come to proper theological conclusions pertaining to theology without divine revelation, such revelation is (he thinks) a more expedient way of communicating such lofty truths. And, in addition, human ratiocination without the corrective of divine revelation is liable to turn up falsehoods mixed in with true theological claims. 'Even as regards those truths about God which human reason could have discovered', he maintains, 'it was necessary that man should be taught by a divine revelation; because the truth about God such as reason could discover, would only be known by a few, and that after a long time, and with the admixture of many errors'. (*ST* 1.1.1.) So, revealed theology is a way of guarding against theological mistakes as well. Given that our salvation depends on rightly apprehending these things, as Aquinas puts it, it was expedient that God provide a more secure route to understanding matters of theology, and that is provided by divine revelation in Scripture.

Now, setting to one side the rather optimistic account of human cognition that this approach presumes, and focusing on the matter in hand, it seems clear from the foregoing that in answer to the question of whether there is an area of philosophy that is properly theological, Aquinas answers in the affirmative. Theology is not discipline-specific in his view any more than mathematics belongs to mathematicians to the exclusion of physicists. On the matter of sacred doctrine, he avers that revealed theology is a fitting – indeed, expedient – means of communicating the truths of the Faith that otherwise might be difficult for human beings to arrive at through sheer ratiocination alone. Thus, the importance of revealed theology is in the delivery of the truths that comprise sacred doctrine, and that would not be communicated as effectively, or without the likelihood of significant error, if the means of arriving at these truths was via philosophy alone. So, it appears that according to Aquinas in *ST* 1.1.1 there is philosophical theology, which is just the philosophical discussion of that which falls under the description of theology done using the natural endowments provided by reason independent of divine revelation. The subject matter of philosophical theology according to Aquinas is what I have called the metaphysics of theism. Presumably, the results of such investigation are theological truths arrived at by philosophical methods. This he contrasts with revealed

---

[5] Later, Aquinas says, 'Sciences are differentiated according to the various means through which knowledge is obtained. For the astronomer and the physicist both may prove the same conclusion: that the earth, for instance, is round; the astronomer by means of mathematics (i.e. abstracting from matter), but the physicist by means of matter itself. Hence, there is no reason why those things which may be learned from philosophical science, so far as they can be known by natural reason, may not also be taught us by another science, so far as they fall within revelation. Hence, theology included in sacred doctrine differs in kind from that theology which is part of philosophy'. ST 1.1.1.

theology, which is a surer way to theological truths because revealed theology is a divine communication of those truths to humanity in Scripture. Thus, the results of revealed theology are theological truths arrived at by means of divine communication. This yields what he calls sacred doctrine.

Put in a more mundane idiom, the idea Aquinas has in view here seems to be something like the difference between learning about some famous person and receiving a written letter from that famous person. If I learned about the King through careful investigation I might learn all sorts of things, but (plausibly) not all of them would be true. It will be an admixture of truth and falsehood, and some things I might not be sure about. For instance, the provenance of the information might be dubious, or based on hearsay, or whatever. However, if I receive a detailed letter from His Majesty, then, other things being equal, I can be much surer of what is communicated in the letter. It is a more expedient, and perhaps more secure way of accessing information that might otherwise be difficult to obtain, if it could be obtained at all.

Now, what is important for our purposes is that this way of thinking about theology, culled from Aquinas, presumes two things. These are, (a) that there are bounds to theology that distinguish it from philosophy, and (b) that theology may be pursued on philosophical grounds as well as on what we might call *confessional* theological grounds, that is, via reflection on the deposit of divine revelation in Scripture as a kind of divine testimony. It is in this context that Aquinas speaks about the subject matter of theology later in Article 7 of Question 1 of Part1of the *Summa Theologiae*, in the familiar terms of 'God and all things in relation to God' when addressing the question of whether God is the object of the science of sacred doctrine. But what does he say there? In providing his resolution to the article, he writes, 'God is in very truth the object of this science'. But in addition to God, the subject matter of theology also includes 'things and signs', the works of salvation, and the *totus Christus*, that is Christ and the members of his Church. 'Of all these things, in truth, we treat in this science', says Aquinas, 'but so far as they have reference to God'. (*ST* 1.1.7.) It is from this that the principle of 'God and all things in relation to God' is derived.

However, and importantly, the scope of theology to which Aquinas is referring in this article is the content of sacred doctrine, which, in turn, is the subject matter of the *Summa Theologiae*. But equally clearly, this is not co-extensive with the subject matter of theology as such, because he allows earlier in his treatment of theology in *ST* 1.1.1 that theology is a broader term that includes both the content of sacred doctrine, which is revealed theology, as well as some of the content of metaphysics, which is first philosophy.[6] If we were to sum up Aquinas's position here, we could say that he conceives of theology as a general, non-discipline-specific area of intellectual inquiry that includes the discipline of confessional theology, as I have called it, which is what he describes

---

[6]Presumably, it is broader than this if we include other areas of philosophy that are pertinent here, such as epistemology, ethics, or logic. But in the context of *ST* 1.1.1, it is the metaphysics of theism that Aquinas is interested in.

as the study of sacred doctrine, as well as philosophy. By contrast, sacred doctrine or confessional theology is a discipline-specific area of intellectual inquiry, which derives from theological reflection on the authority of divine revelation in Scripture.[7]

Thus, even if the claims that theology concerns God and all things in relation to God do properly express Aquinas's aspiration concerning the scope and shape of theology, when this is qualified by what he says about the scope of theology and sacred doctrine, it is clear he does not think this means there are no philosophical grounds on which to make theological claims. Quite the opposite. The confessional theology generated by the study of sacred doctrine is indeed about God and all things in relation to God. But how we arrive at truths about God is a more general question, which is not discipline-specific. It may be done via one of two routes: philosophically and/or theologically. Clearly, this is not the same as claiming that there is no non-theological space from which to assess theological claims, or even that talk of the 'foundations' of theology in some putative metatheology fails to get off the ground because there is no non-theological vantage from which to make that assessment.

Now, up to this point I have been concerned to rebut a particular objection to metatheology, namely, the one mounted by the defenders of what I have called the expansive sensibility. For if I am right, then the expansive sensibility of at least some Thomists is not, in fact, synonymous with what the historical Aquinas says. However, this does not settle the point at issue. To see this, suppose for the sake of argument that I am right about what the historical Aquinas says in *Summa Theologiae*. The defender of the theologically expansive sensibility may simply regroup by saying that, whether the historical Aquinas said so or not, the right way to understand the principle that theology concerns 'God and all things in relation to God' is in terms that exclude the prospect of metatheology *a priori*. In other words, the objection against metatheology still has force even if it turns out it does not have its source in the authority of Aquinas.

Let us explore this second line of objection. For reasons that should be obvious, it depends on what I shall call a *recalcitrant theologically expansive sensibility* – recalcitrant because it involves setting Aquinas to one side and digging in one's intellectual heels to reframe the point at issue. According to this way of thinking, metatheology is a non-starter because the scope of theology includes matters that fall under prolegomena. This is the part of the study of the study of sacred doctrine that provides introductory material and context for the student. The claim here isn't that there are no foundational matters to consider when coming to the discussion of sacred doctrine. Rather, the concern is that the discussion of such foundational matters is already part of the introductory material one would expect within the bounds of the discussion of matters theological. Returning

---

[7] In fact, matters are more complicated than *ST* 1.1.1 suggests. For Aquinas appeals to more than one source of authority in coming to judgements about sacred doctrine. Alongside the foundational role of Scripture, there is the testimony of tradition, especially the Fathers of the Church, to which he appeals on a regular basis as a kind of subordinate norm. He is also willing to appeal to the authority of Aristotle as The Philosopher when it seems appropriate. But this is not the place to pursue matters of more general Aquinas interpretation.

to my initial characterization of metatheology, the advocate of a recalcitrant expansive sensibility claims that the study of the conceptual foundations of theology, comprising its nature, aims, methods, scope and bounds, obtains *within the domain of theology* as such. It is a properly theological task, not a philosophical one. The fact that Aquinas disagrees (if indeed he does disagree), alters this point not one whit.

What shall we say in response to this? Well, given what we have seen Aquinas says about the matter, it should be clear that the recalcitrant theologically expansive sensibility requires some disambiguation. When we attempt this, we quickly discover that it is the advocate of the recalcitrant expansive sensibility who, according to the follower of Aquinas's scheme in *ST* 1.1.1, seems to be guilty of a category mistake. But we begin to get ahead of ourselves. So, let us do what all good scholastic theologians do, and begin to address this concern raised by the advocate of a recalcitrant expansive sensibility by making some conceptual distinctions.

Initially, then, let us distinguish between *theology* as the intellectual domain that is concerned with the study of God and all things in God, and *Divinity* as the study of theology from within a confessional context, specifically, the context of the Christian tradition, broadly construed. Then, the study of what Aquinas calls *sacred doctrine* – which encompasses what today we would think of as distinct sub-disciplines like biblical studies, the history of doctrine, as well as systematic theology and practical theology – falls within the bounds of Divinity. For it is the study of theology from a particular vantage, namely, the vantage of the Christian tradition in which it is believed revealed theology is the principal source of authority. Given this way of carving things up, the mistake of the defender of the recalcitrant version of the expansive sensibility is to think that Divinity is a domain that encompasses within its bounds *all* reflection on theology. It would be like the golfer who claims that the Eden estuary in St Andrews contains all the water of the river Eden which empties into it. Clearly, that cannot be the case; the golfer is mistaken or misunderstands that at any given time there is water running downstream from the mountains through the river Eden as well as the water that empties into the estuary. *Mutatis mutandis*, the theologian who claims Divinity encompasses within its bounds all reflection on theology is guilty of a kind of intellectual overreach. In fact, Divinity encompasses only the parts or aspects of theology that fall under the description of Divinity as a confessional discipline. It may be that a given Divinity school also has professors who study religion from a social science perspective, or who study the philosophical foundations of theology, or whatever. That is well and good. But it should be clear from this way of thinking that such approaches to the matter of theology do not fall under the description of Divinity, strictly speaking. They are ancillary to Divinity understood in this broadly Thomistic fashion as a kind of confessional theology done from within a given tradition.[8]

---

[8] As an aside, it seems to me that this comports well with experience. Often, scholars of biblical studies distance themselves from the perceived 'confessionalism' of colleagues in, say, systematic theology, precisely because

Given these distinctions, we may return to the objection of the defender of the recalcitrant expansive sensibility. It should now be clear that the objector is right that theology is expansive in nature, but wrong to deny that there is no place from which we may reflect on the foundations of theology that is not already theological. Once we distinguish between theology as such, and Divinity as the confessional approach to theology, it should be clear that the confessional study of Divinity is more restricted than theology as such, and that theology as such can be done outwith Divinity by those of other faiths or no faith, including philosophers.

Let us take stock. I have argued that the defender of a theologically expansive sensibility who thinks that theology concerns 'God and all things in relation to God' has things at best half right, if this principle is thought to be culled from Thomas Aquinas. When we consider what Aquinas says, it is clear he thought theology is a subject that comprises the subject matter of sacred doctrine and methods associated with its study in revealed theology (which includes what today we might call biblical studies, the history of doctrine, and dogmatics, or systematic theology, as well as practical theology). But, says Aquinas, theology is also studied in metaphysics. So, theology is not the same as the study of sacred doctrine, and the study of theology may be pursued outside the bounds of the study of sacred doctrine in philosophy. I have suggested that a key difference that seems to inform Aquinas' way of thinking is between what I have called a confessional approach to theology and a non-confessional approach. The confessional approach is, in important respects, tradition-specific (as we postmoderns would say). The non-confessional approach is not tradition-specific. That seems to be a principled way of distinguishing the study of theology as such from the confessional approach to theology. I then considered the recalcitrant expansive sensibility of those who argue that metatheology is a non-starter because there is no non-theological 'view from nowhere' from which to reflect on the conceptual foundations of theology irrespective of what Aquinas says. This, I argued, depends on a category mistake, which is ironic given that this is the mistake that the defender of the recalcitrant expansive sensibility accuses the metatheology advocates of committing. The category mistake in question is, as I have outlined it, to conflate theology as a broad reflection on God and all things in God with a particular intellectual discipline, namely, Divinity. Once we see this, we see that the study of theology is not co-extensive with the study of Divinity and that it is possible to study theology outside of the confessional bounds of Divinity and its concern with revealed theology – in philosophy. (An aside: presumably, and by extension, this is also true of the modern social-scientific study of theology where theology is the object of study, rather than the study of religious phenomena, practices and beliefs. Such developments postdate Aquinas, but it would not be difficult to adjust our description to include them.)

Suppose this is right as far as it goes. It still does not address the question of whether metatheology is a desirable, appropriate, or even feasible activity. That is, even if the

---

they maintain that their own approach to the biblical text is non-confessional and social-scientific. They do not want their work tarred with the brush of what I am here calling Divinity.

objector is willing to concede the point about Aquinas' exegesis and concede the point about the distinction between Divinity and theology as such, this in-and-of-itself does not show that metatheology is desirable, appropriate or feasible.

To see what I mean, consider an example from the social sciences. In the study of law, we have a division between those who study black letter law in order to pursue particular legal cases and those who study the philosophical foundations of the law, that is, jurisprudence or legal theory. The practitioner of jurisprudence is concerned with the philosophy of law.[9] There are many scholars who work in this field, but not all of them are qualified lawyers. Many are what we might call *theoretical lawyers* as opposed to *practical lawyers* – those who practice the law daily as advocates, solicitors, barristers or attorneys. (Think of the difference between theoretical magicians and practical magicians adopted by Susanna Clarke in her sublime novel, *Jonathan Strange & Mr Norrell*. It is just such a distinction that I have in mind here.) One could be both a practical and a theoretical lawyer, of course. But the point is that there is a distinction to be made between the two, one that depends on a real division of labour within the study of law itself. This division is between those concerned with the practice of the law as we have it and those concerned with the theoretical foundations of the law.

Now, it seems clear to me that those who study jurisprudence are normally theoretical lawyers. Or at least, when they are engaged in the activity of jurisprudence, they are theoretical lawyers, not practical lawyers. What is more, jurisprudence concerns itself with the theoretical foundations of law in a way that the practising lawyer normally does not. There is a place for both sorts of lawyer, but they do different (though related) tasks. When pursuing a criminal case that relies on black letter law, one turns to the services of a practical lawyer, not a theoretical one, and with good reason. We need the advice of one who deals with black letter law in prosecuting criminal cases, not with the philosophical assumptions and ideas that underpin black letter law.

Transpose this to the study of theology. Divines study theology; but so too do philosophers. Those studying theology as Divinity students study theology in a confessional manner, presuming the content of sacred doctrine. Those who study theology as philosophers do not. They are only concerned with arguments concerning the philosophy of theology. (Recall, theology in this context is not the same as Divinity. Theology is a general term that is shared between philosophers and divines; Divinity is the discipline studied by divines. Theologians may be divines, but theologians may also be philosophers doing philosophical theology. This is a distinction that used to be observed in the distinction between natural theologians and divines.) Thus, in this way of thinking, it is perfectly appropriate for philosophers to study the subject matter of theology.

---

[9]In contemporary legal theory, a distinction is sometimes made between jurisprudence, legal theory, and the philosophy of law. For present purposes, I am ignoring these distinctions and using these three terms as synonyms.

Metatheology

So far, so good. What then of metatheology? Where does that land? Here we pass decisively from ground-clearing to theological construction. In my view, it lands at the borderlands between Divinity and philosophical theology. That is why it is a disputed topic. Like anything that straddles the borders between two disciplines, its provenance will be the subject of dispute. But in my way of thinking, not only is theology properly studied by scholars outside Divinity. The study of the foundations of theology is also a matter that is properly a philosophical matter. It is, as I intimated earlier, the philosophy of theology. Return to Aquinas again. His concern was with sacred doctrine, or what I (from the vantage of an ancient Scottish university) am calling Divinity. It is appropriate to investigate the subject matter of Christian doctrine from within Divinity. But reflection on the foundations of Divinity takes us outside the discipline, strictly speaking. To put it in the terms used by Aquinas, the practitioner of metatheology reflects on the subject matter of sacred doctrine from the vantage of philosophy.

Now, here is a complication: metatheology is practised by both Divines and by philosophers. In a similar manner, jurisprudence is practised by practical lawyers as well as theoretical lawyers. One can be a practical lawyer and reflect on the foundations of the law! In a similar manner, one can be a Divine and have an interest in philosophical theology or in first philosophy. Our intellectual promiscuity as scholars – which is surely something to be celebrated and embraced rather than denigrated and eschewed – nevertheless tends to occlude the difference on which metatheology depends. I am suggesting that metatheology is in fact the philosophy of theology, and that such an intellectual activity can be both helpful and productive for practitioners of Divinity, just as theoretical legal study can be helpful to practical lawyers trying to measure up to standards of justice in the way they practise the law. This does not amount to an argument in favour of the conclusion that metatheology is the philosophy of theology. Rather, it is an attempt to recommend a particular conception of metatheology as the philosophy of theology. To do so we have had to clear some conceptual space of alternatives to make room for this way of conceiving the matter.

Thus, in my way of thinking, we have the following distinctions:

THEOLOGY
The study of God and all things in relation to God.

DIVINITY
The confessional study of THEOLOGY from within the Christian tradition that is concerned with the content of sacred doctrine in revealed theology. The study of sacred doctrine includes aspects of biblical studies, historical theology, systematic theology or dogmatics, and practical theology.

PHILOSOPHICAL THEOLOGY
A non-confessional approach to questions of THEOLOGY that is concerned with the application of non-confessional philosophical methods to theological topics, e.g. the metaphysics of theism.

METATHEOLOGY
The study of the conceptual foundations of THEOLOGY, namely, its nature, aims, methods, scope and bounds.

As a final thought on this matter before turning to the question of progress in theology, it might be thought that one could have a stipulative definition of theology as the study of God and all things in relation to God, and hold that metatheology is merely *the study of the conceptual foundations of theology, namely, its nature, aims, methods, scope and bounds,* and leave it at that. In other words, one might leave open the question of whether the study of the conceptual foundations of theology is a properly philosophical or theological task that falls within the purview of first philosophy or Divinity. My own thought is that this still betrays a conceptual muddle. We would, I think, be better off saying that divines may do metatheology and philosophers may do metatheology while acknowledging that metatheology is, in point of fact, the philosophy of theology, not Divinity strictly speaking.

Analytic theology and metatheology

At this juncture, the discerning reader may be wondering how this conception of metatheology fits with analytic theology. For, it might be thought, metatheology sounds a lot like analytic theology. Yet, given my characterization of it, metatheology is not confessional theology or Divinity, but the philosophy of theology. Analytic theology is also sometimes described in these terms.[10] Does that mean analytic theology is not a species of confessional theology after all, contrary to some claims I have made in print?[11]

No. In earlier publications, I have argued that analytic theology *may* be practised as what John Webster calls 'theological theology',[12] which is another way of saying confessional theology or Divinity. But analytic theology *may also* be practised as philosophical theology by philosophers. In fact, my (previously published) way of thinking about analytic theology underscores the point I have been making here about metatheology. The point is this: theology is not a term that designates a subject-specific discipline. It might be characterized, as per the expansive sensibility, as the study of God and all things in relation to God. But this, as Aquinas points out, includes aspects of philosophy as well as much of the theology done in theology departments and faculties in universities, as well as Divinity schools and seminaries. In a similar fashion, analytic

---

[10]See, e.g., the subtitle to the original volume of essays that traded under the name 'analytic theology', vis. Oliver D. Crisp and Michael C. Rea, eds, *Analytic Theology: New Essays in the Philosophy of Theology* (Oxford: Oxford University Press, 2009).
[11]See, e.g., Oliver D. Crisp, 'Analytic Theology as Systematic Theology', *Open Theology* 3 (2017): 156–66; and Crisp, James Arcadi, and Jordan Wessling, *The Nature and Promise of Analytic Theology.* Brill Research Perspectives in Humanities and the Social Sciences (Leiden: E. J. Brill, 2019).
[12]See Crisp, 'Analytic Theology as Systematic Theology', 157.

Metatheology

theology is just a method of doing theology, which does not commit its practitioner to substantive theological claims. So analytic theology can be done *qua* philosopher, as philosophical theology in the way that Aquinas suggests in the case of theistic metaphysics. It can also be done (and is being done!) by those interested in other areas of philosophy, such as philosophical ethics, epistemology, logic and so forth. I applaud this work. *Floreant professores, floreat academia*! But analytic theology may also be done *qua* divine. It is unfortunate that in modern English we commonly use the term theology to demarcate a particular intellectual discipline because that leads to confusing theology as such with its practice in a particular context – that of Divinity.[13] Nevertheless, as I understand it, theology is practised in the discipline of Divinity as a confessional mode of studying theology that is beholden to the authority of the Christian tradition and Scripture. Analytic theology can be done in this manner too, by systematic theologians who use the tools, methods, sensibilities and literature of recent Anglo-American philosophy in pursuit of the goals of theology under the aegis of Divinity. Thus, analytic theology tracks the more general term theology. This is because analytic theology is just a mode of studying theology using the tools, methods, sensibility and literature of the analytic philosophical tradition to do so. Is it still philosophy if such a method is transposed from the groves of the Academy into the hallowed halls of Divinity? I say: not if in the process of doing so the philosophical tools, methods, sensibility and literature beloved of analytics are being brought in as ancillary to the study of sacred doctrine. And, after all, isn't that just the sort of thing Aquinas has in view at the beginning of his great *Summa*? There is nothing stopping the student of sacred doctrine from using philosophy. The point is that it has a subordinate role in such contexts, under the authority of divine revelation. Thus, analytic theology may be pursued in Divinity as a species of systematic theology. If that were not the case, then no systematic theology would be possible in Divinity because *all* systematic theology borrows philosophical concepts to furnish its arguments. The question is not whether systematic theologians help themselves to philosophical tools, methods, or arguments when it suits them; they clearly do so as a matter of course, borrowing whatever they need to pursue their theological goals. The question is whether in doing so the systematic theologian does anything untoward. In my view, they do not do anything inappropriate provided the philosophy they borrow has a handmaidenly role – which is precisely the kind of role envisaged by Aquinas in *ST*.

Theological progress

With that, we turn from the demarcation of metatheology to the vexed and disputed question of progress in theology. One important (some might say, perennial) question

---

[13] It is also problematic because theology is a subject studied in other world religions. The study of God and all things in God is clearly not synonymous with the study of *Christian* theology. For I presume that many people of non-Christian faith could say the same thing, e.g., Jews and Muslims, among others.

for metatheology concerns whether there is progress in theology, or even what progress in theology would look like. This is a metatheological concern provided it falls under the description of METATHEOLOGY given in the previous section. And I presume that discussion of progress in theology does, at least in part, raise issues about the conceptual foundations of theology (i.e. whether it is a progressive discipline that accumulates knowledge over time), as well as about its nature, aims, methods, scope and bounds. Here, as in the previous section, and following Aquinas's lead, I will distinguish between theology as such, which is a broad category that is not discipline-specific, and philosophy and Divinity as particular subject areas in which theology may be studied.

Now, it might be thought that theology as such is not progressive in the same way that, say, the natural sciences might be thought to be progressive. On this way of thinking, the natural sciences are progressive because they amass data through hypothesis and experimentation that generate a body of knowledge about the physical world that is cumulative. The idea is that the natural sciences examine physical data about the world around us that can be tested and subjected to experiment and measurement based on the scientific method. Natural scientists see something puzzling in the world, form a predictive hypothesis to explain the puzzle, test the hypothesis through experiment, draw appropriate conclusions from the experimental data in relation to the hypothesis, and adjust or refine the hypothesis considering their findings.

This rather neat way of characterizing progress in the natural sciences is, to say the least, contested. In the past few generations, great volumes of ink have been spilt by philosophers of science, and sometimes by practising scientists reflecting on their own disciplines, which have made this rather simplistic picture of scientific progress appear problematic.[14] Here is not the place to pursue that matter. Instead, I will use this toy version of scientific progress because it is still often trotted out in popular culture as an exemplar of intellectual progress that theology cannot hope to emulate.[15]

Our analysis of the lie of the land in theology presumes that theology is a truth-aimed and truth-apt enterprise. In this sense, it is a realist discipline in a way that, say, astrology is not. That is, theology is aimed at truth about God and all things in relation to God, and it is an apt way of getting at matters of theological truth.[16] However, truth in theology is very much a matter of attending to the object of theology, which is God. In philosophy, this is pursued in philosophical theology, which includes some work done in analytic theology. Philosophical theology uses ratiocination to arrive at truths about God (e.g. whether God exists, what the nature of God consists in, and so on). Divinity pursues

---

[14] A – dare I say? – *paradigm* of this is Thomas Kuhn's work, *The Structure of Scientific Revolutions* (Chicago: University of Chicago Press, 1962). For two more recent studies that make this point from rather different directions, see Nancey Murphy, *Theology in the Age of Scientific Reasoning*, Cornell Studies in Philosophy of Religion (Ithaca: Cornell University Press, 1990), and Bas C. van Fraassen, *The Scientific Image* (Oxford: Oxford University Press, 1980).

[15] A good example of this is the recent work of the New Atheists.

[16] This is a matter that is also disputed. I have attended to the dispute elsewhere, e.g. Crisp, 'Analytic Theology as Systematic Theology' and *Analyzing Doctrine*, and will not repeat myself here.

the claims of truth via divine revelation communicated in Scripture and refracted through the Christian tradition. This yields Aquinas's 'sacred doctrine' (among other things). But notice that in both philosophy and divinity, the pursuit of theological truth involves the attempt to get at, or understand, the object of theology better. If that is right, then progress understood in terms of the accumulation of more knowledge or a greater number of truths concerning the object of theology should, in principle, be an anticipated outcome. For, other things being equal, it seems reasonable to presume that a truth-aimed discipline has the ambition of accumulating truths over time.

Nevertheless, theology as pursued by philosophers and divines is not calibrated like the natural sciences. It does not proceed on the basis of hypothesis and experimentation; there is no theological analogue to the scientific method. But that is not terribly surprising. After all, (as our discussion in the previous section has demonstrated) methodological concerns are usually discipline-specific in important respects. Thus, at least some of the social sciences do not necessarily proceed based on a scientific method either, but we do not think they are any the worse for that. To see this, let us return to our earlier example of law. As previously indicated, in the Anglo-American tradition the law is a body of material, much of which is written down in statute and black letter law, to which the (practical) lawyer must attend. The body of law in each jurisdiction is a collection of testimony, commentary and judgements that functions as the main source of authority for drawing legal conclusions, and for making further law. This textual tradition can be amended and changed, and does to some extent evolve over time so that legal codes become more sophisticated or are refined, or in some cases laws are removed or held in abeyance. Laws from previous eras can sometimes seem hopelessly arcane or immoral to the modern ear. Think of penalties that used to be applied to those who stole a loaf of bread, or who were thought to be witches or discovered to be practising homosexuals. Nevertheless, plausibly there is a kind of stable core to the law built around certain principles about what we take to be appropriate behaviour in our societies (much of which has a religious basis, despite the protests of some modern legal positivists). Yet it is also clear that new law and revisions to the law are made not because of something like the scientific method, but by something more like trial and error, as well as changing social mores. Thus, we no longer think homosexual behaviour between consenting adults should be illegal, or that those who are pagans or Wiccans should be prosecuted for their religious practices, and so forth. And we have come to these views because as communities and societies we no longer consider such practices to fall under the description of criminal behaviour.

Theology as such is much more like this, I think. This is true in how it is practised in both philosophical theology and Divinity, but particularly in the latter. Like the law, Divinity is a discipline that attends to an authoritative tradition, much of which is written down. And like the law, Divinity has to do with the way in which the tradition is expressed institutionally. In the case of the law, the institutions are the legal and political organs of the state, that is, the courts and parliament, and ancillary entities such as inns of court, faculties of advocates, legal chambers, and the like. In the case of Divinity, the institution is the Church and her liturgies. Although there are also associated institutions like seminaries that serve the Church, it is principally the Church and her liturgies that represent the institutional heart of Christianity as it has been expressed from the earliest times to the present.

Well, then, where might progress be found in the study of theology? In a sense, the answer is implicit in what Aquinas says at the beginning of *Summa Theologiae*. If the subject matter of Divinity is sacred doctrine (broadly construed), perhaps progress can be measured in terms of developments in our understanding of the deposit of revelation, which is the major source of authority for sacred doctrine, and in the doctrines that are developed based on revealed theology, as well as in the reception and development of sacred doctrine in catechesis and tradition. Then, like the law, Divinity makes progress through interrogating and engaging a body of tradition, some of which is written down. Progress is measured in relation to a complex of things: our understanding of that tradition and our development of ways of relating and reflecting on it in tension with other non-theology-specific considerations such as those provided by broader culture and other related disciplines that bear on the subject matter of Divinity, such as the natural sciences, and so on. It seems to me that there is good evidence of such progress. To take just one example: the way in which the dogma of the Trinity developed in the first five centuries of the life of the Church, culminating in the Nicene-Constantinopolitan dogma of AD 381 (a matter to which we shall return in Chapter 6). But though this provided a kind of dogmatic framework for subsequent discussion of the Trinity, our understanding of the mystery of the Trinity has continued to develop through further theological reflection and the proposal of new ways of thinking about key aspects of the dogma, and even new models for thinking about the Trinity, such as the hylomorphist-constitution model recently produced in analytic theology by Jeff Brower and Michael Rea.

But suppose it is the study of theology from a philosophical perspective that is in view. There is no formal body of authoritative texts on which philosophers reflect in formulating arguments about God and all things in relation to God. And in many cases philosophers are still discussing versions of philosophical arguments that have an ancient pedigree – think, for example, of standard arguments for the existence of God in an introduction to the philosophy of religion course. Yet where philosophy pays attention to theological traditions in philosophical theology, it may be that progress is more obvious because it tracks developments in the tradition. So, in a sense, it seems to me that although philosophical reflection on theology can be (and is) done without paying much attention to data from a given religious tradition, in practice, philosophical theology is often parasitic on data provided by the tradition in view. Thus, the prospects for metatheological progress depend in some respects on progress in a religious tradition such as that provided by the study of theology in Divinity.

Conclusion

In this chapter, I have given some account of metatheology in dialogue with several alternative ways of thinking about reflection on the foundations of theology. Using

Metatheology

Aquinas' discussion in *Summa Theologiae* 1.1 as a point of departure, I argued that we can distinguish between theology as such, which is a non-discipline-specific approach to the question of God and all things in relation to God that spans Divinity and (some aspects of) philosophy. Divinity is the confessional study of theology from within the Christian tradition. Metatheology is the study of the conceptual foundations of theology, namely, its nature, aims, methods, scope and bounds. This, it seems to me, is best understood as the philosophy of theology, that is, as philosophical reflection on the foundations of theology. Thus, practitioners of metatheology may be philosophers or divines.

I then applied this thinking to analytic theology to show that the analytic theologian can be engaged in metatheology even though (a) metatheology is the philosophy of theology, and (b) not all analytic theologians are philosophers or are practising philosophy when they do analytic theology. One can do both analytic theology and metatheology. This, despite the fact that analytic theology can be pursued from within the bounds of Divinity whereas metatheology cannot.

Finally, I applied this reasoning to the question of progress in theology. I argued that the study of theology as such may be progressive depending on how it is pursued. Progress in disciplines that are organized around authoritative traditions is different from progress in disciplines that use the scientific method. But that does not mean there is no progress in such disciplines. We talk of progress in the study of law, and in a similar manner we can talk of progress in Divinity based on dogmatic reflection on the deposit of divine revelation, and the associated practices of the Church in its liturgy. Thus, dogma is in principle capable of a progressive analysis and the Christian tradition itself can be analysed in similar terms, as I have already indicated. Progress in philosophical reflection on matters theological is less apparent, although philosophical theology that tracks the content of a given theological tradition may benefit from having access to developments in the tradition that may be the subject of philosophical analysis. Nevertheless, it is not clear (to me at least) that philosophical theology is progressive in the same way as Divinity is – at least in principle.

This is hardly the last word on the topic of metatheology. If anything, I hope it might be a stimulus for further work in this area (I hear scholarly quills being sharpened even as I write these words). For, so it seems to me, we all benefit from a greater understanding of the way in which we approach a subject as expansive, and as existentially vital, as the question of God and all things in relation to God.

CHAPTER 2
USING MODELS

In the previous chapter, I provided an account of metatheology. I argued that it is equivalent to the philosophy of theology and may be practised by divines as well as philosophers. In this chapter, we turn to consider a particular methodological tool that can be utilized in the pursuit of the theological task. The 'conceptual tool' in question is the use of models in theology. Analytic theologians have become known for their use of model building in theology.[1] There are other modern non-analytic theologians who use the language of models, for example, the constructive feminist theologian Sally McFague, or, in the religion and science literature, Ian Barbour.[2] Yet it is true to say that one important way in which analytic theologians have approached the constructive task of theology involves setting forth particular models for given doctrines as a way of 'picturing' the view clearly so that it may then be subjected to criticism. But what is meant by a theological model in the analytic literature, and why should we think that models are an appropriate way to think about going about the task of setting out constructive versions of a given doctrine?

This chapter addresses these questions in the following way. In the first section, I give some account of what I mean by a model in this context, drawing on some of the recent literature in this area. Armed with this information, the second section focuses on the different sorts of models used in theology. These include instrumentalist, anti-realist and realist accounts. I shall also touch on arealist accounts. The third section briefly considers two case studies of models in analytic theology: the Trinity and the incarnation (both of which we shall return to in later chapters). Finally, the conclusion draws together the different threads of the foregoing and offers some reflection on how this analytic penchant for model-building may be of use to systematic and constructive theology more broadly.

---

[1] See, e.g., William Wood, 'Modeling Mystery', *Scientia et Fides* 4, no. 1 (2016): 39–59. Wood also discusses this in the broader context of analytic theology in *Analytic Theology and the Academic Study of Religion*. Oxford Studies in Analytic Theology (Oxford: Oxford University Press, 2020).
[2] See Sally McFague, *Metaphorical Theology: Models of God in Religious Language* (Minneapolis: Fortress Press, 1982), and Ian G. Barbour, *Religion and Science: Historical and Contemporary Issues* (San Francisco: HarperCollins, 1997).

Metatheology

Models

In this chapter, I am particularly concerned with conceptual models, though of course there are physical models as well – a point to which we shall return presently. So, we may begin by distinguishing between a *model*, as a kind of conceptual structure or framework for understanding a particular thing and its *target* phenomena.

As an initial pass at giving a rough and ready account of what models are – one that is relevant to the theological task – we might say that they are *simplified conceptual frameworks or descriptions by means of which complex sets of data, systems, and processes may be organised and understood*. Call this rough and ready account, MODEL.[3] On the basis of MODEL we might then describe some of the most important characteristics such models possess. They are representational, analogous, are hermeneutical in nature, have a certain fidelity to aspects of the thing they represent, and take different forms. Let us consider each of these characteristics in turn. Often, models are used to *represent* some aspect of another thing, simplifying a more complex entity or system in such a way that the model is a kind of *analogue* to the phenomena it represents, being both like and unlike it.[4] Consider the example of a model aircraft made of wood. It has a shape that is recognisably that of an airplane. We see it and immediately think of it in this way. However, we do so knowing that it is also significantly unlike a real aircraft, not just in scale but also in many other respects(e.g. it is made of solid wood, does not fly, has no moving parts).

There is an important sense in which the way models represent a given thing is a hermeneutical decision made by those formulating the model. We must understand how the model in question is being used to represent the phenomena of which it is a simpler description to grasp in what way it is a model and what phenomena it is modelling. This is sometimes referred to as the *fidelity* of the model to the thing represented. For instance, if the model aircraft is a child's toy, we know that its role dictates what aspects of a real aircraft it models. It looks like an airplane, having a fuselage, wings and a tailplane. But the likeness is limited to certain superficial physical characteristics because it is a toy, not, say, a working scale model of an aircraft (so it has no engine, is incapable of flight, etc.). This is a point that has been made elsewhere in the recent philosophical and theological literature.[5]

But models need not be of actual things, that is, concrete items in the world around us. We can also model imaginary things, like a model of the Millennium Falcon. The model itself does not need to be some physical artefact either. It can be conceptual, like

---

[3] This way of thinking about models in theology was first articulated in Oliver D. Crisp, *Analyzing Doctrine*, 89.
[4] A similar point is made by Roman Frigg and Stephan Hartmann in, 'Models in Science', *Stanford Encyclopedia of Philosophy*, located at: https://plato.stanford.edu/entries/models-science/ (last accessed May 13, 2020). And Wood observes, 'In a sense, all models are analogies—or, more precisely, all models represent their targets in virtue of analogical relations'. See 'Modeling Mystery', 45.
[5] Thus, philosopher Michael Weisberg says that a model is 'an interpreted conceptual structure that can be used to represent real or imagined phenomena'. Michael Weisberg, *Simulation and Similarity: Using Models to Explain the World* (Oxford: Oxford University Press, 2013), 15, cited in Wood, 'Modeling Mystery', 45.

the model of an atom in a physics textbook, or a mathematical model like a graph of an asymptote. It may be an idealized picture of some phenomena such as a frictionless plane, or it may be a toy model, like the toy airplane – one that is simplified, limiting fidelity to certain stripped-down aspects of the phenomena in view. Thus, models have different forms or can be expressed in different ways, whether physical, conceptual, fictional, ideal, or some combination thereof.

Secondly, and more briefly, a word about the *target* of a particular model. The target is the phenomenon or thing that the model is supposed to help clarify. So, in the case of, say, the scale model of a car that is used to test aerodynamics in a wind tunnel for a proposed new model vehicle, the car is the model, and the proposed new vehicle is the target.

The hermeneutical function of models, and the fact that the model and target phenomena can both be real or imaginary, is not formally expressed by MODEL but is commensurate with it. In fact, MODEL is a conceptually thin description, and deliberately so. It is consistent with a range of different views about the nature and purpose of models as these things have been understood in recent theology. For theologians have rather different accounts of the sort of things models are (where they are willing to countenance such conceptual structures) and what the target of such models should be.

Theological models

It might seem obvious that theologians should adopt the language of models that has been so successful in the natural sciences. But not everyone sees things that way. Some theologians are hostile to what they regard as a kind of Trojan horse – bringing in ways of thinking alien to theology, or that may somehow assimilate theology to a kind of philosophical project – perhaps even a kind of rationalism. (Some, motivated by Barthian concerns about the shape and place of theology, might have this worry.) Others think that the purpose of theological statements is distorted or mischaracterized if we adopt the language of models. (Here I have in mind theologians who think that theology is primarily concerned with producing a coherent grammar for Christian praxis, which is a view often associated with post-liberalism. On this view, models might be thought a distortion of theology—a kind of category mistake, if you will.) Still others may be concerned that models simply fail as conceptual tools in theology because the target of theological statements, namely, the Deity, is not accessible to human ratiocination in a way that would be necessary for us to be able to construct a model. (For instance, one might think that God is not a being that can be modelled by creatures, or that we know too little about the divine nature to model it, or that model-making is a kind of incipient idolatry because all it can hope to achieve is the formation of a kind of golem, rather than a verisimilitude of the divine. Theologians who are drawn to strong versions of apophatic theology might think something like this.)

There are various reasons for these worries. One might be to do with *the cognitive function of models* in relation to their targets, which is an epistemic concern.[6] Here the

---

[6]For discussion of this point, see Frigg and Hartmann, 'Models in Science'.

objection might be: what do models in theology deliver? What help can they provide us in making theological statements? What is their cognitive value? And does the cognitive value of the model track some value in the target? (In other words, is the cognitive value we ascribe to the model a value to be found in the target as well, or only in the model?) Another concern might have to do with the *ontological status* of the model in relation to its target. Then the worry might be: what do we think our models commit us to (if anything), theologically speaking? Do they map onto reality in some way so that we may track things about the divine, or do they have a merely instrumental value? Perhaps they are fictions of a sort along the lines of fictional characters like Sherlock Holmes and the worlds they inhabit. Here too, we can distinguish between the ontological commitments entailed by the model and the extent to which these ontological commitments track some property of the target. For instance, suppose I favour a social model of the Trinity which entails that in God there are three centres of consciousness and will. Does this imply that there *really are* three centres of consciousness and will in God's nature, which is the target of this model? Is the relation of the model to the target isomorphic in this respect, or is the model merely a kind of approximation to its target in this respect and therefore does not require strict fidelity?[7]

With these semantic, cognitive and ontological concerns in mind, let us consider three broad theological approaches to models construed along the lines of MODEL, finessed with the comments we have culled from Weisberg concerning the interpretive aspect of models and the fact that they may target real or imagined phenomena. The three principal ontological commitments in this context are: *instrumentalism, antirealism* and *realism*. These I take to be broad categories that include a range of different possible options. They may not be the only logically possible options. But they do represent what I take to be some of the most important live options (to borrow William James's famous phrase) that are the subject of theological discussion, and that are relevant to analytic theologians.

To begin with, let us consider the prospect of adopting MODEL along with an instrumental view of theological statements. On an instrumental view, as with instrumentalism in the philosophy of science, one is not committed to the reality of the entities posited in the model. It is merely a useful way of conceiving the matter that has a certain instrumental value – that is, as a means to some further end, such as the construction of a coherent grammar by means of which churches and Christians may govern their liturgies and praxis. Such instrumentalism may be anti-realist in nature. That is, it may bottom out as a way of thinking about models that does not commit the theologian to the existence of the target entities posited in the model. For, according to theological anti-realism, such entities do not actually refer to anything that is mind

---

[7] For instance, is the model a fictional one? It models an imaginary entity, rather than a real one – much as one might offer a model of a Greek god or a member of the Asgardian pantheon. Theological fictionalists might take this sort of view. See, e.g., Robin Le Poidevin, *Religious Fictionalism*. Cambridge Elements in Philosophy of Religion, ed. Yujin Nagasawa (Cambridge: Cambridge University Press, 2019).

independent.⁸ On one way of reading her work, this appears to be how Sally McFague thinks about models. They are, on her view, extended metaphors. But they are metaphors all the way down, so to speak.⁹ Of course, one can have a realist account of metaphors. But often in theological discourse, the use of metaphorical language has been opposed to realist language (and that is often how it seems McFague uses such language).¹⁰ Those who think of models in instrumentalist terms may take this way of thinking in an anti-realist direction. Then, the entities posited in the model are literally constituents of a mental world built by the theologian. Gordon Kaufman is one recent theologian who seems to think that such imaginative ways of thinking about doctrine are the right way to conceive of the theological task, and of model-building in theology. He writes,

> Theologians should attempt to construct conceptions of God, humanity, and the world appropriate for the orientation of contemporary human life. As we have been observing, these notions are (and always have been) human creations, human imaginative constructions; they are our ideas, not God's. What is needed in each new generation is an understanding of God adequate for and appropriate to human life in the world within which it finds itself, so that human devotion and loyalty, service and worship, may be directed toward God rather than to the many idols that so easily attract attention and interest.¹¹

Allowing that doctrines are human constructions does not necessarily imply anti-realism. Many theological realists would claim that all doctrine is the product of human creativity, being ectypal. The difference is that such theologians would also want to say that theological creations should be modelled as far as possible after the divine archetype given in revelation. By contrast, Kaufman seems to be committed to a kind of anti-realism: human conceptual constructions in theology and theological model-building are brought forth anew for each generation in pictures and metaphors that communicate religious truth in changing circumstances. Although this too might be understood along critically-realist¹² lines, it appears as a matter of fact that Kaufman was more of a thoroughgoing anti-realist.

---

⁸For discussion of this, see Michael C. Rea, 'Realism in Theology and Metaphysics', in *Belief and Metaphysics*, ed. Conor Cunningham and Peter Candler (London: SCM Press, 2007), 323–44; John A. Keller, 'Theological Anti-Realism', *Journal of Analytic Theology* 2 (2014): 13–42; and Alvin Plantinga, 'How to Be an Anti-realist' (Presidential Address), *Proceedings of the American Philosophical Association* 80 (1983): 47–70.
⁹"Models are dominant, comprehensive metaphors with organizing, structural potential". McFague, *Metaphorical Theology*, 193.
¹⁰Although for a realist account of metaphor in theology in modern theology, see Janet Martin Soskice, *Metaphor and Religious Language* (Oxford: Oxford University Press, 1987).
¹¹Gordon D. Kaufman, *In the Face of Mystery: A Constructive Theology* (Cambridge, MA: Harvard University Press, 1993), 31.
¹²By critical realism, I mean (very roughly) the notion that there is some mind-independent entity to which particular human conceptualizations point, although no one conceptual picture gets at the whole truth of the matter. Imagine several viewers of a sculpture reporting their views of the work. The particular vantage

There is more than one way to be an anti-realist about model-building in theology, however. One could also be a fictionalist about the entities posited in a given model.[13] As Robin Le Poidevin has recently characterized it, according to the religious fictionalist, 'religious statements are propositional, and so evaluable as true or false. But they are only true within a fiction – the Christian fiction, or Buddhist fiction, and so on. Insofar as they are fact-stating, they are only fictional fact-stating, and so not answerable to a reality which is independent of our beliefs, attitudes or conventions'.[14]

Le Poidevin is concerned with religious belief and religious doctrine, as well as religious practice. But we can extend his point to theological model-building as well. On this way of thinking, anti-realism is consistent with propositional attitudes towards the content of theological models, provided one thinks of the entities posited in the model as being part of a fiction. In a similar manner, one might adopt propositional attitudes towards models of, say, the metaphysics of Star Wars, while acknowledging that the entities treated by such models are themselves aspects of a fiction, in this case, the science-fiction world first imagined by George Lucas.

However, theological world-building need not be anti-realist or even instrumental in nature. I take it that many theologians think that there is a mind-independent world, that we can successfully refer to that world in our theology, and that theological model-building is consistent with these theologically realist commitments. This may be true even if, as I think is the case, theological models are merely proxies for the truth of the matter. One can be committed to the (mind-independent) truth of, say, the Trinity, and yet think that at best our theologizing about the Trinity will inevitably yield models that are approximations to the truth of the matter, rather than the truth plain and simple. On this way of thinking, theological models are proxies that stand in for the truth of the matter.[15] Though strictly speaking false, they point toward something that is true. There may be principled theological reasons for thinking this is the case, reasons having to do with commitments that are, at root, realist in nature. For instance, one might think that

---

they have will shape their view of the artwork in important respects and (plausibly) no one vantage yields a complete account of the work of art, though each offers some partial account of it. Critical realism (as I am using the term here) presumes that something like this picture is true with respect to different accounts of a given entity – in this case, theological entities like the Trinity or incarnation, and the doctrines that express these truths. A thorough account of critical realism in theology can be found in the unpublished PhD dissertation of Jesse Gentile, *Bridge Building in Theological Method: Critical Realism and Analytic Theology in Conversation* (Pasadena: Fuller Theological Seminary, 2023).
[13]There is a lively debate about fictionalist accounts of models in the philosophy of science literature. See, e.g. Fiora Salis, 'The New Fiction View of Models', *British Journal for the Philosophy of Science* 72, no. 3 (2021): 717–42.
[14]Robin Le Poidevin, *Religious Fictionalism*, 25.
[15]Compare Ian Barbour: 'Models and theories are abstract symbol systems, which inadequately and selectively represent particular aspects of the world for specific purposes. This view preserves the scientist's realistic intent while recognizing that models and theories are imaginative human constructs. Models, on this reading, are to be taken seriously but not literally; they are neither literal pictures nor useful fictions but limited and inadequate ways of imagining what is not observable. They make tentative ontological claims that there are entities in the world something like those postulated in the models.' Barbour, *Religion and Science*, 115.

the Trinity is a mystery that no created intellect can penetrate, and that our theologizing should be done apropos of this assumption. One way in which the theologian might build a model of the Trinity on this basis is to begin with the supposition that all our theologizing about the Trinity is fallible, fragile and liable to fail and fall conceptually short in significant respects.[16] We are, so it might be thought, fallen human beings incapable of apprehending God. Yet we can approach God, so to speak, by attempting to provide constructive approximations to the truth of the matter that reflect the teaching of Holy Writ and other sources of theological authority, such as conciliar and credal pronouncements. Much Trinitarian model-building in recent analytic theology attempts to do just that.[17]

So, commitment to the MODEL is consistent with instrumentalism in theological model-building, with anti-realism in theological model-building, and realism in theological model-building. These are not necessarily all the logically possible options. For instance, one might think that some sort of theological *arealism* is the right approach to such meta-theological matters. In this context, arealism involves the refusal to make metaphysical commitments one way or another on whether the entities posited in a particular theological model are, in fact, mind-independent or not. Some traditional theologians seem to speak of the divine nature in a way that suggests such an approach. One example of this is the sort of high-octane apophaticism one finds in much of the Christian tradition, which maintains that fallen human beings are incapable of apprehending the divine essence and can only fallibly and incompletely theologize about the nature of God, or about how God appears to us – how the Deity is mediated by means of revelation or signs, such as the burning bush, or the words of a prophet, or by means of the incarnation.

Two case studies: Trinity and incarnation

This completes our overview of theological models. I now want to illustrate the points made in the previous section with two examples of how models have been used in recent analytic theology. For it is one thing to consider how models function at the metatheological level. It is another to see whether that maps onto how things work in a

---

[16] I have attempted to do something like this in *Analyzing Doctrine*, ch. 4. This approach has been recently critiqued by Sameer Yadav. We will return to this matter, and to Yadav's criticisms, in Chapter 7.
[17] Some highlights in chronological order: Richard Swinburne, *The Christian God* (Oxford: Oxford University Press, 1994); the essays collected together in Thomas H. McCall and Michael C. Rea, eds, *Philosophical and Theological Essays on the Trinity* (Oxford: Oxford University Press, 2009); Thomas H. McCall, *Which Trinity? Whose Monotheism? Philosophical and Systematic Theologians on the Metaphysics of Trinitarian Theology* (Grand Rapids: Eerdmans, 2010); and William Hasker, *Metaphysics and the Tripersonal God*. Oxford Studies in Analytic Theology (Oxford: Oxford University Press, 2013). See also the relevant essays in Michael C. Rea, ed., *Oxford Readings in Philosophical Theology: Volume 1: Trinity, Incarnation, and Atonement* (Oxford: Oxford University Press, 2009).

given literature. Thus far, I have argued that models are simplified conceptual frameworks or descriptions by means of which complex sets of data, systems and processes may be organized and understood. They have an important hermeneutical function. Moreover, the model and target phenomena can both be real or imaginary. I have indicated that there is a cognitive and epistemic aspect to understanding models, and an ontological aspect as well. And I have attempted to give a rough-and-ready taxonomy of different options consistent with this account of models in Christian theology. This includes instrumentalist, anti-realist, realist and arealist approaches.

Now, in principle, an analytic theologian could take any one of these approaches because (in my view, at least) analytic theology does not commit its practitioners to any substantive theological views. It is a set of methodological commitments, or a sensibility of a sort, supported by a particular intellectual culture. There are analytic theologians from most of the different strands of the Christian tradition. In this respect, it is an ecumenical enterprise – perhaps because its methodological commitments are so open-textured. Nevertheless, it transpires that there are very few analytic theologians who are anything other than theological realists. The vast majority of analytic theologians are, in fact, traditional theists who maintain that God is a mind-independent reality, the creator and sustainer of the world.[18]

This is reflected in the sort of models analytic theologians have developed in their work to date. Two notable examples in the literature of the past two decades are the work that has been done on the Trinity and on the incarnation, two central and defining Christian dogmas. I will touch briefly on each in turn.[19]

There has been work on a number of different accounts of the Trinity among analytic theologians, as well as helpful work done in classifying various extant views of the Trinity.[20] Unlike recent non-analytic systematic theology, much of the focus of this work

---

[18]*Caveat lector*: some analytic theologians are theistic personalists. They think God is a maximal person, on analogy with human persons. Other analytic theologians are what we might call classical theists, such as Thomists. For many Thomists, theistic personalism may be a species of theism, but it is also a kind of idolatry because its practitioners imagine that God is an individual person like created persons, only perfect and unlimited in power and knowledge. But, say the Thomists, God is not in a genus; he is not a being like creatures, and there are no distinctions to be had between his essence and his attributes. Thus, theistic personalism rests on a grave theological mistake. For their part, theistic personalists are quick to point out the fact that there seem to be serious conceptual problems with aspects of Thomistic classical theism (e.g. divine simplicity, the pure act account of the divine nature) that are not easily resolved. Thus, when I say that most analytic theologians are traditional theists, I mean by this that most presume God is a mind-independent reality, the creator and sustainer of the world. There are still significant differences of view on how these claims should be construed, as the recent debate between theistic personalists and classical theists among analytic theologians attests. For a classic theistic personalist account of the divine nature, see Richard Swinburne, *The Coherence of Theism*, 2nd ed. (Oxford: Oxford University Press, 1993 [1977]). For a contemporary version of classical theism of the Thomist variety, see Eleonore Stump, *Aquinas* (New York: Routledge, 2003).
[19]There are other places in the recent analytic theology literature that discuss these issues and that are relevant here. See William Wood, 'Modelling Mystery', who does a terrific job of assessing the merits of the constitution model of the Trinity; and James M. Arcadi who provides an overview of recent work on the incarnation in 'Recent Developments in Analytic Christology', *Philosophy Compass* 13, no. 4 (2018): e12480.
[20]See the studies in McCall and Rea, *Philosophical and Theological Essays on the Trinity*.

has been on how to understand the relation between the divine unity and triunity – what is often referred to as the threeness-oneness problem. It is usually thought to be the sign of a successful research programme that it generates new ways of thinking about old problems. Analytic theology has already generated new models of the Trinity. This is no mean feat, given the number of minds that have tackled the dogma of the Trinity, and the length of time that it has been the subject of intellectual inquiry. One particularly striking example of such new model building is the *constitution account* of the Trinity that has been put forward by Michael Rea and Jeff Brower, building on some earlier work in relative identity and the Trinity by Peter van Inwagen and Peter Geach, among others.[21] Rea and Brower suggest that we apply a version of Aristotelian hylomorphism to the Trinity, so that the divine persons of the Trinity are 'constituted' by the 'stuff' of divinity, rather like an Aristotelian form relative to some parcel of matter. They use the example of a block of marble fashioned into a statue that is also a pillar in a building. There is the marble stuff that composes each of these items, and then there are the 'forms' of the block, the pillar and the statue that organize the same parcel of matter in three distinct ways. Thus, we have sameness and difference in a way that is relevant to the dogma of the Trinity. Three distinct 'forms', one parcel of matter that is composed by these forms, and each form having different persistence conditions. For instance, if the statue is effaced, the block may still stand as a pillar. Apply this to the doctrine of the Trinity. The marble stuff is like the divine nature; the different 'forms' like the divine persons each of whom is distinct and yet 'composed' by the same divine stuff. We have sameness of substance, but difference of persons.

Inevitably, this view has come in for some criticism, but we need not pursue that here.[22] What is important for our purposes is that we can see in this example how the application of a new model of the Trinity to a long-standing fundamental problem in the doctrine of the Trinity may help illuminate important issues about the divine nature that are the mark of a vibrant research programme. Although Rea and Brower are theological realists, one could take their model and adapt it to the needs of an instrumentalist, an anti-realist, a fictionalist or even an arealist.[23] (I leave this task as homework for the reader.)

---

[21]See Michael C. Rea and Jeffrey Brower, 'Material Constitution and the Trinity', *Faith and Philosophy* 22, no. 1 (2005): 57–76, Peter van Inwagen, 'And Yet They Are Not Three Gods But One God', in *Philosophy and the Christian Faith*, ed. Thomas V. Morris (Notre Dame: University of Notre Dame Press, 1981), 241–78, and Peter Geach, *Reference and Generality*, 3rd ed (Ithaca: Cornell University Press, 1980).

[22]Interested readers may like to consult the following responses to the constitution account (in order of appearance): William Lane Craig, 'Does the Problem of Material Constitution Illuminate the Doctrine of the Trinity', *Faith and Philosophy* 22, no. 1 (2005): 77–86; Christopher Hughes, 'Defending the Consistency of the Doctrine of the Trinity', in McCall and Rea, *Philosophical and Theological Essays on the Trinity*, 293–313; William Hasker, 'Constitution and the Trinity: The Brower-Rea Proposal', *Faith and Philosophy* 27, no. 3 (2010): 321–9; and Brian Leftow, 'The Trinity is Unconstitutional', *Religious Studies* 54, no. 3 (2018): 359–76.

[23]An option that may be worth further consideration in this regard: combine the constitution account of the Trinity with the kind of theological arealism expressed by Jonathan Jacobs, an Orthodox Christian philosopher, in his paper 'The Ineffable, Inconceivable, and Incomprehensible God: Fundamentality and

Metatheology

The doctrine of the incarnation has been another topic that has exercised analytic theologians. Here too, several different models of the incarnation have been mooted, most of which are explicitly attempts to express the teaching of classical Christology, as summarized in the two natures doctrine of the Council of Chalcedon of AD 451. On this way of thinking, Christ is the divine person of God the Son, subsisting in two natures: his divine nature, which he has essentially, and his human nature, which he assumes at the first moment of incarnation. One recent model of the incarnation that has been developed by analytic theologians is the compositional account. There is more than one way to construe the compositional account. Here is one of them.[24]

Suppose we think of Christ as composed of different 'parts'. He has his human nature and his divine nature. And yet there is only one person 'in' Christ, so to speak, that is, the person of God the Son. How are we to make sense of this? Perhaps we should think of Christ as a concrete particular with a concrete human nature which comprises a human body and soul rightly related. This human nature is assumed at the incarnation by God the Son. Thus, we have a view according to which in Christ there are the following concrete parts: his human nature, comprising his human body and soul, rightly related; and the person of God the Son, who is hypostatically united to this concrete human nature. One oddity of this view is that *Christ* is a name that refers to the mereological whole comprising these various parts. A second oddity is that God the Son is not identical with his human nature. Having said that, one potential advantage of this view is that it doesn't necessarily compromise divine simplicity, for no substantive change occurs to God the Son at the first moment of incarnation. What is more, it doesn't mean that God the Son is encumbered by physical parts that are somehow 'part' of him either.

The analytic theologians associated with this view seem to think of it in a theologically realist sense, as an attempt to track with fidelity central claims concerning the metaphysical relation between the divinity and humanity of Christ. But one need not construe it in this way. With some minor adjustments, it could be used by an instrumentalist, anti-realist or arealist. As with the constitutional account of the Trinity, there have been objections to this version of the compositional view of the incarnation. But, once again, we need not pursue those worries here.[25] It is sufficient that we have drawn attention to one important use of theological modelling in the recent discussions of the incarnation in the analytic-theological literature that is illuminating and that helps illustrate how analytic discussion of this topic has borne fruit.

Apophatic Theology', in *Oxford Studies in Philosophy of Religion* 6, ed. Jonathan L. Kvanvig (Oxford: Oxford University Press, 2015), 158–76.

[24]See, e.g., Brian Leftow, 'A Timeless God Incarnate', in *The Incarnation*, ed. Stephen T. Davis, Daniel Kendall SJ, and Gerald O'Collins (Oxford: Oxford University Press, 2002), 273–302, and Oliver D. Crisp, *Divinity and Humanity: The Incarnation Reconsidered* (Cambridge: Cambridge University Press, 2007).

[25]Interested readers might like to consult the following: Thomas Senor, 'The Compositional Account of the Incarnation', *Faith and Philosophy* 24, no. 1 (2007): 52–71, and Jonathan Hill, 'Compositionalism, Nestorianism, and the Principle of No Co-member Parts', *Religious Studies* 59 (2023): 261–75.

The value of theological models

What, then, is the value of theological models as I have outlined them here? What is achieved in the use of such models? To my way of thinking, the use of models in theology is like the use of models in the sciences. That is, theological models provide us with helpful ways of making sense (to the extent that we can make sense[26]) of complex material, so that we can use this material in hypotheses, constructive argument and theorizing. I have suggested we think of theological modelling along the lines of

> MODEL: a simplified conceptual framework or description by means of which complex sets of data, systems, and processes may be organised and understood.

This may be construed in various ways, as we have seen, because MODEL is metaphysically underdetermined. But that reflects how models are used in theology. I have also suggested that models, including theological models, are representational, analogous, hermeneutical in nature, have a certain fidelity to aspects of the thing they represent, and take many forms. I suggest that much of the unhappiness about the use of models in theology stems from a rather flat-footed way of thinking about models, which does not take into sufficient account the different ways in which models are understood and construed in the current literature. In the case of the two sorts of theological models I have considered from recent analytic theology, I was careful to note that these are only two of a range of different models that have been put forward, and that these models may also be thought of as underdetermined in important respects that bear upon the question of the fidelity of these models to their target phenomena.

There is nothing to stop a particular theologian from taking the constitutional model of the Trinity and thinking of it in, say, fictionalist terms as a model that clearly articulates an account of the dogma consistent with the letter of Nicene orthodoxy so that its fidelity is to the propositional content of the creed as traditionally understood. However, being a fictionalist account, it would not make the additional claim that the bare propositional commitments of Nicene orthodoxy expressed in the creed refer to some mind-independent phenomenon. It is an open question why someone might approach matters in this way, and it is certainly true to say that very few analytic theologians working today would be sympathetic to such a move. As I have already said, the intellectual culture of analytic theology is broadly traditional and orthodox in its theological commitments – including commitment to some sort of theological realism. Still, that is not to say a fictionalist interpretation of these things cannot be had; it can. The more important question is whether such an account is the best approximation to the truth of the matter.

---

[26] As William Wood and Sameer Yadav, among others, have argued, model building in theology is consistent with a high tolerance for apophaticism. See Wood, 'Modeling Mystery' and Yadav, 'Mystical Experience and the Apophatic Attitude', *The Journal of Analytic Theology* 4 (2016): 17–43.

Metatheology

For the vast majority of practising analytic theologians, the answer to that question will be in the negative. But, in a way, the use of doctrinal models makes that judgement easier to arrive at by clarifying some of its central conceptual commitments. That, it seems to me, is one good reason to think the use of models in theology has an important, and helpful, place.

CHAPTER 3
THEOLOGICAL AMBITION

What are the ambitions of theology? Put differently, what do we think we are doing when we do theology – what is its goal? Having set out an account of metatheology and examined an important conceptual tool in the use of models, in this chapter I shall address myself to this metatheological question about theological teleology. It is an important one. For, although it may seem rather abstract and removed from the concrete matters of religious beliefs or doctrines, it gets at what the theologian thinks she is doing when she sets about trying to explicate particular beliefs or doctrines – which is a central question about the rationale of theological inquiry in the Christian tradition.

The argument proceeds as follows. The first section considers the general question of the ambitions of theology. Building on the previous chapter, I argue that theology is a realist enterprise. This has several components, including that it is a truth-apt and truth-aimed intellectual discourse that seeks to give an account of some mind-independent thing, namely, God. Yet, theological arguments are frail reeds. For, given our limited epistemic vantage, God remains a mystery to us as creatures. For this reason, so it seems to me, theological argument should proceed with caution. We must calibrate our ambitions to our capacity to know and understand the object of our inquiries. In the case of God, this capacity is severely restricted in at least two respects. The first has to do with our intellectual capacity, which is limited and finite. We are ill-suited to understand, let alone comprehend, the Deity. Second, there is the limitation of data on which to base any theological theories. This is true even if Scripture is or contains divine revelation. What the Bible says about God does not yield a single, unambiguous conceptual picture of the Deity. Thus, a chastened theological realism that concedes the provisionality and fallibility of all theological statements seems to be the right sort of approach for theologians to adopt.

How then should the theologian go about the task of theological construction? In the previous chapter, we saw that the theologian is concerned with conceptual world-building, often by way of constructing models. I return to the question of the use of theological models in the second section. As I indicated in the previous chapter, the use of such conceptual models can be realist provided we think that the target of our model is mind-independent. That said, this realist ambition seems problematic if our models are merely proxies for the truth of the matter. For on the one hand, the theologian with a theologically realist ambition aims to better understand the mind-independent target of the model she constructs. But on the other hand, the model is usually a kind of simplified stand-in for its target. I will argue that one can hold both theological realism and utilise theological models if we properly calibrate our theological efforts, have an appropriate

Metatheology

expectation of what our theologising can achieve, and are clear about the way our theological models exhibit fidelity to their target.

In the third section, I show how the combination of chastened theological realism and the use of models yields an approach to theology that is both coherent and appropriate, given the epistemic constraints that apply to the ambitions of theology outlined in the first section. Once again, I illustrate the theoretical virtues of this account with reference to the central and defining dogma of the Christian faith, namely, the Trinity.

Theological realism and its limits

Let us begin by borrowing a well-worn phrase from Plato. Does theology carve nature at its joints as he proposed his theory of forms did?[1] We might think our best theories ought to be like that – they ought to give us a true account of the world. Some will deny this, of course. There are those who think that all our theorising about a particular domain of intellectual inquiry is at best a way of construing certain phenomena or categorising entities according to conceptual devices of our own making. Some empiricists take this approach. There is the data as it appears to us, and then there is our attempt to organise that data into something that seems coherent in order to make sense of what appears to be the case.[2] But one need not be an empiricist in order to think that our theories about a given domain are purely instrumentalist rather than realist.[3] Instrumentalism is one thing; anti-realism is another. The instrumentalist aims at the provision of adequacy in her theories. Her concern is to ensure that her conceptual frameworks are sufficient to the purpose for which they have been devised. Anti-realism is something different, being a family of views that are wholly constructive. The anti-realist in theology denies that God names a creaturely mind-independent reality. Instead, God is the construction of human minds projected onto the clouds, so to speak. That said, an anti-realist about a particular domain may not necessarily deny that a particular statement that refers to something in that domain lacks a truth value. Such an anti-realist might say something like the following: 'It is true in the world of Sherlock Holmes that Holmes and Watson reside at 221b Baker Street'. After all, there are truths in fiction, including the fiction of Conan Doyle, and there may be truths relative to a particular game or practice even if that practice involves a certain kind of make-believe — such as participatory and immersive role playing games.[4] The same may be true, *mutatis mutandis*, with respect

---

[1] Plato, *Phaedrus* 265e.
[2] Thus, Bas C. van Fraassen, *The Empirical Stance* (New Haven: Yale University Press, 2002), who argues that empiricism should aim at adequacy, not truth.
[3] Nancey Murphy discusses rather different examples in *Theology in the Age of Scientific Reasoning*.
[4] Examples include Dungeons and Dragons and Live Action Role Play (LARPing). An interesting and wide-ranging recent symposium on this topic is Sebastian Deterding and José Zagal, eds, *Role-Playing Game Studies: Transmedia Foundations* (London: Routledge, 2018).

to the domain of theology and its practice in liturgy.[5] Then, there are truths about the practice of theology. There are also truths about doctrines of theology so that the anti-realist can say 'this is orthodox doctrine, whereas this is not for it does not conform to the right norms of Christian doctrine'. But all this is done on the presumption that Christian theology is a kind of immersive and participatory 'game' of a sort – or if not a game, then a practice whose object – God – is fictional.

But let us set questions about theological instrumentalism and theological anti-realism (as well as arealism) to one side in order to focus on theological realism. As I see it, theological realism has the following three fundamental features. The first is that the object of theological inquiry, God, is creaturely mind-independent. In other words, God is not a fictional character, and God is not the creation of human imagination. This blocks theological anti-realism. The second is that at least some of our theological statements about God are apt to predicate objectively true things about God. The third is that true statements about God have realist truth conditions. In other words, saying things like 'God is the creator of the world' is true provided realism about such theological claims, and theological realism itself, is true.[6] The second and third features represent the core constructive components of theological realism and block the theological arealism described in the previous chapter. (Recall that theological arealists prescind from making judgements about realism or anti-realism in theology. They refuse to make metaphysical commitments one way or another on whether the entities posited in a particular theological view or model are, in fact, mind-independent or not.)

Now, a problem with realism in theology is that God is not immediately accessible to human ratiocination. We cannot set about examining God in a theological laboratory to test a hypothesis we have about some aspect of the divine nature. Nevertheless, based on data gleaned from Scripture, tradition, reason and experience, God is usually thought to be invisible, essentially incorporeal, and yet (somehow) omnipresent. God is also traditionally thought to be transcendent. That is, the Deity is above and beyond what we can apprehend. Indeed, in much traditional Christian theology and liturgy, God is said to be ineffable, inconceivable, and incomprehensible.[7] Ineffability means incapable of being expressed in words; inconceivable means incapable of being conceptualised; and incomprehensible means incapable of being comprehended. Strong claims indeed!

---

[5] As Robin le Poidevin argues in *Religious* Fictionalism,

[6] For similar conditions for theological realism, see Michael C. Rea, 'Realism in Theology and Metaphysics', in Rea, *Essays in Analytic Theology, Vol. 1*. Oxford Studies in Analytic Theology (Oxford: Oxford University Press, 2020), 19–35; 19.

[7] An example (borrowed from Jonathan Jacobs): after the confession of faith in the Greek Orthodox Liturgy of St John Chrysostom, the priest intones 'It is proper and right to hymn You, to bless You, to praise You, to give thanks to You, and to worship You in every place of Your dominion. For You, O God, are ineffable, inconceivable, invisible, incomprehensible, existing forever, forever the same, You and Your only-begotten Son and Your Holy Spirit'. The text of the liturgy can be found online at the website of the Greek Orthodox Archdiocese of America, located at: https://www.goarch.org/-/the-divine-liturgy-of-saint-john-chrysostom (last accessed 18/01/24).

Metatheology

All of this raises an obvious epistemic concern. If God is above and beyond us, invisible, inexpressible in words, incapable of being comprehended, and incapable of being conceptualised, then how can we know this? Can theological realism even get off the ground if much of the Christian tradition posits such things of the Deity? Perhaps we need a third option. Thus far, I have mentioned three broad approaches to the theological task, which we have already met in the previous chapter. These are: realist, anti-realist, and arealist approaches. But these can be distinguished from a further position, which we may call *theological nonrealism*.[8] This is the view that God is a mind-independent reality, although we cannot know very much, if anything, about the intrinsic qualities of the divine nature. The Deity is literally beyond our ken, being wholly ineffable, inconceivable, and incomprehensible.[9] What we can say about the divine nature must be done by way of negation — that is, saying what God is *not*. Such an apophatic approach to theology has a long history. One of the fountainheads of high-octane apophaticism is the anonymous medieval divine, Pseudo-Dionysius, who not only delights in theological ascent by negation but in fact thinks of the divine as beyond any ascription. Of God, he writes, 'we should posit and ascribe . . . all the affirmations we make in regard to beings, and, more appropriately, we should negate all these affirmations, since . . . [God] surpasses all being'. What is more, 'we should not conclude that the negations are simply the opposites of the affirmations, but rather that the cause of all is considerably prior to this, beyond privations, beyond every denial, beyond every assertion'.[10]

Upon reading passages of apophatic theology like this one for the first time, the uninitiated is likely to be at something of a loss. How can one predicate things of the divine while at the same time claiming that the divine is beyond all predication? On the face of it, such paradoxical language seems liable to collapse into confusion or even self-referential incoherence. For surely one cannot claim that *S is p, S is not-p, and S is beyond the ascription of p or not-p, including the affirmation that 'S is p, S is not-p, and S is beyond the ascription of p or not-p'* in the same breath and expect to be taken seriously. So, what is the theological neophyte to do?

Thankfully, help is at hand. One plausible way of construing such theological nonrealism is as second-order claims about first-order theological discourse. That is, as claims about claims concerning God. Then, a claim about the ineffability of God would turn out to be a claim about claiming anything substantive of the divine nature. Far from being

---

[8] This is what I called the third option in *Analyzing Doctrine*. Theological non-realism is distinct from arealism in that defenders of this view do make judgements about what we can predicate of the divine nature, whereas arealists prescind or suspend judgement regarding whether God is mind-independent and what the divine nature is like.
[9] For two recent studies of the sort of apophaticism presumed by theological non-realism, see Simon Hewitt, *Negative Theology and Philosophical Analysis: Only the Splendour of Light*. Palgrave Frontiers in Philosophy of Religion (Cham: Palgrave Macmillan, 2020), and Susannah Ticciati, *A New Apophaticism: Augustine and the Redemption of Signs*. Brill Studies in Systematic Theology, Vol. 14 (Leiden: Brill, 2013).
[10] Pseudo-Dionysius, *The Mystical Theology*, I. 2 in *Pseudo-Dionysius: The Complete Works*, trans. Colm Lubheid (Mahwah: Paulist Press, 1987), 136.

incoherent, such strong apophaticism is a means of facilitating our saying *something* meaningful about the reason why we are incapable of saying anything substantive about the divine nature. Such an approach might be thought to be a way of preserving the grammar of Christian Theology, which is a claim about religious language. But the strategy of distinguishing first-order from second-order theological statements could be transposed into a different, and more metaphysical, register.

A version of just such a metaphysical approach has recently been championed by the Christian philosopher, Jonathan Jacobs.[11] He proposes that when we say 'God is ineffable', we mean that statements about the divine nature do not actually refer to something purely fundamental about the divine nature. For, strictly speaking, the divine nature is incapable of being expressed in words. This does not necessarily mean we can say nothing about God. It is just that what we say about God will not be intrinsic to the divine nature. At best, we may say certain things that pick out derived rather than fundamental properties of God. To take a quotidian example, a table has certain derived and apparent properties such as being made of solid wood, being hard to the touch, having a certain fixed shape, and so on. But physicists tell us that such objects are in fact composed of a cloud of particles too small for the naked eye to see. The fundamental properties of the table are not accessible to us and are very different from the derived properties we encounter when we sit at the table to work or to eat. Yet both sorts of properties pick out truths about the table; it is just that not all those truths are (purely) fundamental; some are derived.

When applied to the theological task, this appears to be a promising strategy for addressing concerns about God being above and beyond us, invisible, inexpressible in words, incapable of being comprehended, and incapable of being conceptualised. It turns out that on the metaphysical non-realist view, our theological claims about the divine nature do not have to do with fundamental but derived qualities – those which we may apprehend and experience, like the hardness or solidity of the table. But this strategy does come at considerable cost. For on this way of explicating non-realism, we can say very little about that which is theologically fundamental. As Jacobs observes in summarising this view, 'Every true proposition about how God is intrinsically is non-fundamental. There are no true, fundamental propositions about how God is intrinsically'.[12] This resonates with the high-octane apophaticism of theologians like Pseudo-Dionysius. But it has potentially devastating consequences. For it means that theological statements we normally think of as being fundamentally true of God turn out to be merely derived, including such things as the dogma of the Trinity. And it is surely a high cost to any Christian metatheological theory worthy of the name that it entails God is not essentially and fundamentally triune.

That said, it is important not to mischaracterize such views. They are non-realist rather than anti-realist precisely because those who hold them do indeed think human

---

[11]See Jonathan D. Jacobs' proceeds in 'The Ineffable, Inconceivable, and Incomprehensible God'.
[12]Jacobs, 'The Ineffable, Inconceivable, and Incomprehensible God', 165.

creatures are capable of making true statements about God. It is just that – to reiterate the point – any such statement will not be purely fundamentally true of the divine nature. Jacobs again:

> We can, using non-fundamental propositions, describe God correctly. We can say lots of true things about how God is intrinsically. He is wise, loving. He is three in hypostasis, one in ousia. Such propositions need not be metaphorical. They can be strictly, literally true. And they can be importantly true. We can know them, and understand them. Some may be more fundamental than others, but God is ineffable because no matter what we say truly, we have failed to assert a perfectly fundamental truth. God is non-fundamentally effable, and fundamentally ineffable.[13]

From my point of view, and I think from the point of view of many in the Christian tradition, this is a sophisticated way of trying to tackle the issues raised by the claims that God is above and beyond us, invisible, inexpressible in words, incapable of being comprehended, and incapable of being conceptualised. But its costs are too great. For by my lights, Christian theologians ought to confess that the Trinity is an essential and fundamental feature of the divine nature.

However, all is not lost. Perhaps we can help ourselves to some of the key insights of non-realism while remaining within the bounds of theological realism – an approach that we might call *chastened theological realism*. On this view, what we can know of the divine nature is very meagre, but not negligible. To an extent, then, the cautious approach of the non-realist is warranted. Yet, according to the chastened theological realist, we *can* know some things that are intrinsically true of the divine nature, such as that God is triune. In order to motivate the argument, let us turn to a thought experiment familiar to those whose leisure is at least partly spent in the consumption of science fiction. Call it the *first contact story*. It goes like this:

> FIRST CONTACT STORY: Humanity establishes first contact with an alien species via a strange obelisk that appears in orbit around Earth. The artefact is visited and studied by human astronauts but its nature, and its makers, remain a mystery. It is impervious to attempts to penetrate it, has no obvious openings, and appears to be composed of materials unknown to human natural science. Nevertheless, what is clear is that the species in question is far beyond human intelligence with advanced technology that is incomprehensible to the human scientific community.

No doubt we have all come across some version of this fictional trope, courtesy of great writers of science fiction such as Ursula K. Le Guin, Arthur C. Clarke, Carl Sagan, or Isaac Asimov. What is salient for our purposes is that such first contact stories have an

---

[13]Ibid., 167.

affinity to chastened theological realism. The chastened theological realist believes she encounters God. Yet God is deeply mysterious and is impervious to our attempts to penetrate and understand the divine nature, which is in important respects beyond our ken. Does that mean we can know nothing intrinsic to the divine nature? No, it does not. Consider the strange obelisk once more. Suppose that after remaining suspended in orbit for some days, it disappears from radar screens without human scientists ever getting a chance to properly analyse the interior of the object. Even with so little known of it, we can still predicate certain qualities of the obelisk that would seem to be fundamental to it. For one thing, it is clearly the product of some extra-terrestrial intelligence' and has a certain mass, configuration, and power source. For another, it is clearly an object that has been deliberately transported to an Earth orbit from some great distance and then removed. Both of these are fairly important claims about basic and fundamental qualities of the obelisk.

Now, return once more to the question of the divine nature. The chastened realist thinks we can know a number of things about God that imply fundamental divine qualities. This includes the claim that God is a creaturely mind-independent necessary being. But in addition to this, we can know certain things about the nature of God because God *reveals* certain things about Godself. One of these, so most Christians think, is that Jesus of Nazareth is God Incarnate. Another is that God is triune. A third is that God has certain essential attributes such as being good, loving, and faithful. These are non-trivial and essential qualities of God that feature in Christian doctrines built in part upon a deposit of testimonial evidence found in the teachings of the Apostles and Prophets in Scripture as witnesses to the incarnation and to divine revelation.

Thus, chastened realism has certain advantages over non-realism when it comes to knowing at least some of the essential or fundamental qualities of God. Even so, it seems appropriate for those who opt for this approach to bear in mind that our epistemic grasp of theological matters is fragile and provisional at best. In other words, the chastened realist will also hold to *theological fallibilism*, according to which the doctrines that ecclesial communities form and defend are incomplete and potentially mistaken. For they are the doctrines of fallen human beings. This goes for all Christian doctrine. We cannot be conclusively certain that the two natures doctrine of the incarnation is the right way to understand how God became human in Christ. Nor can we be absolutely certain that our grasp of the triunity of God is the right way to understand the divine nature. The fact that there are other ways of thinking about these nodal issues in the history of Christian theology should give even the most sanguine theologian pause for thought. As Oliver Cromwell famously wrote to the General Assembly of the Church of Scotland in a rather different context, we should always 'think it possible that we may be mistaken'[14] when it comes to our apprehension of a particular doctrine or Christian teaching.

---

[14]Cromwell wrote, 'I beseech thee in the bowels of Christ, think it possible that you may be mistaken'. Letter to the General Assembly of the Kirk of Scotland, August 3, 1650. The text is reproduced on the website of the

Metatheology

Clearly, such provisionality and fallibilism in doctrine do not necessarily mean we can know nothing about the divine nature. But it does mean we should proceed with caution and a certain irenic spirit when it comes to dealing with those with whom we disagree. We can summarise the theologically chastened realist position like this:

> CHASTENED THEOLOGICAL REALISM: Theological realism can be characterised as the conjunction of three claims. First, that God is a (creaturely) mind-independent thing. Second, that at least some of our theological statements about God are apt to predicate objectively true things about God. Third, that true statements about God have realist truth conditions. Theological realism is chastened provided the theologian holds that what we can know of the divine nature is limited, but not negligible. We can know some things that are fundamentally true of the divine nature, such as that God is triune. Core Christian doctrines depend in important respects on the testimony of Scripture. Nevertheless, our grasp of the teaching of Scripture, and our attempts to understand core Christian doctrines may be mistaken in important respects. Thus, our theologising should proceed with caution, cognisant of the fallibilism attending the formation of Christian doctrine.

Models for theological construction

Well then, how should constructive Christian Theology proceed? There are various options, which may depend in some respects on context and audience (a child's catechism is, after all, rather different from the *Church Dogmatics*). Constructive theology often proceeds by way of models.[15] As I argued in the previous chapter, models are simplified conceptual frameworks or descriptions by means of which complex sets of data, systems, and processes may be organised and understood.[16] Usually, such models are presented as a kind of conceptual 'picture', rather like the visual representation of an atom in a physics textbook. But models are only approximations to the truth of the matter. The picture of an atom in a physics textbook approximates to an atom, but it is not strictly speaking a picture of an atom. It represents key features of an atom in a fashion that makes it easily comprehensible, for no-one has seen an atom with the naked eye. This does not make a model useless. But it does mean that we should treat models conservatively. They perform a particular conceptual task by approximating to the truth of the matter. But

---

Cromwell Association, located at: https://www.olivercromwell.org/Letters_and_speeches/letters/Letter_129.pdf (last accessed January 18, 2024).

[15] As I argued in Crisp, *Analyzing Doctrine* and in Chapter 2.

[16] There is some overlap in this section with the previous chapter, but I think there is some virtue in reiterating the issues here.

they are not identical with the truth of the matter. They are, rather, *approximations* to the truth.

Nevertheless, models are representational. The model airplane shares sufficient features with a real airplane that we say that it looks like an actual airplane. Yet, at the same time, we are also aware that the model airplane is only analogous to the real thing. It is like and unlike an actual aircraft. It has stubby wings of the right shape, a fuselage, a tailplane, undercarriage, cockpit and so on. But none of these things are in the right proportion; it is not aerodynamic, and it has no engine or internal space for passengers since it is made of solid wood. There is also a hermeneutical dimension to understanding models. Their fidelity to their target is an important factor in assessing the uses to which they can be put. Thus, the wooden toy plane has characteristics superficially like an actual airplane. But it is not supposed to *fly*; it is a child's toy. Its use dictates how we interpret its role as a model. Of course, models need not be representations of real or physical objects. A diorama of the rooms shared by Holmes and Watson at 221b Baker Street represents a fictional setting; a model of a hylomorphic soul represents something that is immaterial; and so on.

Apply this understanding of models to the theological task. It seems to me that model-building in theology is consistent with theological realism provided one thinks that the target of the model being constructed is some (creaturely) mind-independent thing and that the model bears an appropriate relation of fidelity to its target. In a similar way, the model of an atom in a physics textbook is a simplified description of something more complex, which the scientific realist thinks exists independently of the model. Although the model is only a proxy for an actual atom and is not, in fact, a complete description of an atom, according to the scientific realist it nevertheless refers to actual things called atoms, which are the target of the model. The scientific realist sees the diagram of the atom in the textbook and thinks that in some measure it represents some of the qualities possessed by actual atoms.

Theologians, particularly systematic and constructive theologians, are concerned with conceptual world-building. They set out a case for a conception of the shape of Christian doctrine as a whole or of some specific doctrine. The models they construct to understand Christian doctrine better are only approximations to the truth of the matter. But most theologians believe that there is a truth of the matter, and that truth (at least, with reference to the existence and nature of the Deity) refers to something that is mind-independent (i.e. God). Just as models in the natural sciences are generated in part to facilitate greater conceptual grip on a particular set of data, so in theology the theologian is concerned to generate models that do something very similar. The data in question is rather different, however. For the scientist, it is some aspect of the natural world. For the theologian concerned with formulating Christian doctrine, it is normally some aspect of a putative supernatural world. The scientist considers the 'book of Nature', which supplies the raw data for her work. The theologian focuses on sources or repositories of theological claims and testimony that are authoritative, in Scripture and the tradition.

However, an objection can be raised to this attempt to marry model-building in theology with theological realism. The heart of the objection is that the concatenation of these claims is unstable. For model-building, as I have outlined it, involves the generation of conceptual pictures that approximate to reality whereas the theological realist is interested in better understanding the mind-independent reality of God. So, it looks like the view I am espousing wants to have it both ways: it wants both the conceptual wiggle room to speak about God in terms that are not strictly speaking veridical, and it wants to hold onto a conception of the theological task as a realist one. Though these things appear superficially commensurate, a more careful assessment suggests there are deeper inconsistencies. For, so the objection goes, the person who is engaged in the building of conceptual approximations to the truth is not a theological realist at all — at least, not in terms of the theological constructions for which they argue.

I have already indicated that models can be misused or misapplied when the fidelity of the model to its target is not made clear at the outset. Provided we are clear about the way in which the model exhibits fidelity to its target, we should be clear about how or in what manner the model simplifies the complex data of its target, as is the case with the toy model airplane or the textbook picture of an atom. When constructing doctrinal models in theology, we need to be clear at the outset that our models are approximations and that they target specific things about the divine nature. Although historic theologians do not speak in terms of models and targets, they too understood that our conception of the divine nature and the divine nature are two distinct things, as well as that our limited epistemic vantage means our attempts to conceive the divine nature will only result in approximations to the truth of the matter. We saw this in the non-realism of Pseudo-Dionysius. But we can see a similar perspective at work elsewhere too. For instance, in his *Monologion*, Anselm of Canterbury says that God is 'uniquely whatever he is, having nothing in common with his creatures' so that 'if any word is ever applied to him in common with others, it must undoubtedly be understood to have a different signification'.[17] In other words, human words applied to the divine nature have to be in some measure 'stretched' in their meaning in order to apply to God. In a later chapter in the work, he says of the divine mystery that 'it seems to me to transcend every power of human understanding, and for that reason' he thinks 'one should refrain from attempting to explain how this is true. After all', he goes on, 'someone investigating an incomprehensible thing ought to be satisfied if his reasoning arrives at the knowledge that the thing most certainly exists, even if his understanding cannot fathom how this is so'.[18]

Anselm illustrates the idea that our language and ideas about God are not the same as the divine nature. He also makes clear that God is beyond our comprehension. Indeed, we should not even attempt to 'explain how this is true' precisely because God is an 'incomprehensible thing'. Thus, on Anselm's way of thinking, our theology is indeed a frail and fallible thing that is always attempting to approximate to the truth of something that cannot fully expressed. The language of models may be modern, but the idea that

---

[17] Anselm, *Monologion* 26 in *Anselm: Basic Writings*, trans. Thomas Williams (Indianapolis: Hackett, 2007), 36.
[18] Anselm, *Monologion* 65, in *Basic Writings*, 62–3.

our doctrines might always fall short of complete adequacy is not. Anselm, like Pseudo-Dionysius, was committed to the notion that God is a creaturely mind-independent thing. Neither of them was a theological anti-realist. Yet both understand that there is a gulf between human ratiocination and the divine nature. Transposing this into a contemporary idiom, it is not inconsistent to be a theological realist and to think that our theological doctrines and models about God will only approximate to the truth of the matter. If anything, it is symptomatic of a faith-seeking-understanding approach to theology that acknowledges its fallibilism and conceptual frailty in the task of theological construction.

Carving the Trinity at the joints?

At the beginning of this chapter, I asked whether theology carves nature at the joints, as Plato claimed his theory of forms did. I have argued that theology can get at certain truths about the divine nature, including certain intrinsic truths. Nevertheless, theological statements are fallible and provisional. This is due to the limits of human ratiocination and the epistemic vantage from which we approach matters theological. It is also due to the inaccessibility of the divine nature and to the conceptual limits placed on what is revealed of God in Scripture and tradition. One way of putting such an approach to work is by means of constructive model building. In such conceptual models, the target of the model being constructed is the Deity, who is understood to be some creaturely mind-independent thing. What is more, the model bears an appropriate relation of fidelity to its target. Fidelity comes in different varieties depending on what the model attempts to explicate. A toy wooden airplane is a model of an actual airplane and is none the worse for that. We don't expect to fly in model airplanes, but that is not an aspect of the target that the model aims to replicate. The fidelity of the model airplane depends on it having certain superficial qualities that actual airplanes possess, such as having wings, a fuselage, a tailplane and so on. It is none the worse as a model for not having an interior cabin or engine. For that is not part of its remit as a toy model airplane.

Suppose we put the conjunction of chastened theological realism and the understanding of models outlined above to work. Let us focus on the central and defining doctrine of Christian Theology, the Trinity. By a Doctrine in this context, I mean 'a comprehensive account of a particular teaching about a given theological topic held by some community of Christians or some particular denomination'.[19] In fact, the Trinity is not just a doctrine but a dogma in my way of thinking. For it is a doctrine 'that has a canonical form or definition that is part of the conceptual core of the Faith and that has normative status'[20] for Christian Theology. This is important: I emphasize it because if the account of theological realism plus theological modelling outlined here applies to a doctrine that is a dogma of the Faith (as a central and defining teaching of the Catholic Church), then it is likely to be applicable to other, less central and defining tenets of the Faith as well.

---

[19]Culled from Crisp, *Analyzing Doctrine*, 239.
[20]Ibid.

To begin with, I will give an outline of what I take to be the bare bones of the doctrine. Then I shall say something about how it might be construed on a chastened realist view, before suggesting how that could be made to work in a particular model of the Trinity. We can set out the Trinity in outline as follows:

> TRINITY: The conjunction of dogmatic propositions concerning the divine nature, expressing the claim that God is one in essence and subsists in three persons, that are found in the dogmatic deposit of the ecumenical creeds, especially the Nicene-Constantinopolitan Symbol, and that reflect (a particular way of understanding) the teaching of Scripture and the apostolic faith. The dogmatic core of this conjunction of claims is as follows:
>
> (T1) there is exactly one God;
> (T2) there are exactly three coeternal divine persons "in" God: the Father, the Son, and the Holy Spirit;
> (T3) the Father, the Son, and the Holy Spirit are not identical;
> (T4) the Father, the Son, and the Holy Spirit are consubstantial.[21]

Upon this dogmatic framework, a particular account of the Trinity would need to be grafted like flesh on bones, which is just what has happened in the history of Christian thought. Down through the centuries, different and incommensurate accounts of the Trinity have been offered, all of which are said to be consistent with this dogmatic deposit of Catholic Christianity. Now, recall we said that chastened theological realism is:

> CHASTENED THEOLOGICAL REALISM: Theological realism can be characterised as the conjunction of three claims. First, that God is a (creaturely) mind-independent thing. Second, that at least some of our theological statements about God are apt to predicate objectively true things about God. Third, that true statements about God have realist truth conditions. Theological realism is chastened provided the theologian holds that what we can know of the divine nature is limited, but not negligible. We can know some things that are fundamentally true of the divine nature, such as that God is triune. Core Christian doctrines depend in important respects on the testimony of Scripture. Nevertheless, our grasp of the teaching of Scripture, and our attempts to understand core Christian doctrines may be mistaken in important respects. Thus, our theologising should proceed with caution, cognisant of the fallibilism attending the formation of Christian doctrine.

To this, we may add the notion of theological modelling outlined earlier:

---

[21]Reproduced from Crisp, *Analyzing Doctrine*, 243–4.

MODEL: A simplified conceptual framework or description by means of which complex sets of data, systems, and processes may be organised and understood.[22]

Based on our dogmatic framework, we are after a model of the Trinity that is consistent with chastened theological realism. Here is one such model (though it is by no means the *only* model consistent with the conjunction of the dogmatic framework of TRINITY, plus CHASTENED THEOLOGICAL REALISM and MODEL):

(1) Human beings cannot apprehend the triunity of God absent divine revelation.
(2) In revealing Godself to us, the Deity accommodates Godself to the epistemic limitations of human beings. (This includes some allowance for the noetic effects of sin.)
(3) TRINITY is a dogma (that is, a doctrine that has a particular canonical form).
(4) TRINITY provides a dogmatic framework for understanding the divine nature that is theologically minimal.
(5) The terms 'person' and 'essence,' and their cognates that demarcate the way in which God is three and the way in which God is one in Trinity, are referring terms that are placeholders; we do not have a clear conceptual grip on their semantic content. (This is consistent with the claim that we may have a partial, piecemeal, or analogous sense of these terms.) [23]

Now, this is a version of *Trinitarian mysterianism*. The Trinitarian mysterian is sceptical about the prospects for providing more than a placeholder account of the key terms expressed in TRINITY, preferring instead to adopt a reverend agnosticism about the personhood and essence of the divine Trinity. In other words, the Trinitarian mysterian thinks the theologian possesses an adequate *grammar* for the Trinity, but not an adequate *semantics* (a matter to which we shall return in Chapter 7). In this way, it sounds rather like the theological non-realist. However, unlike the non-realism of Jacobs or Pseudo-Dionysius, Trinitarian mysterianism holds that there are certain objective truths about the divine life that the Christian theologian can know and that are unambiguously fundamental to the divine nature. This includes TRINITY itself, as a dogmatic framework that is the product of revelation and is – to borrow Jacobs's language – fundamentally true of God. On the basis of TRINITY we know that God is essentially triune, and we know something about the relations between the triune persons. These are not trivial conclusions. However, aside from the dogmatic deposit of TRINITY we do not have a firm grip on the notions of essence and person as they apply to God. In other words, the theological flesh that we might put on the dogmatic bones of TRINITY is very thin indeed. We know *that* God is triune. We have the theological grammar by means of which we can articulate this theological claim. However, we do not have a complete

---

[22] *Analyzing Doctrine*, 243.
[23] Adapted from *Analyzing Doctrine*, 244.

Metatheology

explanation of *how* God is triune or even *what it is* to be triune. That is, we do not have an adequate account of Trinitarian semantics. This should not be surprising given that the divine nature is a mystery that is inaccessible to us without divine revelation.

Conclusion

We come to the conclusion. The upshot of the foregoing argument is this: we can know certain fundamental truths about the divine nature, but we cannot know the exact range or extent of some key terms as they relate to the divine nature, for we do not have a complete semantics of Trinitarian doctrine. Our theologising about the divine nature is partial, fallible, and provisional, and, in this model of the Trinity at least, cautious, given that the divine nature is mysterious and inaccessible to human creatures. But we can know something of the divine nature of the God who is independent of us and who is revealed to us in Scripture and tradition, even though God will remain forever beyond our cognitive grasp, a mystery that our finite human intelligences are incapable of fully fathoming. This may be thought a rather convoluted argument for such a modest conclusion. But perhaps one of the most important results of this chapter is that we theologians should be *more modest* in framing our theological ambitions, recognising that when we are faced with the unveiled truth of the matter in the beatific vision of the world to come, all our intellectual outputs will appear, as Aquinas said at the end of his life, like so much straw.

CHAPTER 4
DIVINE IDEAS

Traditionally, Christians have confessed that God is the creator of all things in heaven and earth, visible and invisible. Nothing in all of creation exists without being created and sustained by God. But how are we to understand the *scope* of this claim? Does it mean that God creates literally everything that exists other than Godself? For instance, does that include the creation of abstract objects like numbers, properties, propositions or universals? Or do abstract objects exist independently of God, as Plato thought, in a kind of heavenly realm of perfect ideas or forms? The problem is that the traditional theological notion of God creating 'all things in heaven and on earth . . . all things visible or invisible' that is found in the Nicene-Constantinopolitan Creed is ambiguous between these two sorts of claims. Consequently, it is not surprising that different Christian thinkers down through the centuries have construed the claim about God being the creator of all things in heaven and earth rather differently. Some have taken the latter view and reasoned that God does not create abstract objects. They exist independently of God as necessary beings, much as Plato suggested. Let us call this view *theistic platonism* or just Platonism. Contemporary advocates include Christian philosophers Nicholas Wolterstorff, Peter van Inwagen, and Keith Yandell.[1] An important historic alternative view to Platonism is the *doctrine of divine ideas,* according to which the scope of God's creative act includes what we commonly think of as abstract objects. In this way of thinking, there is literally nothing outside Godself that does not exist through or by means of God because God is metaphysically ultimate; that is, is the source of all that exists. God is sovereign over all created things, including abstract objects. And the Deity depends on nothing outside of Godself (i.e. possesses aseity), so cannot depend on abstract objects like the property 'deity' in order to exist.

The doctrine of divine ideas is the focus of this chapter. It is an important issue in the metatheology of Christian theism because it concerns both the question of the scope of divine power and sovereignty over all that is not God, and, more particularly, addresses foundational questions about the relation of God to abstract objects – an issue that has

---

[1] See Nicholas Wolterstorff, *On Universals: An Essay in Ontology* (Chicago: University of Chicago Press, 1970), 263–97; Peter van Inwagen, "God and Other Uncreated Things", in *Metaphysics and God: Essays in Honor of Eleonore Stump,* ed. Kevin Timpe (New York: Routledge, 2009), 3–20; and Keith Yandell, 'God and Propositions', in *Beyond the Control of God? Six Views on the Problem of God and Abstract Objects,* ed. Paul Gould (New York: Bloomsbury Academic, 2014), 21–35.

enormous theological implications.[2] The main goal is to provide a constructive version of the doctrine in dialogue with several medieval theologians, particularly Anselm of Canterbury. Anselm presents an intriguing account, one that (in the words of two of his recent commentators) transforms rather than transmits the doctrine of divine ideas.[3] For on Anselm's view, in the act of eternally generating the Word of God as the second divine hypostasis, God also generates the exemplar (singular, not plural) that is the divine idea of the world he creates as well as all other possibilities that remain uncreated in the divine mind. Anselm's position is, it seems to me, suggestive, though not without difficulties. However, the hope is that with some repair and extension, a basically Anselmian account may yet be serviceable for contemporary systematic theology.

We proceed as follows. The first two sections provide some theological context for Anselm's views. In the first section, I give a kind of overview of some important distinctions in the recent re-engagement with the doctrine of divine ideas in Christian philosophy. Then, in the second section, I provide some theological context for the discussion of Anselm's account by briefly considering Augustine and Aquinas on the divine ideas, two other members of the medieval 'A' Team whose views on this matter have been particularly influential in subsequent theological discussion. In the third section, I provide a critical reading of Anselm's position with reference to what he says in *Monologion*. In the fourth section, I turn to the task of theological construction, reworking Anselm's account to make it serviceable for contemporary theology. The result is an *Anselmian* doctrine, that is, a view that is deeply indebted to Anselm's view even though it is not the same as Anselm's position.

Some theological distinctions

Discussion of the doctrine of divine ideas has a long and distinguished history, although until recently it had fallen out of favour in contemporary systematic theology.[4] How

---

[2] For instance, whatever answer is given to this question of the relation of God to abstract objects has implications for the theology of things like numbers, properties, the debate about realism vs. nominalism in much historic theology and metaphysics, and so on.
[3] See Sandra Visser and Thomas Williams, *Anselm*. Great Medieval Thinkers (Oxford: Oxford University Press, 2009), 124.
[4] For a helpful account of the history of the doctrine up to Thomas Aquinas, see Vivian Boland, *Ideas in God According to Saint Thomas Aquinas: Sources and Synthesis*. Studies in the History of Christian Thought (Leiden: Brill, 1996). Recent discussions include the work of William Lane Craig in *God Over All: Divine Aseity and the Challenge of Platoninsm* (Oxford: Oxford University Press, 2016); Gregory T. Doolan, *Aquinas on the Divine Ideas as Exemplar* Causes (Washington, DC: Catholic University of America Press, 2008); Paul Gould in several articles and the symposium he edited called *Beyond the Control of God?: Six Views on the Problem of God and Abstract Objects* (London: Bloomsbury, 2016); Mark A. McIntosh, *The Divine Ideas Tradition in Mystical Theology* (Oxford: Oxford University Press, 2021); Thomas M. Ward, *Divine Ideas*. Cambridge Elements in Religion and Monotheism (Cambridge: Cambridge University Press, 2020); and Greg Welty's DPhil thesis, 'Theistic Conceptual Realism: The Case for Interpreting Abstract Objects as Divine Ideas' (Oxford University, 2006), among others.

we should think of divine ideas is a contested matter. However, as I shall characterize them here, divine ideas are *the uncaused, necessary, dependent, immutable, and concrete things that exist in God's mind*. They are uncaused and necessary because they are what we might call the mental content of God's mind, which is eternal and unchanging. His ideas cannot be caused to occur by something, not even by Godself, and they cannot be contingent on anything because God is necessary and unchanging in his nature. The divine ideas are also immutable, being aspects of God's nature, and concrete because they are mental items. The thought here is that mental content is concrete content. Abstract objects are by definition mind-independent, and if all those things we take to be abstract objects are in fact divine ideas, then there are no mind-independent things. Strictly speaking, there are no abstract objects on this way of thinking. Plato's realm of forms is transposed to the divine mind.

The scope of the divine ideas includes all possible worlds, including the contents of the actual world, on the basis of which God creates as God does.[5] A rough analogy may help explain. Suppose an artist stands in front of a large blank canvas. In her mind is a concept of what she wants to express in paint on this two-dimensional surface. She has a *vivid idea*, that is, a clear, complete, mentally occurrent idea in her mind of what it is she wants to convey. It is on the basis of this idea that she picks up her palette, squeezes out the paint, and, taking up her brushes, starts to work, instantiating the idea in her mind on the canvas in front of her. When she is finished, and supposing she has the facility to craft on the canvas an exact representation of the idea she had of the work in her mind, what is presented to viewers is the actualization of the image she had in her mind's eye on the canvas.

According to the traditional doctrine of divine ideas, God creates the world by means of a concept or concepts that God instantiates in an analogous way. It is analogous for a number of important reasons. One of these – often noted in theological literature – concerns the difference between creating and making. It is often said that God alone creates. Creatures are makers, not creators.[6] Creation involves a *de novo* action. The creator takes an idea and generates that thing from nothing. Unlike the artist, God does not have artefacts like canvas and paint, or their analogues, lying around as the medium by means of which God may express divine thoughts concretely. Nor is it the case that God has the thought at one moment, which God then expresses by means of a creative speech act at another moment. For, at least according to the traditional versions of the doctrine of divine ideas, creation does not involve *deliberation* on the part of God.

---

[5] We will make some distinctions about different sorts of divine ideas presently when discussing Thomas Aquinas.

[6] A recent example of this can be found in the work of Ian McFarland, who writes, 'the doctrine of creation from nothing posits a profound disanalogy between God's creation of the world and all creaturely acts of making: creaturely making always requires some factor in addition to the agent who does the making, but God's creating excludes any such factors'. *From Nothing: A Theology of Creation* (Louisville: Westminster John Knox, 2014), 87. It is a common enough distinction in the Christian tradition. For instance, Anselm also makes use of it in *Monologion* 11.

Rather, the thought is that by the word of his power God eternally brings creation from intentionality as a divine idea to formal actuality.

There are other ways in which the artist example is only an analogue, which are just as important for our purposes. For instance, in creating the corporeal world, God generates the world *de novo* on the basis of an idea. No artist does that, because the medium and the environment are given in the case of the artist. They are the corporeal context in which she works. The very idea that she has, which is a concrete thing, exists in her mind, which is intimately related to a particular physical object, namely, her brain. But none of this is true of God. The Deity has no brain, and divine ideas, though concrete, are not the contingent, changeable, ephemeral stuff of human imagination. Rather, God's ideas are uncaused, necessary, dependent, immutable and concrete things.[7]

In the recent philosophical literature, the doctrine of divine ideas has usually been construed in one of two ways. The first of these is *theistic activism*. The second is *theistic conceptualism*.[8] Both views presume that what we commonly take to be abstract objects, like properties and numbers, exist as divine ideas; there are no abstract entities that exist independently of God. The main difference between the two views, as Christian philosopher Michelle Panchuk has recently pointed out, is that 'theistic activism conceives of God's concepts as something eternally created by God via "a causally efficacious or productive sort of divine conceiving" while theistic conceptual realism

---

[7]As I have characterized things here, the doctrine of divine ideas presumes a kind of realism about these ideas. That is, they *really exist* as the concrete mental content of the divine mind. But in another sense, such a view could be thought to be *anti-realist* about abstract objects, in that it denies that there are any objects that are ontologically independent of the divine mind. But this is not the only viable approach to divine ideas. One might, like William Lane Craig, go the nominalist route and deny that the language we use of abstract objects commits us to their existence. This is a different sort of anti-realism, in this case, anti-realism about the existence of abstract objects as such. This will be an attractive option to those worried about the kind of 'bloated' ontology that a doctrine of divine ideas presumes (ideas upon ideas, and ideas of ideas, and ideas of ideas of ideas – enough meta-conceptual worries to motivate a strong version of Aristotle's Third Man argument). But for present purposes, I want to consider the doctrine of divine ideas as it has been traditionally articulated in medieval theology, to see whether it has resources that may be theologically useful today. Not everyone will be worried about ontological bloat. For those willing to go the realist route in entertaining the prospect of a Platonic horde of abstract objects but desiring to transpose this horde to the divine mind, as mental content to preserve the traditional theological claim that God is the creator of all things in heaven and earth, the doctrine of divine ideas is the obvious way to go.

[8]For accessible general accounts of these two ways of construing the doctrine of divine ideas in the recent philosophical literature, see Einar Duengar Bøhn, *God and Abstract Objects*. Cambridge Elements in Philosophy of Religion, ed. Yujin Nagasawa (Cambridge: Cambridge University Press, 2019), William Lane Craig, *God Over All*, and Paul M. Gould, ed. *Beyond the Control of God?* Craig's *God and Abstract Objects: The Coherence of Theism: Aseity* (Cham, Switzerland: Springer, 2016) is the most comprehensive recent account of the field. As I mentioned above, Craig has championed nominalism about divine ideas, which is a third sort of view, and the Gould symposium reflects a broader range of interests in this topic as well. The focus here is on realist accounts of divine ideas in part because this is the sort of view assumed by Augustine, Anselm and Aquinas, with whom we are concerned, and in part because it is the view I currently favour, though I shall not provide independent reasons for preferring it over alternatives here.

conceives of God's concepts as uncreated but metaphysically dependent on him'.[9] We shall circle back to these two different ways of construing the doctrine of divine ideas at the end of the chapter to consider whether Anselm's position is better understood as a version of theistic activism or theistic conceptualism.

Augustine and Aquinas on the divine ideas

With these preliminary matters made sufficiently clear, we can turn to the ideas themselves, beginning with some conceptual context. As is well known, Anselm's thought is deeply imbued with Augustinianism. Nevertheless, on the matter of divine ideas, he takes a rather different view from his theological mentor, the erstwhile Bishop of Hippo. He also has a rather different account from his theological successor, Thomas Aquinas. Given the influence of both Augustine and Aquinas on subsequent discussion of these matters, it is worth first giving some brief account of their respective positions as a kind of intellectual context – theological bookends, if you will – for the discussion of Anselm's doctrine.

Augustine on divine ideas

In 'On the Ideas,' Augustine writes that divine ideas:

> are certain original and principal forms of things, i.e., reasons, fixed and unchangeable, which are not themselves formed and, being thus eternal existing always in the same state, are contained in the Divine Intelligence. And though they themselves neither come into being nor pass away, nevertheless, everything which can come into being and pass away and everything which does come into being and pass away is said to be formed in accord with these ideas.[10]

He goes on to say that God creates all things according to a rational plan that exists 'nowhere but in the very mind of the Creator'. For 'it would be sacrilegious to suppose that he was looking at something placed outside himself when he created in accord with it what he did create'.[11] From which he concludes,

---

[9] See Michelle Panchuk, 'Created and Uncreated Things: A Neo-Augustinian Solution to the Bootstrapping Problem', *International Philosophical Quarterly* 56, no. 1 (2016): 99–112; 100. Cf. Thomas V. Morris and Christopher Menzel, 'Absolute Creation', *American Philosophical Quarterly* 23, no. 4 (1986): 354. My own theistic conceptualist proclivities are implied by my characterization of divine ideas as uncaused, necessary, dependent, immutable, and concrete things.
[10] Augustine, *Eighty-Three Different Questions. Fathers of the Church Patristics Series*, trans. David L. Mosher (Washington, DC: Catholic University of America Press, 1982), 80.
[11] Ibid., 81.

if these reasons of all things to be created or [already] created are contained in the Divine Mind, and if there can be in the Divine Mind nothing except what is eternal and unchangeable, and if these original and principle reasons are what Plato terms ideas, then not only are they ideas, but they are themselves true because they are eternal and because they remain ever the same and unchangeable. It is by participation in these that what is exists in whatever manner it does exist.[12]

Elsewhere in *Confessions*, Augustine writes that God does not create heaven and earth by means of some pre-existing matter, or via some other medium. Rather, 'you spoke and they were made. In your Word alone you created them'. God creates the world *ex nihilo* in a single divine eternal act so that 'there was no material thing before heaven and earth; or, if there was, you must certainly have created it by an utterance outside time, so that you could use it as the mouthpiece for your decree, uttered in time, that heaven and earth should be made'. Indeed, as he goes on to say, 'In your Word all is uttered at one and the same time, yet eternally'.[13] In the course of his discussion of these arcane matters of God's relation to time and creation, Augustine distinguishes between the earth, which is all visible created things, and the heavens above, as well as what he calls the 'Heaven of Heavens', which is not a visible part of creation, but something more like a kind of divine archetype existing in God's mind. He writes 'clearly the Heaven of Heavens, which you created "in the Beginning," that is, before the days began, *is some kind of intellectual creature*'. Although it is in no way co-eternal with you, the Trinity, nevertheless it partakes in your eternity'.[14] Commenting on this passage, the British philosopher Paul Helm writes, 'The heaven in question appears to be a sort of ideal, divinely-willed archetype which exists in complete form in the mind of God'.[15] He goes on to suggest that one plausible interpretation of Augustine's rather obscure notion of the Heaven of Heavens is as a kind of template or conceptual framework – something like a blueprint for the created order – on the basis of which God brings about the creation. Coupled with what Augustine says about divine ideas in 'Of Ideas', it seems that in creating all things, God brings into existence everything apart from himself. God creates on the basis of an existing eternal blueprint, something like a collection of ideas or forms that exists eternally in the divine mind.

Aquinas on the divine ideas

Aquinas's doctrine of divine ideas draws on Augustine and Pseudo-Dionysius to develop a sophisticated and nuanced way of thinking about these matters. Here I can only provide

---

[12]Ibid.
[13]Saint Augustine, *Confessions*, trans. R. S. Pine-Coffin (Harmondsworth: Penguin Classics, 1961), Bk XII. 5–7, pp. 257–9.
[14]Augustine, *Confessions* Bk. XII. 9, 286. Emphasis added.
[15]Paul Helm, *Faith and Understanding* (Edinburgh: Edinburgh University Press, 1997), 95–6.

the barest thumbnail sketch of his work, which spans many of his voluminous writings, though I shall privilege his later, more developed attempts to state his view on the matter.

Thomas thinks of divine ideas on analogy with a human artisan, like the imaginary artist mentioned earlier. Just as the artisan has an idea on the basis of which she forms the object she is making, say a portrait of a young woman, so God has an idea of the creation that God brings about in the act of creating.[16] There are complex issues associated with how Aquinas characterizes divine ideas, and some differences in terminology and of concepts, in the various places at which he writes about the matter that reflect some narrowing of his position over time.[17] But broadly speaking, it seems that Aquinas makes a distinction between ideas that are of practical import, that is, are made concrete or actualized in some likeness, and ideas that are merely cognitive. He tends to think that ideas of the first sort, which are actualized, are exemplars. It is here that the analogy with the artisan is apt. Just as the artisan forms her work based on an idea, so God forms the world on the basis of his idea of it. There are also other ideas that are not made concrete, including things that remain mere possibilities in the mind of God. These Thomas calls 'types'. As Doolan summarizes matters, 'Thomas presents' ideas 'as having a twofold function: as cognitive and as productive principles. In this respect, the various texts are as a whole consistent.'[18] The differences between texts are, he maintains, mainly semantic in nature although there is a sense in which Aquinas uses the term exemplar particularly in his later writings that restricts it to that idea in virtue of which a particular likeness is made—which is the analogy with the artisan. Thus, in *Summa Theologiae* I, Question 15 'On Ideas', Article 3, entitled 'Whether there are ideas of all things that God knows'? Thomas writes this:

> an idea has this twofold office, as it exists in the mind of God. So far as the idea is the principle of the making of things, it may be called an 'exemplar,' and belongs to practical knowledge. But so far as it is a principle of knowledge, it is properly called a 'type,' and may belong to speculative knowledge also. As an exemplar, therefore, it has respect to everything made by God in any period of time; whereas as a principle of knowledge it has respect to all things known by God, even though they never come to be in time; and to all things that He knows according to their proper type, in so far as they are known by Him in a speculative manner.[19]

However, this is not to suggest that there are exemplars in God as distinct things. For Aquinas thinks God is metaphysically simple. Rather, these different ideas, including exemplars, exist virtually or eminently in God as aspects of his metaphysically simple

---

[16]See Aquinas, *Quod* 8 a. 2, cited in Doolan, *Aquinas on the Divine Ideas as Exemplar Causes*, 1.
[17]This is set out with admirable clarity by Doolan, *Aquinas on the Divine Ideas as Exemplar Causes*.
[18]Doolan, *Aquinas on the Divine Ideas as Exemplar Causes*, 23.
[19]See Thomas Aquinas, *Summa Theologiae*, 5 Vols., trans. Fathers of the English Dominican Province (New York: Benzinger Brothers, 1911).

nature, and only concretely, and distinct, in the creature. This is spelled out in ST 1. 15. art. 2, 'Whether ideas are many'? where Thomas writes,

> it is not repugnant to the simplicity of the divine mind that it understand many things; though it would be repugnant to its simplicity were His understanding to be formed by a plurality of images. Hence many ideas exist in the divine mind, as things understood by it . . . Inasmuch as He knows His own essence perfectly, He knows it according to every mode in which it can be known. Now it can be known not only as it is in itself, but as it can be participated in by creatures according to some degree of likeness. But every creature has its own proper species, according to which it participates in some degree in likeness to the divine essence. So far, therefore, as God knows His essence as capable of such imitation by any creature, He knows it as the particular type and idea of that creature; and in like manner as regards other creatures. So it is clear that God understands many particular types of things and these are many ideas.

The thought seems to be this: God knows all things through an act of eternal self-reflection, including all divine ideas. So, although in one sense there may be many divine ideas, there are not many images in the divine mind as there would be in a creaturely mind, which are distinct things. Rather, there is the divine mind, and what we might call the mental content of the divine mind, which we may distinguish formally or virtually, as it were, but which is not really or truly distinct in God. It seems to be rather like the way in which a human person can take in a whole situation in a glance, including all the various elements or parts of the situation, though these are not distinguished as distinct things in the mind of the person perceiving; they are understood in one gestalt. God knows all things immediately and eternally through self-reflection, and in doing so, God knows all ideas including both types and exemplars. This is underlined in the first article on ideas (*ST* 1.15.1, 'Whether there are ideas'?) where Thomas has this to say, 'Although God knows Himself and all else by His own essence, yet His essence is the operative principle of all things, except of Himself. It has therefore the nature of an idea with respect to other things; though not with respect to Himself'. Moreover, 'God is the similitude of all things according to His essence; therefore an idea in God is identical with His essence'.[20]

Divine ideas themselves are, says Thomas, 'the form of things, existing apart from the things themselves' (ST 1.15. art. 1.). Some forms pre-exist in the natural being of a thing, thinks Thomas, such as the generation of one human being by another. Other forms pre-exist cognitively in the mind of the knower, such as the likeness of a house that pre-exists

---

[20] Compare Dominic Legge, O.P., who, in writing about the Trinitarian register of Aquinas's Christology, says this: 'In God, the Father "understands himself" by a single eternal act and so generates an eternal Word – as a conception proceeding from his act of understanding – that "expresses the Father."' *The Trinitarian Christology of St Thomas Aquinas* (Oxford: Oxford University Press, 2017), 15.

in the mind of its builder. He concludes, 'As then the world was not made by chance, but by God acting by his intellect . . . there must exist in the divine mind a form to the likeness of which the world was made. And in this the notion of an idea consists'. These ideas are contained within the divine mind.[21]

To summarize: four doctrinal claims emerge from our brief overview of Thomas's work. First, there are divine ideas, which exist concretely in the divine mind; there is no Platonic horde of abstract objects independent of the divine mind. Second, these ideas are identical with the divine nature, which is metaphysically simple. Third, all created things are exemplars made in the likeness of a divine idea. Fourth, there are types, which are ideas that are possibilities not realized concretely in the world. Presumably, things like propositions and numbers fall under the description of types. Thomas does much to clarify an Augustinian account of the divine ideas, especially in what he says about the difference between ideas as exemplars and as types. As helpful as this is, it falls short of the imaginative rethinking of the doctrine provided by Anselm, to whom we turn next.

Anselm on divine ideas

There are several different ways one could approach the topic of the divine ideas in Anselm's work, depending on one's philosophical or theological proclivities. Nevertheless, it is the theological implications of his way of thinking about divine ideas that are the focus of our attention here. Obviously, Anselm's views on this matter are bound up in important respects with certain philosophical assumptions, and one cannot really extricate his theology from his philosophy without doing violence to both. This is particularly evident in the way he set about the theological task. In his Prologue to the *Monologion,* Anselm explains that the work was written at the instigation of the brothers in his priory, who placed upon him certain methodological constraints. These were that he did not directly appeal to the authority of Scripture to establish any point, and that he used reason and plain, direct argument and disputation to demonstrate his conclusions on each topic. He was also to ensure he tackled all objections, even those that appeared foolish.[22] Clearly, these constraints are unusual in a work of Christian theology,

---

[21]In *De Veritate* (On Truth) Art. 4 'Is there only one truth by which all things are true'? reply 6, Aquinas writes 'Although there is one uncreated truth from which all created truths take their model, these truths are not modeled on it in the same way. For while it is true that the uncreated truth has the same relation to all, all do not have the same relation to it – as pointed out in The Causes [vis., the four Aristotelian causes]. Necessary and contingent truths are modeled on the uncreated truth in quite different ways. But different ways of imitating the divine model cause diversity among created things. Consequently, there are many created truths'. This gets closer to the Anselmian picture (and he is responding to some Anselmian concerns in this section of the work). But it is still not quite the same as Anselm's notion of the Word as the Divine Exemplar. I am grateful to Fr. Emmanuel Perrier, O.P. for drawing my attention to this passage.

[22]Anselm, Prologue to *Monologion,* 1. All references to Anselm in English are taken from Thomas Williams, *Anselm: Basic Writings.* I have also consulted *S. Anselmi cantuariensis archiepiscopi opera omnia, volumen primum,* ed. Francis S. Schmitt (Edinburgh: Thomas Nelson & Sons, 1946 [1938]), hereinafter cited as *opera*

as opposed to, say, a work of philosophy. But Anselm was at pains to point out that he thought his arguments *consistent* with the Fathers, especially Augustine's *De Trinitate*, as well as Holy Writ (MPrologue, 2), even if his arguments did not appeal directly to these theological authorities. And, although his understanding of the relationship between faith and reason is a vexed matter that is the subject of ongoing scholarly dispute, at least this much is clear: the sort of reason Anselm has in mind is a kind of sanctified reason, the reason of a person of faith standing within the ambit of that faith, not the reason of an infidel or a pagan. That is, it is not the reasoning of someone outside the faith dispassionately considering the conceptual content of the faith. This is evident in the original title he chose for the *Monologion*, which was *Exemplum meditandi de ratione fidei*,[23] that is, 'A pattern for meditation on the reason of faith'. As Sandra Visser and Thomas Williams have argued, this *ratione fidei* is not the same as a kind of *praeambula fidei*, or preamble to the faith, which would make it closer to philosophical discussion of the content of the faith that comes logically prior to any treatment of the doctrine of the faith. Rather, it is a pattern of meditation on the reason of faith. They write, 'Anselm regards the doctrines of the Christian faith as intrinsically rational because they concern the nature and activity of God, who is supreme reason and exemplifies supreme wisdom in everything he does. Because human beings are rational by nature, we can grasp the reason of faith'.[24] Later they add that the sort of believers Anselm has in mind, 'prayerfully exercise their rational powers in order to understand what they already believe'[25] – which is the faith seeking understanding programme Anselm sets out in *Proslogion*, his sequel to the *Monologion*. I suggest that the rationale Anselm himself provides for his work, especially his work in *Monologion*, is fundamentally a theological not a philosophical one. His meditation on the reason of faith in *Monologion* is just that: a theological reflection on the conceptual content of the faith, particularly the dogma of the Trinity in imitation of Augustine, but carried out (unlike Augustine) without appeal to sources of authority, using plain argument alone – the plain argument of the person of faith who seeks to better understand the conceptual content of that faith.[26]

With this methodological caveat in mind, we can turn to Anselm's argument. He takes the notion of divine ideas and the idea of a kind of blueprint of creation (Augustine's 'Heaven of heavens') and recombines them in a startling manner in the *Monologion* so as to make of his treatment of the divine ideas the first step in an argument about the divine

---

omnia, followed by page reference. I refer to passages of the *Monologion* in the body of the text as M, followed by the chapter number, and then the location in the Williams translation, e.g. 'M4, 10'.

[23]Anselm, *Proslogion*, Prologue, 75. Cf. *opera omnia*, 94.

[24]Visser and Williams, *Anselm*, vi.

[25]Ibid., 7.

[26]At one point in her recent study of Anselm's work, Eileen Sweeney notes, 'We also see what theologians always notice but philosophers tend to miss (the few who read the *Monologion* at all rather than stick to the *Proslogion*): that this is a work on the Trinity'. See *Anselm of Canterbury and the Desire for the Word* (Washington, DC: Catholic University of America Press, 2012), 129. Anselm makes it plain that his work is on the Trinity in the Prologue to the *Monologion*.

processions in the Trinity that occupies a substantial part of the work, from M29 to the end of M65. It is a fascinating treatment. But our focus is narrower. We are interested in the claim, set out and argued for in M29-36, that the eternal generation of the Word of God is the means by which God generates an exemplar of the divine ideas, so that by means of this eternally generative act not only does the Son proceed from the Father, but also God comes to know Godself and comes to know all possibilities, including all things created. (Of course, we are stretching human language almost to breaking point, as Anselm himself does in the *Monologion*. God does not 'come to know' anything strictly speaking, because the act of generation he is concerned with is an eternal act that has no beginning.) Thus, on his account, the eternal procession of the Son is also how God knows what God knows. It is an act that is generative in more than one sense and that brings about self-knowledge through a kind of eternal locution (*locutio*) or speech-act.

This claim requires some expansion and discussion in order that we may better see its logical form to assess its theological merits. Up to this point in the work, Anselm has been explaining that God is the supreme essence through whom all things exist and are sustained. Let us call this *the ultimacy thesis*, since it amounts to the claim that God is the thing through which, or by means of which (*per aliud*), all other things exist.[27] God himself uniquely exists independent of all other things as an eternal substance or substance-like thing (*a se*). Anselm claims in Chapter 1, for example, that there is, therefore, 'some one thing that is supremely good and supremely great – in other words, supreme among all existing things'. (M1: 8). He then argues for the claim that this supreme thing is the sole thing that exists 'through himself', whereas all other existing things exist through this one supreme thing (M3: 9). This in turn is grounded in a more fundamental notion about the scale of being common to perfect being theologians. Anselm believed that certain entities are greater than others, with God as the greatest being. He writes that anyone 'who doubts that a horse is by its very nature better than wood, and that a human being is more excellent than a horse, should not even be called a human being' (M4: 10.). This metaphysical thesis includes a kind of status principle, according to which certain entities have a greater dignity than others, with God the greatest being in this regard.

So, God is metaphysically ultimate. The Deity is that by means of which all things other than Godself exist and have their being (the ultimacy thesis). God exists independently of creatures in a metaphysical sense, for God does not depend on them for continued existence. God is also independent of creatures in a psychological sense, in that God does not have a need for creatures. This we may call *the aseity thesis*. We might add to this that Anselm thinks God is sovereign over creation. God creates everything from nothing (M7-10) and conserves all that exists thereafter. This is *the sovereignty thesis*. This triumvirate of claims undergirds what Anselm says about the divine ideas in important respects. For it marks off Anselm's doctrine as a successor to the tradition of Christian theology that thinks of the domain of quantification over which God is said to

---

[27] As Anselm says later in M13, 'Therefore, it has been established that whatever is not the same as the supreme nature was made through him'.

be the maker of all things, visible and invisible, as unlimited.[28] He is no Platonist when it comes to thinking about abstract objects.

Now, although Anselm is committed to the doctrine of creation out of nothing, like Augustine he sees that there must be a kind of pattern or blueprint for the creation of particular objects that correspond to an idea in the divine mind. As he puts it, 'there is no way anyone could make something rationally unless something like a pattern (or, to put it more suitably, a form or likeness or rule) of the thing to be made already existed in the reason of the maker' (M9, 17.). Clearly, logically prior to creation the things that were made do not exist as concrete objects in the world. But, as Anselm points out, they must exist logically prior to creation as items of mental furniture in the mind of the creator. These items of mental furniture he calls utterances or locutions. These utterances are the ideas that are held in the mind's eye by the artisan before making a thing as either mental images or concepts, such as the concept of a horse, or the mental image of a horse held in the mind's eye prior to carving a horse-shaped ornament from a block of wood.[29] But caution must be registered at this juncture, as Anselm is quick to point out. For God is significantly unlike the artisan. God does not collect forms or concepts from outside Godself to form a given artefact, as does the craftsman. This is the distinction between *making* and *creating* mentioned earlier (see M11). For the ideas God has of a thing, like a horse, are eternal items of mental furniture in the divine mind. God does not find them lying around and imitate them or form a concept from concrete examples. Instead, the idea of a horse is eternally present as an idea in God's mind.

But if God's ideas are eternally and immediately present to Godself, then God did not make them like the artisan, through some other thing or some other medium like the existing block of wood from which the artisan carves the horse ornament. Instead, 'whatever he made, he made it through his innermost utterance' (M12). This is important for Anselm's argument concerning the procession of the Word, which he picks up again in M29 after some chapters spent discussing the divine nature. In M29 Anselm claims that 'if the supreme spirit made nothing except through himself, and whatever was made by him was made through his utterance, how can that utterance be anything other than what he himself is'? The divine locution cannot be a creature since it is the medium by means of which all creatures come to be (presumably in the very act of divine fiat). He writes, 'every subsistent created thing was made through it, and it could not have been made through itself'. Consequently, 'the only remaining possibility is that it is nothing other than the supreme spirit'. To this he adds that the divine locution must be the understanding of the supreme spirit by means of which he understands all things. For uttering in the sense Anselm has in mind includes the notion of understanding or comprehension of the thing uttered. God cannot fail to understand what he utters. Moreover, 'that supremely simple nature is nothing other than what his understanding is', says Anselm. So, the utterance and understanding must be the same thing. Or as he

---

[28] I borrow this phrase from Craig, *God Over All*, 40.
[29] In M10 Anselm writes of 'corporeal images' or 'understanding of reason', but the point is the same.

puts it, 'he is nothing other than what his utterance is'. The utterance and the supreme spirit are, in fact, consubstantial.

Anselm thinks he can avoid positing the divine locution as something distinct from the supreme spirit in three conceptual steps. First, by making it the instrument by means of which all creatures come to exist; second, by assimilating it to the divine understanding; and third, by appealing to divine simplicity according to which divine understanding, as an attribute of God, is not distinct from the divine nature. For, to quote the Roman Catholic dogmatician, Ludwig Ott, in God 'all is one where there is no opposition of relations'.[30] And, as Anselm goes on to say in M30, once it has been established that the divine locution is consubstantial with the divine nature in this three-step process, it should be clear that the divine utterance is simple as the divine nature is simple – to which we may add, *because* it is an aspect of the divine nature.

There is something very appealing about this reasoning, theologically speaking. For it neatly joins up the divine locution to the divine nature in such a way that Anselm's readers are left with one, simple divine utterance as an aspect of the one, simple divine nature. But there is something about this that seems odd, some sleight of hand that appears to have been performed though we are not exactly sure where. (Aficionados of Anselm will acknowledge that this is a common experience in reading his work). Of course, once one has conceded that the divine locution just is the divine understanding, which is the move from his second to third conceptual step, then the argument is all but over. For if God is metaphysically simple in the way that classical theists like Augustine, Anselm and Aquinas thought, then divine attributes like understanding are identical with the divine nature. But why think that the divine locution includes within itself divine understanding? Why not think that God understands, and then speaks as two distinct things, the first being a necessary and intrinsic aspect of the divine nature, and the latter being an extrinsic, contingent divine act? One obvious way to provide motivation for this sort of conceptual move is to appeal to biblical authority. Here the motivation would be something like this: Why think that the divine locution is divine or even that the divine locution is assimilated to divine understanding? Well, because this is a revealed doctrine, given to us in Scripture. God has revealed this about Godself, in Scripture which we take to be theologically authoritative. So, we have a good reason based on authority to hold to this notion.[31] For instance, the Johannine prologue suggests that the Logos is divine

---

[30] This is the 'Basic Trinitarian Law' set out by Ludwig Ott in *Fundamentals of Catholic Dogma* (Rockport, IL: Tan Books, 1950), 70. This in turn, is taken from Anselm's treatment of the individuation of the divine persons in his work *On The Procession of The Holy Spirit*, Section 2.

[31] There are well-known philosophical worries with arguments from authority. I take it that the sort of theological argument I have in mind here does not fall foul of the informal fallacy of arguments from authority because God is mysterious and beyond our ken, such that without some act of divine revelation, the connection between the divine locution and divine understanding would not be apparent. The notion I have in mind is something like this: where some item of knowledge is beyond our ken absent some act of revelation on the part of another agent, it is appropriate to appeal to revelation as a kind of special testimony when seeking to know the thing in question.

Metatheology

and is intimately related to the divine understanding. But this appeal to the testimony of revelation is not an option open to Anselm given the theological constraints with which he is working in *Monologion*. Without some such motivation, however, it is difficult to see why one would concede the step from divine locution to divine understanding – even if Anselm's interlocutor stands within the faith, rather than outside it.

Having established to his own satisfaction that the divine locution is identical with the divine essence, Anselm turns next to consider the relationship between the Word and the likenesses of created things. Whereas we creatures have ideas of things that are not the same as the thing itself but merely approximate to that thing as a kind of mental likeness (such as my idea of the green dinosaur toy Rex and the actual toy Rex), the likenesses of creatures had by the Word are identical with the truth of that creaturely essence. In other words, the likeness of the toy Rex in the divine utterance of the Word is the truth of the essence of Rex. It is tempting to smooth out the rather complex language Anselm employs to say that the divine idea of Rex is the exemplar on the basis of which the concrete Rex is exemplified. Anselm does say something like this when he writes that the essence of creatures is to be found in the divine utterance, whereas creatures only have a likeness of other concrete things in their minds when conceiving them (M31, 41). But he is also committed to a kind of participatory metaphysics according to which 'every essence exists more greatly and is more excellent to the extent that it is more like the essence that supremely exists and is supremely excellent' (M31, 41.). This is rather more obscure and depends on his idea of something like a great chain of being from the simplest creatures to the supreme divine nature – a notion that sounds much more objectionable to modern ears than to medieval ones.

We come to the heart of Anselm's argument. In M32, he argues that the supreme spirit utters himself by uttering his Word. If there were no creatures at all, the divine utterance would still exist as the divine self-understanding. For, thinks Anselm, 'if he understands himself eternally, he utters himself eternally'. (M32, 42.) To this he adds the idea that by the one utterance, the supreme spirit utters both himself and his creatures in M33. We can set out his reasoning in that chapter as follows:

1. '[W]hen the supreme understands himself by uttering himself, he begets a likeness of himself that is consubstantial with himself: that is his Word.'
2. This Word 'is not a likeness of creation but rather its paradigmatic essence.'
3. Hence, 'he does not utter creation by a word of creation.'
4. 'Now, if he utters nothing other than himself and creation, he cannot utter anything except by his own Word or by a word of creation.'
5. He utters nothing by a word of creation.
6. So 'whatever he utters, he utters by his own Word.'
7. 'Therefore, he utters both himself and whatever he made by one and the same Word.'[32]

---

[32] From Anselm's *Monologion* in *Anselm: Basic Works*, 43–4.; cf. *Opera Omnia I.* 52–3.

In M34, he expands a little on this central argument by indicating that the ideas of creatures 'always exist in him [i.e., God]' even before they are made as divine ideas, or more precisely, they are aspects of the one idea, the divine utterance. For, he says, 'they always exist in him, not as what they are in themselves, but as what he himself is'. (M34, 44.)

This transforms rather than transmits the doctrine of divine ideas.[33] For, on this view, the exemplar from which God creates the world is identical with the Word, the second divine hypostasis, and is somehow eternally generated in the self-same act in which the Word is eternally generated. If it is asked *how* it is that the supreme spirit knows or utters the things that are made, Anselm is at a loss for explanation. Such matters are, he avers, incomprehensible to creatures (M36, 45).

Reflection on Anselm's doctrine

Let us take stock. By his own admission, Anselm is concerned in the *Monologion* with the *reason of faith*. Proceeding by plain argument, and without appealing to theological authority, Anselm sets up his position in this section of the *Monologion* by way of three principles: divine ultimacy; divine aseity; and divine sovereignty. God's ideas are eternal. God creates out of nothing based on (what Aquinas would call) an exemplar of all creatures that is 'contained' eminently or virtually in the divine understanding. This divine understanding is identical with the divine nature, given his understanding of divine simplicity which admits of no real distinction between God and God's attributes. And this divine understanding is identical with the divine word or locution by means of which God utters creatures. So, the divine utterance is also simple. Thus, in an eternal speech-act God speaks Godself (more precisely, God's eternal understanding of Godself), and God speaks the exemplar (singular) of all creatures. God also speaks the creation of these creatures, though this is consequent upon the eternal utterance of the exemplar in the Word. The picture seems to be that the eternally simple supreme essence eternally generates a second hypostasis, an utterance or word, in something akin to an eternal speech-act. In performing this speech-act the supreme essence understands Godself, and thereby understands the exemplar of every creature. It is also part and parcel of this self-same eternal divine speech act that in uttering it, the supreme essence utters the creation of all things other than Godself. Thus, divine ideas are collapsed into the one eternally generated Word: in Anselm's mind, divine ideas and the procession of the Second Person of the Trinity meet.

There is much more to Anselm's account than I have discussed here, and M37-M48 spell out more clearly the relation between the First and Second Persons of the Godhead, how they are distinct and yet share in the same essence, and how the Son can be said to

---

[33]This is the point made by Sandra Visser and Thomas Williams in *Anselm*, 124, which was mentioned in the opening of this chapter.

be the understanding of God in particular. These too are fascinating arguments, and a complete summary of Anselm's attempt to spell out the divine processions would have to take account of these chapters, as well as those that succeed them, and that tackle the individuation of the Spirit. But for our purposes, we may stop at M36, for this is the end of his argument for the conclusion that the divine utterance is both the second divine hypostasis and something like the instantiation of divine understanding, as well as the exemplar of divine ideas of all created things.

Dogmatic sketch of an Anselmian account of divine ideas

We have seen that Anselm developed themes that can be found in the broadly Augustinian tradition of thinking about the doctrine of divine ideas. Anselm takes the doctrine in a radical logocentric direction; Aquinas makes of it a doctrine of divine exemplars. How might Anselm's work in particular help us in thinking about the doctrine of divine ideas today? In this final section, I want to sketch one possible response to that question. To be as clear as I can, I shall give a metaphysical 'just so' story in two parts outlining this constructive account before offering some closing reflections on its main claims.

Here is the first part of the story:

> God the Son is the divine idea. The Son is eternally generated by the First Person of the Trinity. The very act of eternal generation is not merely how the Second Person of the Trinity is said to proceed from the First Person (which is one of the divine processions internal to the life of God that distinguishes one divine person from the others). It is also the act by means of which God comes to know Godself, so to speak. We might say that eternal generation is an act of divine self-knowledge. For in eternally generating a second divine person, the First Person also generates the exemplar – that is, the Second divine Person – who contains, as it were, the knowledge of all things, necessary and possible. This information is 'contained' in a single exemplar, which is identical with the Second Person of the Godhead. The knowledge of all things necessary and possible may be understood on analogy with the way a large number of digital files can be compressed together into a single 'zip' file on your computer – which is just a file of compressed data that can be more easily transmitted because it takes up less computer memory to do so. In a similar fashion, we might say that on this Anselmian way of conceiving the eternal generation of the Son, the act of eternally generating the Son is also something analogous to the generation of a massive zip file containing the ideas of all that is necessary and all that is possible. In a similar manner, generating the email that includes the zip file as an attachment, and sending the email to its intended recipient, is a complex action that, so we might think, includes the attachment of the zipped file as a constituent. There is the message, there is the attachment, and then there is the sending of the message and its attached digital documentation in the zipped file. On the way of thinking about the act of eternal

generation in view here, the sending of the email is like the act of eternal generation. The act of sending the email is also how the attachment containing the zip file is transmitted. Similarly, on this way of thinking, the act of eternally generating the Second Person of the Trinity is also the way the exemplar of the divine ideas – the information concerning all that is necessary and possible contained in the one 'zip file' of the Son – is also generated. We might say that eternally generating the Son is the means by which the exemplar of the divine ideas is also eternally generated.

Thus, the act of eternal generation within the divine life is an act of divine self-knowledge. Aquinas tells us that God knows all things in an eternal act of self-reflection. Anselm doesn't necessarily contradict this. Rather, he provides us with a logocentric lens through which to understand this dogmatic claim.

Call this *the logocentric account of the divine ideas*. This account could be expanded to make its claims about the centrality of the Word in the generation of divine ideas more clearly christocentric. Drawing on my earlier work in Christology in which I developed a version of incarnation, anyway Christology,[34] we could augment our previous logocentric metaphysical just-so story in the following way:

God the Son is the exemplar of the divine ideas, the one who 'contains,' as it were, the multiplicity of divine ideas within himself, in some ways rather like a zip file on a modern computer. Included in this exemplar are the ideas of all possible worlds, including all those worlds at which God creates human beings. Now, suppose that an important motivation for creation is participation in the divine life. God creates us to be united with Godself everlastingly. On one way of thinking about these things, such participation requires a hub between divinity and humanity in order that we may interface with the divine and participate in God's life. It would be too great a metaphysical act of bootstrapping for mere humans to participate in the divine life without such an interface. In a similar fashion, it would be too great a metaphysical act of bootstrapping for a laptop computer to be linked wirelessly with the internet without some wireless hub to connect the computer, via radio signals, to the internet servers to which the hub is hardwired via a cable. Christ is the interface between divinity and humanity, and, plausibly, he is the most fitting means by which God can enable our participation in his divine life. In all those worlds God creates with humans, where one of God's fundamental motivations for creating is union with creatures, it seems reasonable to think that God provides the mechanism by means of which such union may be achieved. And it seems plausible that Christ is a fitting, perhaps the most fitting, means by which this is brought about. Suppose that is right. Then, God has reason to create a world of human creatures who are able in principle to participate in the

---

[34]See Crisp, *The Word Enfleshed: Exploring the Person and Work of Christ* (Grand Rapids: Baker Academic 2016) and *Analyzing Doctrine*.

divine life. And he has a reason to ensure that in such worlds, the incarnation takes place irrespective of human sin.

This is an incarnation anyway argument. It is related to the Anselmian doctrine of divine ideas in this way: God the Son includes or encompasses an exemplar of all those worlds containing humans including those worlds containing unfallen humans – all of which require something like an incarnation in order to provide the means by which human beings can be united to Godself, which is an aspect of God's motivation for creation in the first place. Thus, God the Son contains within himself the information necessary for the creation of any world containing humans, and, plausibly, the information necessary for the generation of an interface between divinity and humanity to make such an interface feasible in worlds containing such humans. And this information about the interface between divinity and humanity concerns the Second Person directly, because he is the divine person who becomes incarnate to provide this interface. For Christ is the hub between divinity and humanity. Thus, in this extended Anselmian account of the divine ideas we have a reason for thinking that God the Son, as the divine exemplar, is the very ground or reason for the incarnation. He himself, as the divine exemplar, makes it true that he is God Incarnate, the hub between divinity and humanity, and the means by which human beings may participate in the divine life irrespective of human sin.

Conclusion

In this chapter, I have offered a critical account of the doctrine of divine ideas in dialogue with the 'A' team of medieval theology, namely, Augustine, Anselm, and Aquinas. I have argued that each of these theologians makes a significant contribution to the doctrine of divine ideas, but that Anselm's logocentric account is a significant recalibration of the divine ideas doctrine and hooks it up to the doctrine of divine processions. In Anselm's account, the doctrine of divine ideas feeds into the doctrine of the procession of the Son and is of a piece with it. Although not without problems, this Anselmian view seems to be very promising. I have attempted to indicate one way in which this doctrine may be taken that would make it potentially serviceable for contemporary theology, shorn of some of its more problematic claims (e.g. the conceit that Anselm makes no assumptions about the divine nature drawn from authority). I have also indicated how this logocentric account of the divine ideas could be linked to a particular way of thinking about God's action in creation, a way of thinking about this that draws on the tradition of incarnation anyway arguments yet without going down the route of conflating God's action in the economy of creation (and salvation) with God's identity – a mistake that Karl Barth and Robert W. Jenson, among others, have made popular in contemporary systematic theology.

At the beginning of the chapter, I mentioned the distinction in recent philosophical discussion of the divine ideas between *theistic activism* and *theistic conceptualism*.

Defenders of both sorts of doctrine have claimed Anselm as a source. And, in one respect, the logocentric account seems to straddle the difference between these two versions of the doctrine of divine ideas concerning whether the ideas are created by God or are the eternal, necessary constituents of the divine mind. That seems to me to be a potential benefit of the Anselmian account: in one respect, God the Father does generate the divine ideas in generating the Son. But we would not want to say that the Son is created. Similarly, we would not want to say the mental content of the Son is created. The divine ideas on the Anselmian account are mental content had by the Son. So, though they are eternally generated with the Son, they are not created. For this reason, it seems to me that we want to say that divine ideas are uncaused, necessary, dependent, immutable, and eternally occurrent concrete things that exist in the mind of God.

CHAPTER 5
SCRIPTURAL INSUFFICIENCY

Traditionally, Christians have proclaimed that Scripture is the Word of God. But they differ among themselves on the question of whether Scripture is *sufficient* for salvation. It is this question of the sufficiency of Scripture that is the subject of this chapter. Given the central place Scripture has in Christian theology, the question of its sufficiency as a theological norm is a fundamental issue for theology that falls within the purview of metatheology.

My argument depends in large measure on a commonplace philosophical distinction between the necessary and sufficient conditions for a thing.[1] For present purposes, a condition is said to be necessary just in case the thing in question cannot obtain without it. For example, the striking of one ball by another is a necessary condition for the moving of the second ball across the green baize of the table's surface in a game of billiards. A condition or conditions is/are said to be sufficient just in case the thing in question obtains or transpires by means of it or them. Thus, conditions sufficient for winning a game of billiards obtain when the black ball is knocked into a pocket on the billiard table, the player having previously successfully knocked each of the other balls into pockets of the table in a certain order.[2]

It is often said by Protestants in the Magisterial Reformation tradition that Scripture is sufficient for human salvation as part of a broader account of the place of Scripture in Christian theology.[3] But without careful qualification, this, I think, is a misleading claim

---

[1] Commonplace, but not straightforward. See the discussion in Andrew Brennan, 'Necessary and Sufficient Conditions', *The Stanford Encyclopedia of Philosophy* (Fall 2022 Edition), eds. Edward N. Zalta & Uri Nodelman, URL = <https://plato.stanford.edu/archives/fall2022/entries/necessary-sufficient/>.
[2] Compare J. L. Mackie's influential notion of an INUS condition. This is an insufficient but necessary condition of an unnecessary but sufficient cause (= INUS). Thus, in the game of billiards, knocking the black ball into the corner pocket ends the game. This is an insufficient but necessary condition for the conclusion of the game because it depends on other conditions, such as the fact that the ball needs to be knocked at the right angle and velocity by the cue of one of the two players of the game, and so on. Yet, without the black ball being knocked into a pocket of the table, the game is not formally concluded. Hence, this action is an insufficient but necessary condition for the conclusion of the game. The sum of the various conditions that contribute to this action of successfully pocketing the black ball is said to be an unnecessary but sufficient cause for the conclusion of the game. They are individually unnecessary aspects of the one complex act, but taken together they are sufficient for its obtaining. See J. L. Mackie, 'Causes and Conditions', *American Philosophical Quarterly* 12 (1965): 245–65.
[3] Some modern Protestant divines have made considerably more expansive claims for the sufficiency of Scripture. Thus, the Dutch Reformed theologian G. C. Berkouwer writes, 'It is not easy . . . to confess the sufficiency of Scripture: it is not a self-evident, handy chapter in systematic theology, but it is the dominating tone for the entire chorus of the church'. Berkouwer, *Holy Scripture. Studies in Dogmatics*, trans. Jack B. Rogers

that is mistaken in several different respects and has been the cause of some theological mischief. First, it is mistaken in that such a claim is not made by the confessional tradition of the churches of the Magisterial Reformation. What they normally claim is that Scripture is, in effect, a necessary but not sufficient condition for a right knowledge of salvation (a matter to which we shall return presently). However, that is a much more modest idea of the role played by Scripture in coming to a right understanding of salvation, according to the Christian faith. In which case, by the lights of their own confessions, Protestants in the Magisterial Reformation tradition cannot claim that Scripture is sufficient for salvation *tout court*. At most, they should claim that Scripture is normally *one* condition for coming to a right understanding of salvation. But it is not a *sufficient* condition for salvation without qualification.

Second, and ironically, whatever the Reformation confessions *state*, the churches that subscribe to them use them as a lens through which to read and understand Scripture. This is true despite the oft-repeated disclaimer that confessions are merely subordinate norms – that is, doctrinal standards that are subordinate to and susceptible to correction by Scripture as the norming norm. For in practice, the very confessional basis of Magisterial Reformation churches provides a hermeneutical constraint on how Scripture is read that is not itself to be found in Scripture or implied by Scripture. This can be seen in the way in which the propositional content expressed by texts of the confessions becomes a dogmatic matrix through which the words of Scripture are filtered and understood in the churches that the confessions were written to serve. We might say that *in practice* the confessions function as a dogmatic constraint on what is thought to be an acceptable reading of the biblical text (e.g. 'this way of understanding original sin is surely mistaken because it conflicts with what is stated in the confession').

Thus, Protestant heirs to the Magisterial Reformation should not be committed to a doctrine of the sufficiency of Scripture but rather to the idea that Scripture is in some sense *normally necessary but not sufficient* for the right understanding of the nature of salvation as it is understood in the confessional tradition of their particular Protestant communions.[4] Scripture is not *strictly speaking* sufficient for salvation according to the churches of the Magisterial Reformation. It is in fact insufficient absent certain other necessary conditions, such as a right understanding of the text of Scripture and, more fundamentally, the agency of the Holy Spirit in regeneration. Thus, it seems to me that this doctrine should be set to one side as an unhelpful and obfuscating notion that detracts from the right use of Scripture in what we might call Reformation or

---

(Grand Rapids: Eerdmans, 1975), 305. Berkouwer's view is repeated and endorsed by Timothy Ward in his more recent monograph, *Word and Supplement: Speech Acts, Biblical Texts, and the Sufficiency of Scripture* (Oxford: Oxford University Press, 2002), 3.

[4] I say necessary 'in some sense' because I presume most Christians would agree that Scripture is only conditionally necessary for an understanding of salvation. It might be that God communicates salvation directly to a given person in special revelation that would be extra-scriptural, though consistent with the message of salvation conveyed in Scripture.

confessional Protestantism, that is, the Protestantism that takes its theological point of departure from the Magisterial Reformation.[5]

But that is not all. Scripture does not seem to be sufficient for a right understanding of core Christian doctrines either – or so I will argue. Thus, in addition to the worry about the sufficiency of Scripture, my argument drives a wedge between the question of what is necessary for an understanding of salvation and what is necessary for an understanding of central and defining doctrines of the Christian Faith. On my way of thinking, it turns out that a complete understanding of central and defining doctrines of the Faith is not necessary for salvation. On its face, this may not appear to be a particularly dramatic or unexpected conclusion – for surely, we may all learn more about the central doctrinal mysteries of the Christian Faith! But, as the sequel will show, this has important implications for what we think about the role of Scripture in making theological judgments as well as what we think the purpose of doctrine is in the life of faith.

These are substantive, and potentially controversial, claims. Put in the form of a positive thesis, I will argue for the two interrelated conclusions that Scripture is a conditionally necessary but strictly insufficient condition both for salvation and for a complete understanding of core Christian doctrines. Let us call this the *Insufficiency of Scripture Thesis*:

> INSUFFICIENCY OF SCRIPTURE THESIS: Scripture contains all that is necessary to an understanding of salvation according to the Christian faith. But it is not sufficient for salvation *per se*. Nor is it sufficient for a complete understanding of central and defining doctrines of the Christian faith.

We proceed as follows. In the first section, I will offer some remarks about the confessional constraints that have historically applied to Protestants in the various branches of the Magisterial Reformation. These provide a kind of dogmatic context for the argument. Such Protestants should take these confessional constraints seriously even if they end up departing from them. If they do depart from them, it seems that some kind of justification would need to be offered if, as has often been the case in such churches, these confessions do in fact act as what we might call communion-specific doctrinal norms – that is, doctrinal norms that represent the historic theological mainstream of a particular communion of churches, such as Anglicans, Presbyterians, or Lutherans. Then, in the second section, I turn to consider the argument for the Insufficiency of Scripture Thesis. This depends in important respects on principles that I have defended elsewhere, namely, that Scripture is metaphysically and epistemically underdetermined.[6]

---

[5] I think it should be a doctrine removed from Christian theology as such, but my concern here is with how this has been understood in Protestant churches of the Magisterial Reformation because they have a particular stake in this doctrine.

[6] See Crisp, *Analyzing Doctrine*.

Metatheology

The conclusion draws the elements of the argument together and poses some questions for further theological exploration.

Confessional constraints

Let us begin with some remarks about confessional constraints. Protestants whose ecclesial affiliation is to one of the churches of the Magisterial Reformation[7] will normally be cognisant of confessional norms that act in some fashion as constraints on what these churches have historically taken to be acceptable theological views. This is certainly true with respect to the matter of the sufficiency of Scripture. To take representative examples from the confessions of several different Protestant traditions, Article VI of the Anglican *Articles of Religion* (1563) says this:

> Holy Scripture containeth all things necessary to salvation: so that whatsoever is not read therein, nor may be proved thereby, is not to be required of any man, that it should be believed as an article of the Faith, or be thought requisite or necessary to salvation.[8]

So, according to the *Articles of Religion*, Scripture contains all that is *necessary* for salvation. Presumably, what the framers of this document had in mind was principally the propositional content of Scripture – that is, statements that express concepts that have a truth value, such as 'God loves his people, Israel'. It is not claimed that Scripture is *sufficient* in this respect. This is perfectly consistent with the claim that someone may be in possession of all the propositions needed to come to a right judgement about a thing, and yet not come to the right judgement about a thing. For instance, many antisemites have claimed to be committed to the truth of the propositional content of Scripture, even though their antisemitism is clearly inconsistent with the teaching of Scripture.[9]

---

[7] A distinction between churches of the Magisterial Reformation and those of the Radical Reformation is a long-standing one. It goes back to the work of historian George Hunston Williams in the latter half of the twentieth century. Churches of the Magisterial Reformation comprise those ecclesial bodies that were reformed hand-in-hand with the political leadership of cities, cantons and states, e.g. Lutherans, Anglicans, Presbyterians. Churches of the Radical Reformation comprise those ecclesial bodies that were reformed without the assistance of the political leadership – and often resulted in the political persecution and suppression of those churches, e.g. the various communions of Anabaptists.

[8] Article 7 of *The Belgic Confession* (1561), one of the Three Forms of Unity in European Reformed thought, says substantially the same thing about the sufficiency of Scripture: 'We believe that this Holy Scripture contains the will of God completely and that everything one must believe to be saved is sufficiently taught in it'. (The text can be readily found in various places, e.g. the website of the *United Reformed Churches in North America*, located at: https://www.urcna.org/threeforms [last accessed October 10, 2023].)

[9] This is a matter that is faced with some honesty in the recent publication of the Faith and Order Commission of the Church of England, entitled *God's Unfailing Word: Jewish-Christian Relations* (London: Church House Publishing, 2019).

Similarly, Chapter 1.6 of *The Westminster Confession* (1648) states,

> The whole counsel of God, concerning all things necessary for His own glory, man's salvation, faith, and life, is either expressly set down in Scripture, or by good and necessary consequence may be deduced from Scripture: unto which nothing at any time is to be added, whether by new revelations of the Spirit, or traditions of men.[10]

The divines of the Westminster Assembly took pains to add in certain caveats lacking in the earlier *Articles of Religion*, specifically the claim that all that is necessary for human salvation is either expressed in Scripture or implied by Scripture. But note that here too the scope of the claim seems most naturally to be about the necessity, not the sufficiency of Scripture with respect to the right *understanding* of salvation. The thought is not that merely by reading Scripture and coming to a right understanding of salvation one is saved.[11]

In the Lutheran tradition, we find these words in the *Epitome of the Formula of Concord* (1577):

> the Holy Scriptures alone remain the only judge, rule, and standard, according to which, as the only test-stone, all dogmas shall and must be discerned and judged, as to whether they are good or evil, right or wrong.[12]

This is more circumspect and, I would add, for this very reason more helpful. It limits the dogmatic role of Scripture to that of a kind of litmus test for right doctrine. The idea is that Scripture is the only norm against which our doctrines will be tested to ensure they measure up. This too is a necessary condition for the formation of *right doctrine*, not a sufficient condition for salvation. For a person can hold right doctrine and not be saved, as Jas. 2:19 is often thought to teach.

---

[10] The earlier Scottish subordinate standard, the Scots Confession of 1560, does use the language of sufficiency in Ch. 19 on 'The Authority of the Scriptures'. This says, 'As we believe and confess the Scriptures of God sufficient to instruct and make the man of God perfect, so do we affirm and avow the authority of the same to be of God, and neither to depend on men nor angels. We affirm therefore that such as allege the Scripture to have no other authority, but that which is received from the Kirk, to be blasphemous against God, and injurious to the true Kirk, which always heareth and obeyeth the voice of her own Spouse and Pastor, but taketh not upon her to be mistress over the same'. But note that the sufficiency in view here is that which makes 'the man of God perfect', that is, it provides instruction sufficient for the Christian life – which is consistent with the insufficiency of a knowledge of Scripture for salvation. I can know a thing and not act upon it or act in a manner consistent with it.

[11] There is an irony here: the Westminster Confession states that Scripture alone is the norming norm for Christian doctrine that is not to be supplanted by human tradition. Yet this claim is not a deliverance of Scripture, but of the Confession.

[12] From *The Book of Concord* website, located at: https://bookofconcord.org/epitome/#ep-rule-and-norm-0007 (last accessed October 8, 2023).

Now, this quick look at several representative confessional documents from the churches of the Magisterial Protestant Reformation is hardly definitive. But it should raise a question in the mind of the impartial inquirer concerning the doctrine of the sufficiency of Scripture understood in terms of necessary and sufficient conditions for salvation. Let us explore this in more detail.

Consider a hypothetical *maximal account of the sufficiency of Scripture*. For present purposes, I will stipulate that a maximal account of the sufficiency of Scripture is one according to which the words of Scripture in both the original languages and in adequate translations of the texts are such that if a person reads and rightly understands them, that person has in her possession all that she needs for her salvation. If someone quibbles about what constitutes the text of Scripture, since this is debated among different communions of the Christian churches, we can say that for the sake of argument the canon of Scripture in question includes at least the sixty-six books of the Protestant Bible. This, we might think, is a kind of threshold for Scriptural adequacy with respect to the question of the Bible's sufficiency for salvation.[13]

But this immediately raises a question, to wit, what is meant by the claim that 'if a person reads and rightly understands them, that person has in her possession all that she needs for her salvation'? On this maximal account, what is meant is that if a person reads and understands the text of Scripture, she will then be in possession of all the information necessary and sufficient for salvation. Of course, it does not follow from this that such a person will rightly understand the information, and still less that this person will be saved. Many readers of the Bible have fundamentally misread and misunderstood it (e.g. Arians, Socinians), and many have read and understood it and rejected its teaching (e.g. Marcion, Servetus). Similarly, someone may read and understand the safety information provided by an airline leaflet in the pocket of the seat in front of her in an aircraft she has boarded. Upon reading it she should be in possession of all the information necessary to exit the airplane successfully if an accident should occur. But this does not guarantee that the traveller will, in fact, exit the airplane successfully if an accident occurs. Being in possession of certain information and understanding and acting upon it in an appropriate way are distinct things.

Now, it might be thought that something like the maximal account of the sufficiency of Scripture is just what the framers of the Reformation confessions meant when they wrote that 'Holy Scripture containeth all things necessary to salvation' or 'The whole counsel of God, concerning all things necessary for His own glory, man's salvation, faith, and life, is either expressly set down in Scripture, or by good and necessary consequence may be deduced from Scripture' or even, 'Holy Scriptures alone remain the only judge, rule,

---

[13] Lutherans will say this is too expansive, given the dubious status of the Epistle of James; Roman Catholics and the Eastern Orthodox communions will say this is too little, given that the Apocrypha is also part of Holy Writ. So be it. I am only after a minimum threshold account of the contents of Scripture for the sake of argument. This sort of argument is discussed in Thomas M. Crisp, 'On Believing that the Scriptures are Divinely Inspired', in Crisp and Rea, *Analytic Theology*, 187–213.

and standard, according to which, as the only test-stone, all dogmas shall and must be discerned and judged'. But, in fact, that is not the case. For the Reformation confessions also make clear that salvation is entirely a work of divine grace, and that saving faith is itself a divine gift provided by means of the Holy Spirit. So, even if we take Reformation confessions like the Anglican *Articles of Religion*, *The Westminster Confession* or *The Book of Concord* at face value, none of these documents, taken in the round, is committed to the idea that an understanding of the content of Scripture is sufficient for salvation *tout court*. For none of these confessions (or other Protestant confessions like them) states that possession of all the information *necessary* for a right understanding of salvation is *sufficient* for salvation. Even if a person does have a right understanding of the texts of Scripture, the salvific action of the Holy Spirit is still required to provide the gift of faith that is normally instrumental in the regeneration of fallen human beings.[14] No amount of reading Scripture or possessing the right information about salvation will be sufficient for salvation without the suasions of the Spirit, according to Protestant heirs of the Reformation. Calvin makes the point clearly in the *Institutes* when he says, 'Scripture will ultimately suffice for a saving knowledge of God only when its certainty is founded upon the inward persuasion of the Holy Spirit'.[15] This claim about prevenient divine agency in salvation is representative of the Magisterial Reformation tradition. For these reasons, having to do with the right understanding and interpretation of the information provided by Scripture and the need for the prevenient grace of God in the secret work of the Spirit in regeneration, possession of the right information to be found in Scripture is not sufficient for salvation. The maximal view is not an accurate view, according to the very confessions themselves.

It might be claimed that this is to conflate several doctrinal notions, namely, the sufficiency of Scripture and the effectual calling and regeneration of the believer. The sufficiency of Scripture has to do with a right understanding of the Faith, whereas effectual calling and regeneration have to do with the transformation that takes place in an individual when they are brought to salvation by the secret work of the Holy Spirit. This does represent an important conceptual distinction. But it is not the issue I am

---

[14] Compare Articles XI and XVII of *The Articles of Religion*; ch. 10 of *The Westminster Confession*; and Article IV of *The Augsburg Confession*. *The Epitome of the Formula of Concord* puts it succinctly: 'God the Holy Ghost, however, does not effect conversion without means, but uses for this purpose the preaching and hearing of God's Word, as it is written Rom. 1:16: The Gospel is the power of God unto salvation to everyone that believeth. Also Rom. 10:17: Faith cometh by hearing of the Word of God. And it is God's will that His Word should be heard, and that man's ears should not be closed. Ps. 95:8. With this Word, the Holy Ghost is present, and opens hearts, so that they, as Lydia in Acts 16:14, are attentive to it, and are thus converted alone through the grace and power of the Holy Ghost, whose work alone the conversion of man is. For without His grace, and if He does not grant the increase, our willing and running, our planting, sowing, and watering, all are nothing, as Christ says John 15:5: Without Me ye can do nothing. With these brief words, He denies to free will its powers and ascribes everything to God's grace, in order that no one may boast before God. 1 Cor. 1:29; 2 Cor. 12:5; Jer. 9:23'. (https://bookofconcord.org/epitome/).

[15] John Calvin, *Institutes of the Christian Religion*, ed. John T. McNeill, trans. Ford Lewis Battles (Philadelphia: Westminster Press, 1960. [1559]), 1. 7. 5; 1. 8. 13.

seeking to address. Rather, my concern is that discussion of the sufficiency of Scripture in Reformation theology is seriously misleading if it is not made plain at the outset that this is restricted to the right understanding of the *teaching* of Scripture regarding salvation, and not to salvation as such.[16]

It is not just that Scripture is not sufficient for salvation on its own absent the secret work of the Holy Spirit or a right understanding and interpretation of what is being read, however. It is also that Scripture must be understood according to the confessions of the Reformation church in question, whether Lutheran or Reformed. Although Protestants of all stripes would baulk at the idea that a confession might be treated as a norm on a par with Scripture, as I have already intimated, for many Protestants whose churches are a product of the Magisterial Reformation, the confessions that form the foundational documents of those communions are the theological lens through which Scripture is read.

For instance, although the Reformed churches pride themselves on being 'reformed and always reforming according to the Word of God' (*ecclesia reformata, semper reformanda secundum verbi Dei*), this itself, along with the confessions of the different Reformed churches, is a theological dictum that is not found in Scripture. (In fact, it is not a dictum found in any of the confessions of the Reformed churches either.[17]) In other words, the notion that Scripture is the norming norm that norms all other theological norms (*norma normans non normata*), and that it contains 'all things necessary for salvation' or even that a given church is 'reformed and always reforming according to the Word of God' are not themselves deliverances of Scripture. Rather, they are hermeneutical principles that are brought to the reading of Scripture by those who hold them.[18] Magisterial Protestants read Scripture in communities formed in fundamental ways by the confessions that bind them together, even when parishioners do not themselves take much notice of the confessions in question or read them. This is one reason why ecclesial communities have a particular theological 'flavour'. Lutherans focus on doctrines that are enshrined in their confessions, but so do Anglicans and Presbyterians. Each is different in this respect, and in substantive, not merely trivial, ways. To take a notorious example: these communions and their confessions understand what is going on in the celebration of the Eucharist in different and incommensurate ways. But this is surely to be expected given that the

---

[16]Kevin Vanhoozer says that Scripture is 'sufficient for everything for which it was divinely given'. John Webster says 'Scripture is *enough*. This is because Scripture is what God desires to teach'. I have no quibble with these claims, but they are consistent with something much less expansive than the traditional Protestant version of the sufficiency of Scripture. (Both citations are taken from Kevin J. Vanhoozer, *Biblical Authority After Babel: Retrieving the Solas in the Spirit of Mere Protestant Christianity* [Grand Rapids: Brazos, 2016], 114.)

[17]It is a phrase that originally appeared in a 1674 devotional by the Dutch Reformed pastor, Jodocus van Lodenstein.

[18]It is not obvious that passages in Scripture like 2 Tim. 3:16 provide internal biblical evidence of the sufficiency of Scripture. Such passages can only have been written with what today we would call the Hebrew Bible in mind – for clearly there was no New Testament at the time the epistles were composed. Besides which, 2 Tim. 3: 16 does not imply that the referent of 'Scripture' (γραφή) is *sufficient* for salvation, only that it is *useful* (ὠφέλιμος) for teaching, training and correcting in righteousness.

teaching of Scripture is contextualized (understood, interpreted) in the very different situations in which communities of Christians find themselves hundreds of years after the events described within its pages.[19]

Timothy Ward's treatment of the sufficiency of Scripture is perhaps one of the most comprehensive treatments in the last few decades. He attempts to defend what he thinks of as the traditional view that Scripture is sufficient for salvation, understood in a robustly Protestant sense consistent with the Magisterial Reformation and post-Reformation Reformed Orthodoxy, while also paying attention to recent debates about issues such as speech-act theory.

Ward distinguishes between the *formal* and *material* senses of the sufficiency of Scripture. While not a distinction made explicitly in the historic material on the topic, it is one that, he thinks, gets at a fundamental issue in the theological trajectory that stems from the Reformation confessions. He writes, 'What is most regularly meant by "the sufficiency of Scripture" is what is being called here its *material* aspect: that Scripture contains everything a person needs to know to be saved and to live in a way which pleases God. The *formal* aspect of sufficiency relates to the authority by which Scripture is interpreted and asserts that Scripture is its own interpreter.'[20]

Now, not all historic Christian theologians have affirmed both aspects of this distinction, most notably the Fathers of the Church (as Ward admits[21]), as well as many post-Reformation voices outside the Magisterial Reformation. But it does seem that the Lutheran and Reformed confessions treat Scripture as both formally and materially sufficient in the sense Ward intends. Suppose we grant this for the sake of argument. It still does not get us the idea that Scripture is sufficient for salvation *tout court*. For Ward admits, as do the Reformers and their successors, that Scripture needs to be understood and rightly interpreted, and requires the internal testimony of the Holy Spirit to be effectual for salvation. What is more, the confessions act in practice as hermeneutical constraints on what is understood to be the right interpretation of Scripture – which looks very much like a denial of formal sufficiency in practice if not in principle, given that the confessions are not themselves the words of Scripture or merely repetitions of the words of Scripture.

---

[19] As Richard Swinburne puts it at one point, 'An effective revelation cannot consist solely of original documents or other proclamations; *continuing* guidance is required, a mechanism which helps translators of the original revelation to get their translation correct'. Swinburne, *Revelation: From Metaphor to Analogy* (Oxford: Oxford University Press, 1992), 81. Emphasis original.

[20] Ward, *Word and Supplement*, 21. I shall not address the formal aspect of sufficiency in detail here, though I think Scripture is not formally sufficient given that there are clear examples of fundamental Christian doctrines that one cannot derive merely from interpreting one scriptural passage in light of another. This includes the doctrine of the atonement, the right understanding of which is still disputed in Christian theology despite all participants having access to the same data in Holy Writ.

[21] Ward, *Word and Supplement*, 28. The Fathers of the Church often deny the formal sufficiency of Scripture, which they understand to require right ecclesial interpretation.

Metatheology

Scripture is conditionally necessary but (strictly) insufficient for salvation

Let us take stock. On the basis of an appeal to some of the representative confessions of the Magisterial Reformation, I have argued that Protestant heirs of the Magisterial Reformation should not claim that they are committed to the sufficiency of Scripture if that is understood to mean something like 'sufficient for salvation' without qualification. For plainly, Scripture is not sufficient for salvation in this sense, as even the confessions themselves attest. Rather, Scripture is understood in the Reformation tradition as conditionally necessary but strictly speaking insufficient for salvation without the agency of the Holy Spirit. It is sufficient in the sense that it provides those who can read and understand it with the information needed for a right comprehension of the shape of salvation according to Christian teaching. But this is a rather Pickwickian sense of sufficiency. We would not normally claim that, say, a manual provided by a car manufacturer was sufficient for the effective running of your car. It may be sufficient for a right understanding of how your car functions if you understand the language of the manual and the concepts and diagrams it contains. But that is hardly the same thing. Yet this is exactly what the Protestant doctrine of the sufficiency of Scripture is often thought to mean. It is unhelpful and obfuscating to claim that Scripture is sufficient for salvation without careful qualification and without the right theological context. To use the language favoured by Ward, Scripture is not materially sufficient for salvation. Nor (it seems to me) is it formally sufficient. At best, it is conditionally necessary for the right understanding of the nature of salvation according to Christian theology.[22]

With this in mind, we may turn to the more constructive section of this chapter. Here I want to defend the claim that Scripture is conditionally necessary but strictly speaking insufficient for salvation, and this for several reasons. First, it is insufficient because salvation requires the prevenient work of the Holy Spirit, mentioned in the previous section. Secondly, it is insufficient because it requires theological contextualization of the sort provided by creeds and confessions, including those of the Magisterial Reformation. Thirdly, and related to this second point, it is insufficient in the sense that it does not deliver a clear and unambiguous account of core Christian doctrines such as the Trinity, incarnation and atonement.

We can present the argument in numbered statements to make its form clear, like this:

1. Scripture is, or contains, or bears witness to, the Word of God.[23]
2. By means of Scripture, God speaks.

---

[22] As I mentioned earlier, Scripture is 'conditionally necessary' for salvation because there are situations in which God confers salvation on a person who has little to no notion of the teaching of Scripture. This is true of almost all the believers recorded in Scripture who would not have had access to the Scriptures since they were not complete and available at that time. It is also true of most believers in subsequent ecclesiastical history who have not had direct access to Scripture either. (Consider the fact that most human beings until recent times were illiterate and owned no books.)

[23] I have deliberately left this first sentence open to several different understandings of the nature of Scripture that might be called 'high' views of Scripture. This includes what is often called a 'plenary' view as well as a 'Barthian' view of Scripture. Subsequent references to Scripture as the Word of God should be taken to be elliptical for this more expansive position.

3. As the Word of God, Scripture is the norming norm that norms all other theological norms this side of the grave.
4. Scripture is conditionally necessary for a right understanding of the shape of salvation.
5. Scripture is metaphysically underdetermined in important respects.
6. Scripture is epistemically underdetermined in important respects.

(Taken together, the metaphysical and epistemic underdetermination of Scripture constitutes a denial of the material sufficiency of Scripture.)

7. Scripture must be understood by its reader and requires correct interpretation.
8. In principle, the right understanding and interpretation of the propositional content of Scripture may provide the reader with a sufficient understanding of the shape of salvation according to Christian teaching.
9. This is not provided by the mere reading of Scripture, including the comparison of one passage of Scripture with another. (Denial of formal sufficiency.)
10. A framework for understanding the propositional content of Scripture is given in creeds and confessions, which act as subordinate theological norms.
11. Thus, Scripture as the Word of God is normally conditionally necessary but strictly speaking insufficient for salvation *tout court*.

Some explanatory notes on this reasoning: it presumes the high place Scripture is accorded in confessional Protestantism with which we began, though it is more expansive than the wording of the historic confessions. That is a stipulation made for the sake of argument, since it is an important motivation for the doctrine of scriptural sufficiency (as per sentences 1–3). Sentence 4 expresses the notion defended in the previous section that Scripture is necessary in the conditional sense that it is brought about by God acting by means of human agents, and that it is *one* means, indeed, the normal or typical means, by which a person comes to a knowledge of the Faith. But it is not the *only* way in which people come to the Faith, for God is free to communicate to people as God sees fit. For example, if someone has no access to Scripture and so cannot read and understand it, that is not necessarily a barrier to their coming to the Faith given the secret working of the Holy Spirit.

Sentences 5 and 6 are crucial for undercutting the notion of material sufficiency. Scripture is metaphysically and epistemically underdetermined in many important ways. For instance, it does not provide the reader with a clear and unambiguous view of God's relation to time – that is, whether God is timeless or temporal. Theological opinion on the topic is still divided at least in part because Scripture is metaphysically non-specific on this issue.[24] Nor does Scripture give a clear and unambiguous view on the paradox

---

[24]It is no argument against this position to claim that Scripture unambiguously depicts God in time, changing, repenting and interacting with creatures. For this is just to read the texts according to a rather naïve hermeneutic

of divine foreknowledge and human freedom. This is a problem that generated so much heat in the sixteenth-century Iberian Peninsula debate between Dominicans and Jesuits that the Pope intervened to suspend further discussion without resolution – a situation that persists to this very day.[25] It is also a perennial debate among Protestants, including confessional Protestants, many of whose work is deeply influenced by the shape of the historic Roman Catholic discussion.

But Scripture is also underdetermined with respect to fundamental Christian doctrine. Take the three cardinal Christian doctrines: Trinity, incarnation and atonement. 'Trinity' is not a biblical term, nor is 'atonement'. More importantly, the concepts to which these terms refer are not clear or well-defined and are not agreed upon by all participants. For this reason, there are multiple doctrines of the Trinity, incarnation and atonement, the vast majority of which are incommensurate with one another. Thus, some take the divine persons of the Trinity to be subsistent relations within a metaphysically simple Godhead. Others take the persons of the Trinity to be distinct centres of will and action that share a trope of Divinity; and there are still other views incommensurate with either of these. Plainly, these two doctrines are incompatible, though both are doctrines of the Trinity that are held by contemporary Christian thinkers – and neither can be found clearly and unambiguously taught or implied by Scripture. Similar things could be said about the incarnation and atonement, both of which have multiple interpretations that are incommensurate with one another but are often thought to be commensurate with what is found in Scripture. (Does Christ have two natures in one person? Does he have two wills, one human and one divine? Does the atonement constitute the punishment of Christ on our behalf, or is such language wholly inappropriate when applied in anything but a metaphorical sense to God's action in reconciling fallen human beings? And so on.)

These differences are the staple of theological debate. Scripture does not have a view on which extant account of each of these core doctrines of the Faith is the right one. In fact, it is not clear to me that Scripture has a clear and unambiguous view on each of these doctrines at all, which is precisely why divines continue to debate their merits. This is not because theologians are inherently vituperative and disagreeable individuals who refuse to acknowledge the plain teaching of Scripture. Rather, it is because Scripture is metaphysically and epistemically underdetermined. It does not provide us with a

---

that takes things predicated of God at face value in many (though not all) respects. Note that such a position is not hermeneutics- or metaphysics-free, however. The person who comes to the text expecting it to deliver an account of a deity who is in time will read the text one way; the person who comes to the same texts expecting to find there some account of divine action accommodated to the limitations of the human intellect will read differently. But both readers make assumptions about how the text should be read and interpreted according to different background assumptions about the divine nature and God's relation to creation, as well as which passages should be read metaphorically or figuratively, and which in a more metaphysically loaded manner.

[25] An excellent account of the *De Auxiliis* Controversy is given in Robert J. Matava, *Divine Causality and Human Free Choice: Domingo Báñez, Physical Premotion and the Controversy de Auxiliis Revisited*. Brill's Studies in Intellectual History, vol. 252 (Leiden: Brill, 2016).

sufficient account of core doctrines any more than, say, *The Lord of the Rings* provides the reader with a sufficient account of the workings of the magic of the Istarii or the Elves, or why it speaks of different races, all of which seem to be variants of white Europeans.[26]

But this appears to cut against the view of some of the Reformation confessions we began with, which state that Scripture contains all that is necessary to salvation. Of the three confessions considered, *The Westminster Confession* was the one that made explicit that this should be understood to mean that the 'whole counsel of God, concerning all things necessary for . . . man's salvation, faith, and life, is either expressly set down in Scripture, or by good and necessary consequence may be deduced from Scripture: unto which *nothing at any time is to be added*, whether by new revelations of the Spirit, or traditions of men'. (Emphasis added.)

At first glance, this seems to suggest that Scripture is materially sufficient for much more than a right knowledge of salvation. It encompasses salvation, faith and life; and is sufficient for these purposes in what it expressly states or implies – to which nothing may be added by subsequent revelation or tradition.[27] This sounds a lot like the maximal account of the sufficiency of Scripture that we already discounted. But is that right? Consider again what the *Anglican Articles of Religion* state. 'Holy Scripture containeth all things necessary to salvation: so that whatsoever is not read therein, nor may be proved thereby, is not to be required of any man, that it should be believed as an article of the Faith, or *be thought requisite or necessary to salvation*'. (Emphasis added.[28]) That which cannot be read or proven by Scripture (i.e. that which is not stated or implied by Scripture based on sound argument) is not required as an article of Faith or as necessary to salvation. Recall also that the Lutherans maintain that Holy Scripture remains 'the *only* judge, rule, and standard, according to which, as the only test-stone, all dogmas shall and must be discerned and judged, as to whether they are good or evil, right or wrong'. (Emphasis added.)

There are at least two ways to understand these confessional claims on the assumption that they form a consistent whole. The key claims seem to be these:

(C1) Scripture contains all that is needed to rightly understand salvation according to the Christian faith.
(C2) No doctrine that is not explicitly set forth or implied by the teaching of Scripture is requisite for salvation.

---

[26]Swinburne comments, 'it is far from obvious how certain parts of the Bible are to be understood –we need a context to make the meaning of the sentences clear – and different readers to whom the truth of Scripture has seemed evident have understood it to mean very different things'. (*Revelation*, 117.) This seems historically indisputable.
[27]Compare Heinrich Heppe, who writes 'The distinction between a *fundamentum Scripturae* and the individual doctrines in it, and the conviction that the latter are essentially present in the former, is so essential . . . to the Reformed system in general, that the latter cannot be understood at all without recognition of the former'. *Reformed Dogmatics*, ed. Ernst Bizer, trans. G. T. Thomson (London: Collins, 1950), 42.
[28]Recall also the similar language of the Belgic Confession on this point, mentioned earlier.

But these two claims are consistent with at least two different views. The first of these states that Scripture contains all that is required for salvation. Presumably, this includes core doctrines like the Trinity, incarnation and atonement, at least in embryonic form. These core doctrines are either explicitly taught in Scripture or may be derived by implication from what Scripture says. Call this the *material sufficiency view of Scriptural doctrine*. The alternative is to say that Scripture contains all that is required for (an understanding of) salvation, but that it does not necessarily explicitly teach or imply a single, complete account of core Christian doctrine; for Scripture is metaphysically and epistemically underdetermined in this respect. Although the right understanding of these doctrines is important, it is not necessary for human salvation. Call this the *material insufficiency view of Scriptural doctrine*.

The material sufficiency view of Scriptural doctrine is the one that authors like Ward and other defenders of the views of Reformed Orthodoxy of the post-Reformation period wish to uphold.[29] But there is much to commend the material insufficiency view of Scriptural doctrine. For one thing, there are a host of those counted as among the redeemed by even the most conservative confessional Protestants who did not hold core Christian doctrines in any shape or form. This includes not just the saints of the Hebrew Bible, such as Abraham, the prophets, and the people of Israel, but many, many individuals who lived during and/or after the life of Christ. So, it cannot be true that either access to the right understanding of Scripture or a right knowledge of core Christian doctrine is requisite to salvation, for that automatically excludes this vast host that even the most conservative confessional Protestant would want to count as among the redeemed.

Nevertheless, it might be argued that the material sufficiency of Scripture can account for this concern. Perhaps the thought is that once the canon of Scripture was complete, the core doctrines it contained in embryonic form became mandatory for salvation. Then, it would be true for those who lived after the time at which the canon was established that Scripture contains all that is necessary for a right understanding of salvation and that includes the core doctrines like the Trinity, incarnation and atonement that are either taught in Scripture or can be inferred on the basis of a right understanding of Scripture and are requisite for salvation. But this cannot be true either. For one thing, it commits its defenders to a view according to which those who live after the closing of the canon are significantly epistemically disadvantaged. They are subject to an epistemic standard that those who lived before the closing of the canon are not – the very text of Scripture that contains all things necessary for salvation including all (core) doctrine. But it would be invidious to commit oneself to a doctrine of salvation that meant those living after the closing of the canon were chronologically disadvantaged in comparison with, say, Abraham, who didn't need to have any views about the sufficiency of Scripture or what

---

[29] A good recent example of this sort of view in a textbook of Christian doctrine can be found in Fred Sanders, *The Triune God*. New Studies in Dogmatics (Grand Rapids: Zondervan Academic, 2017). Sanders's point of departure is the notion that the doctrine of the Trinity is at least implicit in the texts of Scripture.

it implied and yet was saved. Surely God does not make salvation more difficult after the coming of Christ than before!

Behind these concerns is something more fundamental, however. This is that the way in which the material sufficiency of Scripture is used tends to make salvation a very logocentric affair. By that I mean, it ties salvation in important respects to Scripture and to holding certain views about Scripture. That is surely a mistake. When the thief on the cross made his inchoate confession, he was not greeted with consternation for not having a rightly formed understanding of the Faith based on rightly apprehending Scripture and its doctrine. He was told that he would be with Christ in paradise that very day.

Some will worry that the sort of argument being mounted here makes Scripture and/or right doctrine a much less important matter than it was for those who framed the confessional documents of the Magisterial Reformation. But that need not be the case. What it does mean is that a knowledge of doctrine that is not contained in or implied by Scripture is not requisite to salvation. I have said this includes the core doctrines of the Faith. But that is not to make such doctrine unimportant; still less is it to marginalize the importance of Scripture to the life of faith. It is rather to put both Scripture and doctrine in their rightful place. The fact is, most Christians do not know the Bible very well and hold to at least some mistaken doctrines. The Trinity is a notorious example of this, but so are the incarnation and atonement. Most Christians cannot give an accurate account of any of these doctrines as they have been traditionally taught and understood in Catholic Christianity. Most would be hard-pressed to find exegetical arguments in their favour. But this should not be surprising. Similarly, most people living in a particular jurisdiction cannot provide an adequate account of the role of the law or of important ways in which legal doctrines like *mens rea* inform given branches of the law, such as criminal law, either. A failure to understand a thing or to rightly apprehend its importance says nothing about the actual thing itself or about its actual importance. All it speaks to is a person's limited understanding of the matter.

Doctrine is important. This is particularly true regarding the cardinal doctrines of the Faith. But rightly apprehending them is another matter, as is rightly sourcing them (whether in Scripture or the tradition). Scripture does indeed contain what is necessary for a right *understanding* of salvation – the raw data, as it were, on the basis of which we may form a view. But this must be rightly interpreted (normally, in a particular ecclesial community). Even if sufficient comprehension is attained, this does not mean salvation is also obtained. For that is a matter of the secret work of the Holy Spirit. It seems that salvation is consistent with very little knowledge or understanding of core doctrine or even familiarity with Scripture.[30] Yet Scripture is the norming norm to which we turn in trying to understand and make sense of the Faith this side of the grave, under the guidance of the Holy Spirit, and in accordance with creeds, confessions and ecclesiastical

---

[30]Something that even the Apostle Paul seems to acknowledge in Rom. 10:9: 'If you declare with your mouth, "Jesus is Lord," and believe in your heart that God raised him from the dead, you will be saved'. (NIV.)

authority. In other words, Scripture is conditionally necessary but strictly speaking insufficient for salvation according to the Christian faith.

Conclusion

We began by setting out the following thesis:

> INSUFFICIENCY OF SCRIPTURE THESIS: Scripture contains all that is necessary to an understanding of salvation according to the Christian faith. But it is not sufficient for salvation *per se*. Nor is it sufficient for a complete understanding of central and defining doctrines of the Christian faith.

I have argued that this is the right way to think about the authority of Scripture as the norming norm of the Christian faith this side of the grave. However, this is clearly contrary to a widely held view in many churches of the Magisterial Reformation that Scripture is sufficient for salvation and for a complete understanding of central and defining Christian doctrines like the Trinity, incarnation, and atonement. If my argument is right, this view is mistaken. Not only that, retaining it has the potential to cause serious theological mischief. For those who think that Scripture is sufficient for salvation and/or for the right understanding of core Christian doctrines will inevitably misappropriate Scripture or misconstrue the scope and reach of its authority.

As the Word of God, Scripture is the norming norm this side of the grave – or so the churches of the Magisterial Reformation have confessed. Historically, it is the normal means by which participants in these churches have come to understand the shape of salvation according to the Christian faith. Understood in this way, it may be said to contain all that is necessary for a right understanding of salvation according to the Christian faith. But that in and of itself is not sufficient for salvation because other conditions are needed for a person to be regenerated. Nor is it sufficient for a complete understanding of central and defining doctrines of the Christian faith. For in the case of the Trinity, incarnation, and atonement, which are the three cardinal doctrines of Christianity, Scripture theologically underdetermines which of the extant views on these topics is the right view. One needs to go beyond Scripture to articulate adequate doctrines of the Trinity, incarnation and atonement. This is not to undermine the authority of Scripture, but merely to place proper limits on its epistemic and metaphysical functions when it comes to understanding the Faith. Perhaps this may be an aid to those churches that continue to think it important to be reformed and *always reforming* according to the Word of God.

CHAPTER 6
WHENCE TRINITARIANISM?

In Christianity, the doctrine of God is inseparable from the dogma of the Holy Trinity. For God is essentially triune. That is, it is necessarily the case that God is absolutely one and indivisible and yet subsists in three distinct divine persons. This is the central and defining claim of Christian theism. But how this claim has come to be so central to Christianity is a matter that is disputed. Rather than attempting to give a historical analysis of the events that led to its adoption in the early church, I will focus instead on what might be called a dogmatic account of its formation. I am interested in answering the following question: *how should we understand the relationship between the formation of the doctrine and the dogmatic role it plays in Christian thought?* This is surely a metatheological issue.

The chapter proceeds as follows. To begin with, it is important to say something about the fact that the dogma of the Trinity is a mystery. This provides vital context for the explanatory scope of any attempt to specify the doctrine. For, as I have already said in previous chapters, our comprehension of these sublime matters will only ever be partial and incomplete this side of the grave. With this in mind, we turn in a second section to consider sources for the Trinity in Scripture and the tradition. Following on from the previous chapter, I argue that Scripture is insufficient for a doctrine of the Trinity, and that it is only in the broader context of reading the biblical texts in line with later tradition that we come to see that God is indeed triune. The third section of the chapter focuses on the relationship between Scripture, tradition and models of the Trinity, arguing that theologians engage in providing models of the Trinity that are simplified descriptions of more complex data that approximate to the truth of the matter – a truth that is given in outline in the combination of Scripture plus the tradition, but which is not fully specified there (in keeping with the findings of Chapters 2 and 3). Thus, there is still a place for constructive theology with respect to the Christian doctrine of God, for the dogma of the Trinity is not given in full in either Scripture or subsequent tradition.

Divine mystery

Recall that by the word 'mystery', I mean something that is beyond human understanding. I do not mean something that is simply a veil drawn over poor reasoning or, worse still, a contradiction in terms. A mystery in this sense is a matter that we can only grasp partially at best. There are many such mysteries in human life, and not just in theology. The universe is deeply mysterious. We cannot fathom it – literally cannot, given the limitations of human minds. Some of the most fundamental concepts of contemporary physics are deeply mysterious, and not just for laypersons unversed in the mathematics required to understand these matters. (How shall we understand quantum mechanics? There are multiple interpretations and most of them are very difficult to comprehend. Even if they can be comprehended by human intellects, the heart of such concepts is far beyond the mastery of all but a handful of human beings.) Even in philosophy, it may be that some problems are beyond our ken. Take, for instance, the endless debates about human free will – not just about what 'free will' means (if anything), but about what is meant by acts of volition, what sort of freedom of choice human agents have, whether moral responsibility requires some notion of human free choice, and so on. There remain deep divisions on this fundamental matter and no sign that resolution is in sight. Some contemporary philosophers have simply admitted that the whole notion of freedom in this sense is deeply mysterious and unresolvable for humans in our present state of evolutionary development. These two examples could be multiplied. Mystery is part of human existence, something we encounter in many different spheres of life, not something that is necessarily obviously conceptually problematic.

Turning to matters theological, we find mystery at the very heart of our attempts to reason about the divine. We might say that God is mysterious in the sense of being *beyond our ken*. In fact, God will be forever beyond our understanding. The Deity remains mysterious for finite creatures forevermore. As the writer of Deut. 29: 29 puts it, 'the secret things belong to the LORD our God'. That is one reason why the life promised to Christians in the eschaton, or the world to come, is a life full of discovery. For human beings, even in a glorified state, will be forever understanding new things about the God who is so much greater than we are. Something similar would be true if we humans lived forever in this world and spent all our time investigating the cosmos in which we live. We would continue to make new discoveries for centuries to come! In the case of our relationship to God, the journey of finite human beings towards God is one that never yields complete union or complete understanding of the divine mystery. But it does lead to ever greater proximity to the divine and ever greater participation in the divine life. We are everlastingly pilgrims journeying deeper 'into' God, in this life and the next. Even in a glorified state, this will be the case if our knowledge and understanding of the divine is to increase, as it must if we are to forever commune with the one who made us.

Some theologians want to add to this notion about the mysteriousness of God and God's ways additional claims about what we can know of God. They claim that the Deity is *inconceivable, incomprehensible,* and *ineffable*.[1] That is, God is said to be such that we cannot conceptualize the divine nature, which is unintelligible to creatures, and is so

---

[1] There is a long history to this discussion, and we have already had cause to mention these apophatic theological claims in previous chapters. In addition to the works of Pseudo-Dionysius in *Pseudo-Dionysius, The Complete Works* and Jonathan D. Jacobs, 'The Ineffable, Inconceivable, and Incomprehensible God: Fundamentality and Apophatic Theology', one might consult Karen Kilby, *God, Evil and the Limits of Theology* (London: T&T Clark, 2020), especially chapters 2–4.

removed from us that we cannot express anything substantive about the divine essence in words. These are very strong theological claims. For on this way of thinking, it is not just that we human creatures cannot fathom the depths of the divine. It is not merely that we stand before a great mystery, the mystery of divinity which we can only apprehend in a piecemeal and fragmentary way. It is that we cannot know what God is like *in Godself* because there is a massive ontological gulf between ourselves and God that is in principle unbridgeable. We cannot ever reach God through our own reasoning and reflection no matter how hard we try – divinity remains forever inaccessible to us. Thus, if we are to know God, it must be because the Deity deigns to be revealed to us. This certainly chimes with what we find in Scripture. God speaks, draws near to creatures and is revealed to them. But when that happens, it is almost as if, in one sense, God remains as mysterious as before. Consider the revelation of the divine name in Exodus 3:14. In response to Moses' query the LORD is revealed as 'I am who I am', or, perhaps, 'I will be who I will be'. That is, to say the least, enigmatic. In a sense, it reveals that God is beyond the comprehension of Moses and that God is mysterious, which is itself a curious thing. After all, revealing to someone that you are mysterious is an odd sort of revelation! But perhaps this encounter says something more, something about the great gulf that separates us from God. This is a metaphysical rather than an epistemological matter. That is, it is a matter of how things are, rather than how we apprehend or know them or whether we can apprehend or know them.

It seems, then, that we would know next to nothing about the divine were it not for the condescension of God towards creatures. What is more, even when God is revealed to us in some manner, that revelation can only ever be partial and fragmentary because God is transcendent. That is, God is above and beyond us, something we cannot fathom. Indeed, on occasion in the Hebrew Bible those who encounter the divine fear that they will be consumed because mere human eyes cannot apprehend the Creator who is holy as well as transcendent. Thus, Samson's parents fear that they will be consumed upon meeting with the Angel of the LORD in Judges 13, and the prophet Isaiah in the famous courtroom vision of Isaiah 6 is afraid that he will be undone because he has had a vision of the divine court, until he is comforted by the angel who sears his sin away with a coal from the censor before the throne of divine majesty.

This apophaticism, or negative theology, according to which we can know little or nothing about the divine essence or nature of God and must approach thinking about the divine by means of negation or saying what God *is not* rather than what God *is*, has some warrant. In this way of thinking, we can say things like, God is incorporeal, that is, without a body, or that God's nature is incommunicable, that is, incapable of being communicated or understood by creatures. For without revelation, human beings would be groping around in conceptual darkness with no clear idea of God. However, this does not mean that if God reveals Godself to us, the mystery of the divine nature will completely dissipate. Even with revelation, we are presented with a way of thinking about the divine nature that is deeply puzzling and counterintuitive, the supreme example of which is the doctrine of the Trinity. Thus, paradoxically, at the heart of Christian doctrine is a teaching that is revealed and yet is deeply mysterious and beyond

Metatheology

our comprehension. Yet it is with this central and defining dogma of Christianity that we must begin – for to understand anything of Christian teaching we must understand at least something of who it is that we are being taught about. Given that our grasp of these things will be piecemeal and tentative, and dependent in important respects upon divine revelation, where can we look to find the sources for the doctrine of the Trinity?

Sources for the Trinity

It is often said that the Trinity is a biblical doctrine, though it is not a biblical term. The word 'Trinity' postdates the closing of the canon of Scripture. Nor do we find in Scripture the doctrine of the Trinity in embryonic form, implicit in the words of the text just as, in a love letter written between two young people in a secret tryst, the lover may indicate her affection for her beloved without ever explicitly declaring it. It is frequently claimed that this is just what we *do* find in Scripture, however. For many Christian theologians, the doctrine of the Trinity is at least intimated even if it is not explicitly taught in the Hebrew Bible and New Testament.[2] Thus, in the creation accounts of the primeval prologue in Genesis, much has been made of the plural pronoun used by the Deity in creating human beings (Gen. 1: 26–27), as indicating an actual plurality in the Godhead. Moreover, frequent appearances of the Angel of the LORD in various Old Testament narratives are often said to indicate Christophanies, that is, appearances of the Second Person of the Trinity in a kind of quasi-incarnate form prior to his incarnation in Jesus of Nazareth. From the story of Abram's meal with angels (Gen. 19) and Jacob wrestling with God at the Jabbok ford (Gen. 32: 22–30) through to Joshua's encounter with the Commander of the Armies of the LORD (Josh. 5:13–15) and the story of Samson's parents and the stranger they encounter whose name is too wonderful to say (Jud. 13), as well as many other narratives besides these, God is physically manifest in human encounters.

Similarly, in the New Testament, the baptism of Jesus or the appearance on the Mount of Transfiguration, or the baptismal formula given by Christ in the Great Commission of Matt. 28:19, or the coming of the Holy Spirit at Pentecost are often thought to be indicative of the triunity of God. For in the canonical accounts of Christ's baptism, we have the Holy Spirit appearing like a dove above the baptised Christ, and the voice of God the Father approving of the work of the Son. In the case of the Transfiguration, we have the changed appearance of Christ and the disembodied voice of God. When considering the baptismal formula in the Great Commission (Matt. 28:19), we see that believers are to be baptised in the Triune name. And in the case of Pentecost, the tongues of fire that come to rest above the heads of those gathered in the Upper Room after

---

[2]For a recent example of this claim, see Fred Sanders, *The Triune God: New Studies in Dogmatics* (Grand Rapids: Zondervan Academic, 2016).

Christ's ascension are said to speak of the agency of the Spirit distinct from that of the incarnate Son incarnate or of the Father.

These examples are meant to illustrate the point that Scripture is usually traditionally understood to be the principal source of the dogma of the Trinity, a doctrine which the Church gradually came to comprehend through reflection upon the biblical texts and the apostolic witness to the life and work of Christ that was passed down through the generations of the early Christian communities. But is that right? Historical biblical-critical scholarship has tended to be very sceptical of such claims and wary of apparently anachronistic Christian re-readings of various biblical stories, especially in the Hebrew Bible, which are interpreted through the lens of later Christian orthodoxy. Such scepticism is not universal, however. A small but important group of recent New Testament scholarship has argued that Christ is included in the divine identity and in the worship of God from an early phase of the life of the followers of The Way in the New Testament documents. This sort of view has come to be known as *early high Christology*.[3] Yet even if the early high Christologists are right (and I find many of their arguments persuasive), it does not get us a dogma of the Trinity as they themselves are quick to point out. One does not need to be sceptical about the dogma of the Trinity or its importance for Christian belief to maintain that it is not to be found, even in embryonic form, in the writings of the biblical witnesses. To see this more clearly, let us revisit the several biblical passages just mentioned, in each case accepting for the sake of argument the assumption that traditional Trinitarian biblical exegesis has presumed can be found implicit in the texts in question about the divine nature.

Return once more to the primeval prologue of Genesis. In the creation accounts, God is spoken of in the plural ('let us make humans in our own image . . .'). In and of itself, this does not imply Trinitarianism. For instance, in more recent times, it has become a commonplace for princes or potentates to speak of themselves in the plural when making royal pronouncements ('We thank our prime minister for her words . . .'). But we do not think this implies anything more than a kind of royal prerogative. There is certainly something of the potentate in the way God speaks and acts in the world God creates in Genesis. Yet even if we conceded that the creation accounts do indeed suggest there is some sort of metaphysical plurality within the divine life, this in-and-of-itself does not imply Trinitarianism. Plurality falls conceptually short of triunity, as anyone familiar with Vedantic Hinduism will know. So, there is no good reason to think that the use of a plural pronoun to refer to God implies the Trinity as such, though it may indicate something more than royal prerogative – that is, it may suggest something

---

[3] Scholarly names associated with this position include the late Professor Larry Hurtado of Edinburgh University, the late Professor James Dunn of Durham University, Professor Richard Bauckham of the University of St Andrews, and Rt Rev Professor N. T. Wright, also of St Andrews. For a helpful overview and contribution to this literature, see Andrew Tern Loke, *The Origin of Divine Christology*. Society for New Testament Studies Monograph Series 169 (Cambridge: Cambridge University Press, 2017).

about the divine life that lends itself towards later Christian re-readings of these texts in a Trinitarian direction.

If we turn to consider the passages in the Hebrew Bible that speak of the Angel of the LORD, it is even less clear that what is said of these various theophanies, if indeed they are theophanies, should be taken to be Christophanies. A theophany is an appearance of God. Many of the passages in which the Angel of the LORD appears suggest that it is indeed God who has appeared to those who encounter this mysterious figure. (At least, that is how many of those who encounter the Angel in these narratives understand the entity in question.) But an appearance of God is not the same as an appearance of the Second Person of the Trinity in some apparently physical state prior to the incarnation. There is nothing in the passages in which the Angel of the LORD appears that indicates that these theophanic narratives should be understood as specifically christophanic in nature. If anything, such readings of the texts appear to be a kind of anachronistic Christian colonising of the Hebrew culture and context in which the narratives are set.[4]

Next, recall the New Testament passages mentioned above. In the baptism of Jesus, the Spirit of God appears to Christ as a dove and a voice from heaven is heard confirming the work of Christ. But we read into the narrative if we think this *implies* a doctrine of the Trinity. On its face, it commits its readers to no such doctrine. It would be perfectly consistent with the baptismal narratives of the three synoptic Gospels, Matt. three: 13–17; Mk. 1:9–11; and Lk. 3:21–22, to regard them as explaining how God, by God's spirit, is present and confirms God's approval of Christ's ministry by means of the disembodied heavenly voice. Nothing in that way of understanding the passage *requires* Trinitarianism. (The Spirit of God may, after all, simply be a manner of speaking about the presence of God in the narrative, and it is not clear from the text itself, independent of prior commitment to the dogma of the Trinity, why we should understand the image of the dove who appears to Christ, and the voice he hears, as indicative of distinct divine *persons*. That too seems to require the imposition of concepts upon the text that are simply not there.)

This is even more clearly the case in the story of the appearance on the Mount of Transfiguration, versions of which can be found in the three synoptic Gospels in Matt. 17, Mk. 9, and Lk. 9. Although these are remarkable narratives, none of the three canonical versions of the story imply that there are distinct divine persons of the Godhead. Jesus' clothing is transformed, shining brighter than any launderer could whiten them. The two pillars of the prophetic tradition of the Hebrew Bible, Moses and Elijah, appear with Jesus. A voice is heard commending the work of Jesus to the disciples gathered on the Mount with Christ from a cloud that shrouds him in a manner reminiscent of the Shekinah cloud of the divine presence found in the stories of Mount Sinai in Exodus and in the dedication of Solomon's Temple. Nevertheless, extraordinary though the narrative

---

[4] Of course, whether one thinks of such views as the Christian 'colonising' of the Hebrew Bible with Christian tropes or as an appropriate canonical approach to the texts understood from the vantage of greater revelation in the New Testament is a matter that is religiously moot.

is, it is not a sound basis upon which to begin the construction of a doctrine of the Trinity. For the concept of the Trinity is not taught or implied in the narrative.

The baptismal formula of the Great Commission at the end of Matthew's Gospel is more obviously Trinitarian in structure and has led many biblical scholars to wonder if it is a later addition to the text. Let us assume for present purposes that it is not a later addition, to concede as much as possible to the Trinitarian readers of this text in a spirit of charity. What follows for Christian doctrine? Baptism in the triune name is something precious to almost all Christians down through the ages. But the words given by Christ in Matthew's account do not in-and-of-themselves imply that God is triune. For it does not teach or imply that there is one God subsisting in three distinct divine persons. (Once again, and at the risk of testing the patience of the reader, this is said with the proviso that we come to such texts without assuming the dogma of the Trinity at the outset or reading it into the text, which would be to beg the question at issue.) At most, the words of the Great Commission indicate that there is something in God that is plural – something corresponding to the threefold name of Father, Son and Spirit. But that is some way away from the creedal notion promulgated by the Fathers at the First Council of Constantinople, that God is one substance subsisting in three persons.

Not only that: in Peter's address to the gathered crowds on the Day of Pentecost at the beginning of the Acts of the Apostles, he tells them that they should repent and be baptised in the name of Jesus Christ for the forgiveness of their sins – *not* the name of the Holy Trinity. Upon being baptised in Christ's name, they will receive the Holy Spirit. In the text, Peter says, 'Μετανοήσατε, καὶ βαπτισθήτω ἕκαστος ὑμῶν ἐπὶ τῷ ὀνόματι Ἰησοῦ Χριστοῦ εἰς ἄφεσιν τῶν ἁμαρτιῶν ὑμῶν, καὶ λήμψεσθε τὴν δωρεὰν τοῦ ἁγίου πνεύματος·' (Acts 2:38). That is, 'Repent and be baptised every one of you, in the name of Jesus Christ for the forgiveness of your sins, and you will receive the gift of the Holy Spirit.' Later in the same narrative, when the Apostle Paul encounters some of John the Baptist's disciples, he asks if they have received the Holy Spirit, and they concede they have not. He then baptises them in the name of Jesus. (The text reads 'ἀκούσαντες δὲ ἐβαπτίσθησαν εἰς τὸ ὄνομα τοῦ κυρίου Ἰησοῦ' [Acts 19:5], i.e. 'upon hearing this, they were baptised into the name of the Lord Jesus'.) Thereupon, the disciples receive the Holy Spirit by the laying on of his hands (Acts 19:1–7). Oneness Pentecostals have used these texts to justify their teaching that baptism should only be in the name of Christ. They have also cited them as a partial justification for their denial of the doctrine of the Trinity. At the very least, these passages in Acts make problematic the claim that the universal witness of the New Testament authors is to a Trinitarian formula for baptism. The idea that baptism in Christ's name may be elliptical for baptism in the name of the Trinity is, to say the least, to strain the meaning of the texts in question.

Next, return to the story of the coming of the Holy Spirit at Pentecost. Here too there is insufficient evidence to read a doctrine of triunity from the face of the text. The sound of rushing wind in the Upper Room and the appearance of what seem to be tongues of fire suspended above the heads of those gathered (Acts 2: 2–4) are immediately followed by the believers being filled with the Holy Spirit and speaking in foreign tongues to the multinational Jews gathered in the city for the Passover feast. But even if this does speak of the Spirit of God, that in-and-of-itself does not yield a dogma of the Trinity. For it does not imply some distinct divine person *within* the Godhead, so to speak.

What are we to make of all this? Does this mean that the dogma of the Trinity should be excised from Christian doctrine or placed in an appendix in systematic theologies as the nineteenth-century German divine, Friedrich Schleiermacher, did in his great systematic-theological work, *The Christian Faith*?[5] Not necessarily. What this thumbnail sketch of some of the relevant textual data indicates, I think, is that the biblical documents are metaphysically and epistemologically underdetermined. We cannot derive the dogma of the Trinity from the Bible alone, for it is not clearly or unambiguously taught in the Bible. In fact, there is no clear, unambiguous account of the Trinity until its canonical form was disseminated after the First Council of Constantinople in AD 381. The earlier creed of the First Council of Nicaea in AD 325 did not include an explicit identification of the Holy Spirit as the third person of the Trinity, proceeding from the Father and worshipped together with the Father and Son. But this is some hundreds of years after the end of the Apostolic age.

Of course, similar things can be said of other central and defining Christian doctrines. For instance, according to classical Christology, which was bequeathed to the Christian churches after the great upheavals of the debates about the person of Christ in the first few centuries of the life of the Christian communities, the incarnation should be understood in terms of the two natures doctrine. This is the view that Christ is one divine person subsisting in two natures, one divine, the other human. The divine nature is the nature of God the Son, the Second Person of the Trinity. The human nature is acquired upon assumption at the first moment of incarnation when the human nature of Christ is miraculously formed in the womb of the Virgin Mary by the supernatural agency of the Holy Spirit. The two natures doctrine, which is a cornerstone of traditional Christian teaching from the time of the Council of Chalcedon in AD 451, is nowhere taught in the New Testament. Nor is it implied by the New Testament documents. Yet it is fundamental to much historic Christian teaching.

Or consider the atonement. This is a central and defining Christian doctrine that has never had a settled dogmatic form; that is, a theological or doctrinal form shared by all Christians or encapsulated in a creed or confession that all Christians have acceded to or recognize as authoritative. The dogmatic shape of the atonement is still a matter of dispute, with competing views being argued over to this day. Most theologians working on the doctrine of atonement acknowledge that one of the reasons for this plurality of views on the doctrine is that there is no single way of construing atonement taught in the Bible. There are different motifs and metaphors used, and different concepts at work in

---

[5]Schleiermacher is often unfairly thought to have *relegated* the Trinity to an appendix in *Christian Faith*. However, a more sympathetic interpretation of his purpose is that in so doing he treats the Trinity as the climax of Christian doctrine, but not a notion that one can derive merely from experience, as with much of the rest of Christian doctrine discussed in the bulk of his text. The Trinity, on this way of thinking, is a kind of theological postulate that helps explain the grounds of the Christian's experience of a sense of utter dependence upon God.

particular passages that are illuminating and that throw light on aspects of the doctrine. But there is nothing like a complete account of the atonement as the redemptive work of Christ, either according to its nature (what the mechanism of atonement turns out to be) or according to its scope (who it is that the atonement of Christ saves in principle or on fact).

The Trinity, incarnation, and atonement are the three central and defining dogmas of Christianity. They mark out Christian doctrine from other forms of monotheism, such as Judaism or Islam. Yet, so it seems to me, in the case of the Trinity and the incarnation, the particular form of those doctrines that have been bequeathed to subsequent theology by the early church in its conciliar pronouncements is not clearly or unambiguously taught or even implied (at least, in the strict and particular sense, which is the sense we are interested in here) in the biblical documents. And in the case of the atonement, there is no single account of the doctrine in terms of the nature or scope of Christ's redemptive work that is universally agreed upon based on the biblical texts. Yet so it seems to me, these are doctrines that represent a kind of conceptual hard core to Christianity. This seems problematic. For it is a theological commonplace in historic Christianity of whatever stripe to hold that forms of these three dogmas are in fact taught, or at least implied, in the biblical documents. Without such a theological safeguard, it is difficult to see how they can be defended. For, the thought is, rooting them in Scripture is to root them in divine revelation – or at least, to secure witnesses to divine revelation, namely, the canonical writings of the biblical authors. If we decouple the dogma from these texts, we unmoor ourselves, theologically speaking, and set ourselves adrift on a sea of theological speculation that is not anchored in the oracles of God.

However, scepticism and full-throated biblicism are not the only two live options available when it comes to the dogma of the Trinity or, for that matter, the incarnation or atonement. A persistent worry about Christian uses of the biblical texts, especially Hebrew Bible texts, has been that they court anachronism or are even guilty of colonising the texts in question with ideas alien to their original audience or cultural context. But such concerns conflate several things that should be distinguished.

First, there are the texts of Scripture. (For reasons of space, let us set to one side worries about the canonization of the text of Scripture, important and salient though it is for questions of biblical authority.) Traditionally, these have been understood to be the oracles of God, or at least witnesses to the oracles of God, the bearers of divine revelation. Suppose that is right, and the biblical texts are at least the witness to divine revelation they are traditionally thought to be. Such texts can still be metaphysically and epistemically underdetermined. That is just what we find is the case when it comes to central and defining dogmas of the Faith such as the Trinity, incarnation and atonement.

Second, there is the question of the right interpretation of these texts, which is a matter of hermeneutics. Given that they were written by many different authors and editors over a long period of time in very different contexts and cultures and in several different languages, it is not surprising that the right interpretation of these ancient texts presents a significant challenge to modern readers. The two horizons, that of the ancient world and that of the modern reader, must somehow be brought into alignment. Not only that:

we also read these texts within a tradition of interpretation, even if that is not something of which we are conscious. For instance, readers of the New Testament who have been formed in some branch of the Christian tradition come to the texts expecting to find a particular worldview that someone formed in, say, a Confucian context or a secular non-theological context would not. For the Christian reader has received, as it were, a whole history of interpretation in their formation and in how they are taught to read and understand these texts. These are non-trivial contextual differences when it comes to thinking about matters like the Trinity, a doctrine unique to the Christian tradition.

Taken together, these two things, the text of Scripture and its interpretation, present significant challenges to the reader seeking to understand the doctrine of the Trinity. But note that they are quite distinct things. We bring to the text certain assumptions, an understanding of the background to the text, its history, formation and reception. And we expect to find in the text certain things depending on how we read the texts in a particular community of interpretation, context and tradition. Thus, for example, someone who reads the New Testament from the context of a contemporary American Southern Baptist Church community will understand key aspects of the text of Scripture very differently than someone who reads it in the context of, say, a modern German State Lutheran Church community, or a South African independent Pentecostal community, or a Colombian Roman Catholic community. Once again, the differences will often yield non-trivial results. (Consider the difference between Oneness Pentecostal readings of the book of Acts and traditional Roman Catholic readings. The first is non-Trinitarian, the second is decidedly Trinitarian!)

Yet it is true to say that most voices in the Christian tradition, of whatever stripe, have tended to think that the Trinity is a doctrine to be found in Scripture even if it is only in embryonic form. I have given reasons for thinking this is problematic. But I have also cautioned against scepticism with respect to the dogma. So where does that leave the reader of Scripture committed to both a careful, hermeneutically sensitive reading of the texts as witnesses to divine revelation, who is alive to the concerns about metaphysical and epistemic underdetermination and who does not want to jettison the traditional Christian understanding of God as triune? My suggestion is that we think of post-biblical tradition in the Church, especially those aspects of the tradition that yielded ecumenical consensus in the ancient Church about certain doctrinal matters like the Trinity, as providing us with *dogmatic constraints* on how we understand the texts themselves. Put differently, we might say that the reflections and controversies in the early Church about the nature of God that resulted in the Nicene-Constantinopolitan creed and its doctrinal framework for thinking about God in triune terms as one essence subsisting in three distinct divine persons is a hermeneutical framework that should shape how we read the biblical texts.

On this way of thinking, there are the texts of Scripture and then there is the post-biblical tradition. Both are sources of theological authority in making judgements about Christian doctrine. But neither is sufficient on its own. This is not a conclusion reached on the basis of prior theoretical commitments about the nature of theological authority in abstraction, as it were, from history – a kind of armchair dogmatics. Rather, it is a conclusion reached because of what is in fact the case when it comes to the formulation of Christian doctrine. In historic Protestantism, there is the idea that Scripture is the final authority in all matters of doctrine, and a norming norm that norms all other theological norms. I think that this can certainly be preserved on the account being offered here. Scripture is the final authority in matters of doctrine this side of the grave, and it is a norm that norms all other matters of theological importance in this respect: it trumps other sources of theological authority. For instance, if a particular council or synod were to draw up a statement of doctrine or a confession that was plainly contrary to the teaching of Scripture, the teaching of the biblical text would trump the teaching of the council or synod. To take a hypothetical case, suppose a synod decided that there are many gods but that the God of Scripture is the only divinity that should be worshipped. This is a version of henotheism. Plainly, that is contrary to the teaching of Scripture. Although passages in the Hebrew Bible do speak as if there are many gods, the prevailing view in Scripture as a whole, and certainly in the later Hebrew Bible and in the New Testament, is that there is only one true god, and that is the God and Father of Jesus of Nazareth, who is also the God of Abraham, Isaac and Jacob. Other deities are either false gods, idols, or angelic beings.

However, often judgements need to be made in cases where things are not as clear-cut, and at least some of those cases will touch upon matters vital to the shape of Christian doctrine, like the Trinity. Suppose the teaching of Scripture, taken as a whole, supports some form of monotheism, as is commonly thought. Is this consistent with Trinitarianism? Is Trinitarianism taught or implied in Scripture? I have given reasons for thinking it is not clearly or unambiguously taught or implied in Scripture. But these are matters that would need to be argued in detail.

In the case of weighing different sources of theological authority, then, Scripture is the final arbiter of theological matters where it states a clear view on a topic. It is also a norming norm that norms other norms where it provides a clear, unambiguous view of a particular matter such as whether monotheism is true, and whether the God described in Scripture is worthy of worship. But, on the view I am outlining here that develops what was said in the previous chapter, it is not the case that Scripture is a *sufficient* norm in all matters of doctrine. It is also the case that, if Scripture is metaphysically and epistemically underdetermined, it will not always be *perspicuous* either. However, as we saw in Chapter 5 these two claims, about the sufficiency and perspicacity of Scripture, are important ones from the point of view of Reformation Christianity, the tradition that Protestant Christians have inherited. Setting aside these claims makes way for post-biblical tradition to play a larger role in making judgements about theological authority.

This needs some explanation. Let us say that a thing is *sufficient* for a particular purpose just in case it is all that is needed to achieve some particular goal or end. Thus, a spirit level is sufficient to the task of ascertaining whether a particular surface is horizontally aligned. Next, a thing is *perspicuous* just in case it makes that thing conceptually clear. Thus, a 'keep off the grass' sign in the quadrangle is perspicuous to readers of English. It gives a clear directive to those walking by, and no one would mistake its meaning. Finally, a thing is a *norm* if it is a standard by which we measure some other things. Thus, a ruler

Metatheology

is a norm by means of which we measure the length of objects. A *norming norm* is a standard that is used to measure other standards. Thus, the metre bar stored in a vault in Paris is the norm of a metre against which all other metre measurements are measured.

Now, Scripture can be said to be a norm. It is a standard by means of which Christians measure their conduct and beliefs about God. Most Christians also claim that Scripture is a norming norm. That is, it is the theological standard that is used to measure all other theological norms this side of the grave. But something can be a norm, even a norming norm, and not be either sufficient for a particular purpose or perspicuous. Mundane examples of this are not hard to find. Consider, for example, a law code or constitution. Such documents are normative – at least, legally and politically normative for a given state or society. In the case of a constitution, such as the Constitution of the United States of America, the norm is also a political and legal norming norm, with which laws in individual states such as Indiana or California must be consistent. But a law code or a constitution is not usually sufficient in the sense that they are open to interpretation and further elucidation through amendments and annexes. Moreover, they are not always perspicuous, as any law student will tell you.

Something similar is the case with Scripture. It is a theological norm, in fact, the norm that norms other theological norms this side of the grave because it is a witness to divine revelation. However, it is not sufficient because, as I have argued, it does not deliver a clear, unambiguous dogmatic account of the three central and defining doctrines of Christianity, namely, the Trinity, incarnation and atonement. Nor is it perspicuous because it does not make clear the theological scope or content of these three central doctrines. In this way, Scripture is epistemically and metaphysically underdetermined. What is more, in making theological judgments about doctrines like the Trinity, incarnation and atonement, Christians do not look to Scripture alone, though they usually begin there. Other norms come into play in making decisions about what is theologically permissible on these three dogmatic topics – especially the catholic creeds, as well as other confessional norms such as the Anglican Articles of Religion or the Westminster Confession. These in effect act as a kind of theological constraint or 'control' on how we read the texts of Scripture. They provide a means by which we read Scripture in a particular, ruled way. This is why Roman Catholic understandings of, say, the Trinity are different from Oneness Pentecostals or Protestant social Trinitarians. In reading Scripture dogmatically, we are engaged in the complex task of interpretation: reading with (aspects of) the tradition and reading Scripture through the lens of that tradition so that certain ways of thinking about theological topics seem more plausible than others even if both can be supported by a responsible understanding of the texts in question. This brings us back once more to the matter of *models* – this time, models in Trinitarian theology.

Models of the Trinity

Christian theology aims at truth, or at least, it ought to do so. For theology is truth-apt and truth-aimed. It makes truth statements; and it is a discipline aimed at uncovering truths about divinity. To give up on the alethic orientation of theology is to give up on something significant that is part of the very warp and weft of historic Christianity. Martyrs do not go to their deaths for fictions. They are willing to give up their lives because of something that they believe is a transformational truth. Previously, I have suggested that systematic theologians invest in a chastened account of theological realism.[6] This is the claim that God is a mind-independent reality, though our grasp of that reality is only ever piecemeal, partial and fallible because God is transcendent and in important ways ineffable, inconceivable and incomprehensible. For we finite creatures cannot fathom the divine nature and cannot hope to comprehend it. However, it may be that we can grasp some things about the divine nature via divine accommodation in revelation and in the Christian tradition.

In coming to the central and defining dogma of the Faith, namely, the Trinity, the chastened theological realist may proceed as follows. First, she acknowledges the authority of Scripture and the catholic creeds, with the creeds acting as a theological constraint on how to read and interpret Scripture, providing a 'reading strategy' for understanding what is revealed of Godself there. Second, acknowledging that her conceptual and epistemic limitations mean she cannot fully comprehend the dogma of the Trinity, but adopting a faith-seeking-understanding approach to the dogma, she begins from the branch of the Christian tradition in which she finds herself and works from there toward greater understanding. To begin with, that involves apprehending the core theological claims of the catholic creeds regarding the divine nature. The apogee of these creeds as far as Trinitarianism is concerned is the Nicene-Constantinopolitan symbol. *In nuce*, it says that God has one essence that subsists in three persons, the Father, the Son and the Holy Spirit. This provides a core dogmatic structure for thinking about the doctrine of God that is distinctively Christian. The chastened theological realist then applies this structure to the way in which she reads Scripture. This need not result in hopeless anachronism. For the chastened theological realist who is sensitive to the complexities of the biblical texts and their different perspectives and theologies can still hold to the Trinitarianism of the catholic creeds.

In a similar way, someone who comes to consider particular issues in black letter law for the purposes of prosecuting a particular course of action may have a hermeneutical framework by means of which they structure how they think about the nature or shape of the law as such, whilst remaining sensitive to the particular nuance and complexity of law as it appears in the penal code of a particular jurisdiction. Often, such individuals combine both the theoretical and practical in their work as legal scholars and as lawyers or judges – a classic example being Oliver Wendell Holmes, who was both a Supreme Court justice and one of the foremost American Legal Realists.

Hermeneutics is a complex matter. The reading and interpretation of texts involve judgements about provenance, sources, composition, redaction, form, and so on. But,

---

[6] See Crisp, *Analyzing Doctrine*.

in the case of Scripture or other theological texts like creeds and confessions, it also involves theological judgements. We bring certain judgements to the texts, but the careful reader allows the text to test those judgements. So, the interpretive traffic goes in both directions: from theory to text, and from text to theory. This must be the case if we are to be hermeneutically sensitive. But it also means that the hermeneutical frameworks with which we come to the text must be tested by the text, so to speak. If the theory does not hold up because it does not adequately represent what is being said in the text or forces the text into a particular shape that it does not actually have (making it 'say' certain things that are not present in the text, or about which the text in its broader context is clearly not concerned), then the theory must be adjusted accordingly.

This is not a new process. It is precisely this approach – or something very like it – that gave rise to the Catholic creeds and confessions of the Christian churches in the first place. The Fathers of the ecumenical councils were readers of Scripture and saw themselves as guardians of the apostolic faith. They were students of the texts of Scripture as they had them, and they held to the oral traditions and summaries of doctrine such as the Rule of Faith that had been passed down to them as well. They also had other practices that factored into their understanding of Scripture, such as the liturgical practices of the early church, some of which can be seen in early documents like the *Shepherd of Hermas* and *The Didache*. And, of course, they were members of communities of faith that were local and regional sources of traditions and practices that fed into the theologies of different parties and groups. These various elements form what William Abraham calls a 'canonical symphony'[7] that, as he puts it, had its own intellectual harmony in the early church and acted as a complex of theological authorities and structures that were canonical. In this way, and taken together, they provided structures for preserving the faith and passing it on. He writes,

> When we expand our conception of what is constituted by the canonical traditions of the Church, then the evidence for this claim [that canonical material is diverse, and not restricted to Scripture] is overwhelming. Sacraments, doctrinal summaries, particular forms of internal structure, liturgical materials, the designation of certain individuals as Fathers, saints and teachers, ecclesiastical regulations about fasting – all these constitute canonical material and practice, in that they are acknowledged as binding within the life of the Church across the board.[8]

Thus, reducing the Trinity to a doctrine that is found in Scripture and extrapolated by later tradition is a rather simplistic way of thinking about matters. There was a symphony of canonical material that, when taken together, yielded a particular vision of the Christian faith that culminated in the formal articulation of the dogma of the Trinity.

---

[7] William Abraham, *Canon and Criterion in Christian Theology. From the Fathers to Feminism* (Oxford: Oxford University Press, 1998), 21.
[8] Ibid., 40.

I have argued that the doctrine of the Trinity is not taught in Scripture, strictly speaking, but that it may be read and understood through the lens of a Trinitarian hermeneutical framework. The early church did this via the 'canonical symphony' of different authorities that, taken together, meant that the doctrine of the Trinity came to be understood as the right way to think about the god of Christianity. The leaders of the early Church came to understand that theirs was a monotheism with an important conceptual twist in the direction of plurality, yet without collapsing into polytheism. That is a significant theological development by any standard, and one that has proven decisive for the shape of Christianity.

Having said all that, the dogmatic framework provided by the Catholic creeds is just that, a framework. It does not fill in the gaps to provide a complete *theory* of the Trinity, for the Trinity is a mystery, as we have already indicated. Mysteries, by their very nature, defy complete theoretical analysis. By definition, one cannot have a mystery that is fully understood. Yet one can formulate a model for understanding the Trinity. That, in effect, is just what has happened down through the centuries. Different theologians have attempted to put flesh on the dogmatic framework provided by the Catholic creeds by filling out the framework with accounts of how to construe the framework. Such models are simplified descriptions of more complex data. They are approximations to the truth of the matter. Models can be truth-apt and truth-aimed. It is just that they are not the complete truth. They are an attempt to get closer to the truth by theorising about what that might look like.

In some of my earlier work, critics have indicated that talk about doctrinal models that are only proxies for the truth of the matter means that the views to which the theologian comes are not necessarily the truth.[9] There is a big difference between saying 'this is the truth of the matter' and 'this approximates the truth of the matter'. Worse still, such an approach may have the consequence that the theologian is not, in the end, in search of the truth with respect to a particular doctrine, but rather a plausible fiction that is consistent with what we do know. 'For all we know, the doctrine of the Trinity should look something like this . . .' says the theological model builder; or so the critics think. But that is not what I have in mind here.

It is true that theological models, like models in the natural sciences, are proxies for the truth. They are simplified descriptions of more complex data. In the case of central mysteries of the faith like the Trinity, such a result is inevitable. The reason is obvious: we cannot fathom the Trinity, so we cannot expect to have a complete understanding of it. All our theologising about the Trinity will come up short. The best we can hope for is that our theology approximates the whole truth of the matter, which will forever remain beyond our creaturely ken. However, that does not mean we are engaged in a grand fiction, projecting different theories onto the clouds, so to speak, in the hope that our picture of the divine nature seems more attractive than another – as if we are all

---

[9] See, for instance, *Analyzing Doctrine*.

latter-day Feuerbachs. Nor does it mean we have no criteria for distinguishing different approximations to the truth of the matter. The right way to think about the use of models here is as theological attempts to make sense of the dogmatic framework of canonical ways of thinking about the divine nature, especially (for the purposes of dogmatic theology) that found in the Catholic creeds.

We take the creeds to be a source of theological authority. They provide a way of thinking about the divine nature that is the culmination of the canonical symphony of the early church, which includes Scripture. They, alongside the Rule of Faith, liturgies and other early records of church practice such as *The Didache*, provide the Trinitarian structure to Christian theology. However, this dogmatic structure is not sufficient. It requires extrapolation; it needs further elaboration to be serviceable in Christian theology. In a similar way, a skeleton is no good on its own; it needs flesh and a working nervous system to move. Models of the Trinity provide the theological flesh to the dogmatic framework of the Catholic creeds and the other aspects of the canonical symphony of the early church.

This, as I suggested in Chapter 2, is why subsequent theological reflection on the Trinity has turned up a variety of different accounts of the divine nature that are consistent with the Catholic creeds but are inconsistent with each other. They are all attempts to better understand how the dogmatic framework provided by the creeds in the context of the larger canonical symphony works. The dogmatic framework tells us that God is one in essence, preserving monotheism. Yet God subsists in three persons. These divine persons are distinct yet are all one God sharing in the one divine essence. This is Trinitarianism. But upon reading this, the theologian immediately asks, How is God both one and three at one and the same time? How can God be one in essence and yet subsist in three persons? How can both claims be true? How are they compossible? Mindful of the fact that we cannot hope to fathom this mystery, the theologian seeks something more modest: a model. Providing a model is a way of construing the dogmatic framework that attempts to answer things like the threeness-oneness problem, which is just the problem that God is said to be in some sense both one and three at one and the same time.

Summary and conclusion

Let us take stock. The Christian has various sources of theological authority to which she can appeal in making theological judgments. These are ordered according to their relation to Scripture, which is the norming norm this side of the grave. Let us call this the first tier of norms. The catholic creeds are second-tier norms that all Christians should take seriously. They provide interpretative frameworks for the right understanding of Scripture. In the case of the Nicene-Constantinopolitan creed, this includes the outline of the dogma of the Trinity. This is not a doctrine that is explicitly taught in Scripture. Nor is it a doctrine that is implied by Scripture, strictly speaking. Nevertheless, through reflection upon the life and ministry of Christ in relation to God passed down to the early generations of Christians in various forms including creedal fragments, liturgies and traditions of the apostles, the early church came to see that Christ was included in the divine identity. Further reflection and disputation eventually led to an understanding of the divine nature that preserved the historic monotheism of Christianity's Jewish heritage, while adding to this the differentiation of three divine persons, the Father, the Son, and the Holy Spirit. The beginnings of this new understanding of God can be found in Nicene Christianity. It comes into full view in the Nicene-Constantinopolitan symbol, with the differentiation of the Holy Spirit. It is not surprising that it took the early church some time to reach this conclusion. After all, the dogma of the Trinity represents a theological revolution in the doctrine of God that is unique to Christianity. It is also not surprising that this dogma is not evident in Scripture. For the biblical documents were composed by strict monotheists. Even those who, like the Apostle Paul, appear to have come to new and radical views about Christ's relation to God did not find their way to the doctrine of the Trinity as we know it. That came later.

This does mean that when it comes to the Trinity we need to read Scripture with the tradition. The canonical symphony of which William Abraham speaks indicates just how rich the tradition was in this respect. Protestants often have rather caricatured views about Scripture in relation to the tradition, as if there was a body of documents dictated by God to various authors and then deposited in the churches for all to read and understand. Subsequent church history represents episodic departures from this norm and occasional renewal movements that take the Church back to Scripture. But this narrative of a pristine Bible, and the decline and fall of the Church once the apostolic age came to an end, must be cast upon the bonfire of vanities. For it has led to much mischief. The story of how we came to have the Bible alongside other sources of theological authority is a much more complex, messy, and politically fraught story than this neat narrative suggests.

Scripture says much that is fundamental to Christian belief and practice. But it does not say everything, nor does it say what it does say with one voice. As biblical scholars know only too well, there are many different theologies in Scripture. Reading it canonically and reading it with the tradition, especially in light of the Catholic creeds, is, it seems to me, the right way to go about understanding the role of Scripture. Doing this will yield a dogma of the Trinity. Reading the Bible without this richer context, as if we can simply intuit its meaning, is hermeneutically naive. It is also plainly insufficient for the formation of a dogma of the Trinity.

So, we read Scripture in its proper theological context, which is the canonical symphony of the wider tradition. When we do this, paying particular attention to the creedal formulation of the dogma, we find ourselves in possession of a dogmatic framework for making sense of the relevant biblical data. This yields the idea that God is one in essence and subsists in three persons, the Father, the Son, and the Holy Spirit. But, as with any framework, this needs further specification in order to generate a working doctrine of the Trinity. It is this task of further specification that subsequent theologians have taken up in their attempts to provide what I am calling models of the Trinity. These theologians have not usually understood their task as setting forth models;

Metatheology

they speak instead of dogmas and doctrines. That is all well and good. They are indeed in the business of articulating dogmas and doctrines. However, the doctrines that they arrive at, though normally consistent with the dogmatic deposit of the catholic creeds, say much more than the creeds in specifying how we should understand the divine essence and persons of God. Not only that, but there are also various such doctrines, and they are incommensurate with one another. They cannot all be true. As I suggested earlier in this volume, it seems to me that it is better to think of these specifications of the Trinity that put flesh on the bones of the catholic creeds as models, for they are approximations to the truth of the matter. Or, if you prefer, they are one way in which the dogmatic framework of the Trinity can be specified. But judging which extant model of the Trinity is the right one (if any of the extant models are in fact the right one) is a much more difficult task. But it is here – in the proposing and defending of such models – that constructive theological work begins.

CHAPTER 7
TRINITARIAN MINIMALISM

In this chapter, we turn from the question of the origin and development of the dogma of the Trinity to questions of a metadogmatic nature about its articulation. The focus of attention here is on the notion of *Trinitarian minimalism* that has been hinted at in previous chapters but not fully explored until now. According to the Trinitarian minimalist, we can say very little about what it means for God to be triune. We can say *that* God is triune because of the historic confession of the Trinity in the Nicene-Constantinopolitan Creed. But we cannot give a complete account of *how* God is triune.[1] Put another way, we have a grammar for our theology of the Trinity provided for us by the credal tradition, which represents a particular interpretation of the biblical data. In light of this, we can express the doctrine adequately; with the ancient Church, we can confess the Trinity. But we do not have a complete semantics of the Trinity. That is, we do not have a complete grasp of the meaning of the terms we use in Trinitarian theology. Their semantic content outstrips our understanding.[2]

This is not a new idea. At the beginning of the *Summa Theologiae*, Thomas Aquinas writes in the preamble to the article on divine simplicity that 'because we cannot know what God is, but rather what He is not, we have no means for considering how God is, but rather how He is not'. On its face, this appears to be a manifesto for a kind of apophatically oriented mysterianism about the divine nature. That is, God's essence is a mystery the content of which we creatures cannot penetrate or comprehend, much less explain. The best we can do is say what God is not. In response to the objection that we can know *whether* God exists but not *what* God is (ST 1. 3. 4, obj. 2) Aquinas says, 'we cannot understand God's existence nor His essence'. For we cannot access the 'act of essence', that is, the pure act that is the divine essence. What we can do as creatures, he says, is form subject-predicate propositions about the divine nature, the content of which we know to be true from God's effects—that is, divine action in creation (ST 1. 3. 4, reply to objection 2). Later, he makes it clear that this epistemic limitation is removed for those in the world to come who enjoy the beatific vision, and who can, in some sense, 'see' the essence of God (ST 1. 12. 1). Nevertheless, this side of the grave, God's essence cannot be known except by way of negation, stating what God is not. Nor can the Trinity

---

[1] This distinction can be found in Sameer Yadav's essay, 'The Mystery of the Immanent Trinity and the Procession of the Spirit', 55–67.
[2] Compare the concept of infinity with an instance of an infinite series, such as the infinite number of points in a line segment. Our concept is finite, but names something that is not finite. We can grasp the idea that something is 'not-finite'. Yet we cannot grasp the series of points in the segment all at once.

be known by natural reason; it is a revealed doctrine (ST 1. 32. 1) that we can only know on the basis of authority, that is, Scripture and tradition. It is an oddity of Aquinas's account that, despite this apparent reticence to speculate about the divine nature, he is willing to say quite a bit about the divine persons in relation to one another and the divine essence. This, it seems to me, represents a tension in his thought. It is a tension one can find elsewhere among medieval theologians who want to give some cataphatic account of the triunity of God whilst wrestling with a deeply held apophaticism about the divine life.[3]

In the late twentieth century, a superficially more sanguine approach prevailed in mainline Protestant theology in the United States, with the emphasis on the use of religious language rather than metaphysics and epistemology. This was the idea that theology provided the grammar for our talk about God but not always a complete semantics. It was associated with the postliberalism of Yale theologians like George Lindbeck, Hans Frei and David Kelsey.[4] Lindbeck in particular was associated with the cultural-linguistic account of what might be called metadogmatics – that is, the discussion of the meaning of Christian doctrine.[5] The cultural-linguistic account presumed that Christian doctrine was formed to provide a grammar for Christian thought, so that people of faith could adequately express their theological views in the Christian community. The use to which Christian doctrine was put was primarily linguistic rather than the expression of propositions aimed at truth. This is not to say that the Yale divines were uninterested in questions of truth or even in theology articulated in the form of propositions. Rather, they saw themselves as attempting to give an account of what it is Christian communities do when they articulate and deploy Christian doctrine, which is to say, they were interested in the task of metadogmatics.

As is well known, the linguistic philosophy of the later Ludwig Wittgenstein was an important impetus for this Yale approach to metadogmatics. Famously, Wittgenstein claimed that it is in its use that we find the meaning of a word, situated in a particular form of life, and often used in a particular language 'game'.[6] In other words, we use particular words in a given context and community in which they take on a concrete

---

[3] A similar tension exists in the thought of Anselm of Canterbury, who combines an 'ontological argument' concerning the existence of God at the beginning of the Proslogion with a prayerful approach to theology that is fully cognisant of its epistemic fallibility. For a helpful recent discussion of the shape of the Proslogion, see Gavin Ortlund, *Anselm's Pursuit of Joy: A Commentary on the Proslogion* (Washington, DC: Catholic University of America Press, 2020).
[4] For an account of postliberalism, see Paul J. DeHart, *The Trial of the Witnesses: The Rise and Decline of Postliberal Theology* (Oxford: Blackwell, 2006). An interesting recent reassessment can be found in Michael Root, 'What is Postliberal Theology? Was there a Yale School? Why Care?', *Pro Ecclesia* XXVII, no. 4 (2018): 399–411.
[5] See George A. Lindbeck, *The Nature of Doctrine: Religion and Theology in a Postliberal Age* (Louisville: Westminster John Knox, 1984). One motivation for Lindbeck's work was his interest in ecumenism.
[6] See Ludwig Wittgenstein, *Philosophical Investigations*, 2nd ed., trans. G. E. M. Anscombe (Oxford: Basil Blackwell, 1958 [1953]).

meaning, and are used in order to give syntactical rules by which we can be understood in the conceptual framework used by that community.

In theology, we might think that the community in question is the Church, and the 'game' that is played, the liturgy and life of the Church. The language used to give a framework of meaning for the community of the Church is, of course, theological in nature. It is directed by the members of that community to the object of its worship, which is the triune God. Thus, the use to which the language of theology is put in the life of the Church gives it its shape. Believers learn how to use that language, how to generate well-formed sentences that can be expressed in appropriate ways and times in, say, the liturgy or in other meetings of the community. People of faith also learn that there are ways the language should not be used, ways that are unorthodox or mistaken or malformed, such as speaking of three 'parts' to God. But all this is consistent with having a particular theological grammar without a complete semantics. For we can know that it is improper to speak of divine persons as 'parts' of God even if we do not have a complete understanding of how we should refer to the divine persons in the Godhead. For to know that something lacks a particular quality is not the same as knowing a quality it does have.

We may come to know enough to use theological language appropriately in the context of a Christian form of life in the Church. But even if we become masters of such language and its appropriate use, we do not thereby become masters of its *meaning*. This is not just because the meaning of the language of theology is context-dependent, requiring us to attend to the subtle changes of nuance in each community and context that may change over time. (A good example of this might be the way in which the Western Church came to think that the *filioque* clause that they unilaterally added to the Creed was an important way of extrapolating the meaning of the Trinity in the Creed, though this was rejected by the Eastern Church, leading to the separation of East and West that persists to this day – a matter to which we shall return at the end of this chapter.) It is also because the semantics of theological language outstrips our comprehension. Put plainly, we do not fully understand the mystery of the Trinity, for God is greater than we can apprehend or imagine. But we can say certain things about the Trinity that are appropriate and helpful, even if in doing so we confess things that we do not fully grasp.

The idea that language may play such an ambiguous role in a community is not restricted to ecclesiastical life, of course. Wittgenstein's ordinary language philosophy was not primarily aimed at theologians but sought to give an account of how language is used in everyday situations. He was interested in the quotidian. What is more, we can think of other communities and contexts in which this distinction between well-formed structures of language and the meaning of the terms used in that language is clearly at work. For instance, in the natural sciences, the language of 'waves' and 'particles' and so forth is routinely used. But their semantic content is not always fully understood, one notorious example of which is the collapse of the wave function in quantum mechanics – a conceptual puzzle that has given rise to multiple interpretations. Some philosophers of science even claim that the language of the natural sciences is aimed at adequacy, not necessarily truth.[7] On this way of thinking, the value of the language used in the natural sciences depends on its theoretical or experimental usefulness, not necessarily whether it is tracking some mind-independent truth of the matter.

Such linguistic instrumentalism has its uses, as the ironic philosopher might say. But does it track how we really deploy such language? For that matter – and to return to the Yale divines once more – is the purpose of theological language principally to be found in its appropriate *use*? Should doctrinal theologians be concerned with the grammar of theology, so to speak, or should they also attend to its semantics? Is our theology largely a matter of confessing that the object of our worship is a mystery that we cannot penetrate, the Deity of Sinai shrouded in clouds of darkness, illuminated from within by the divine presence – Pseudo-Denys' 'brilliant darkness'? Or are we able to say at least some things about the nature of the Deity in the doctrines that we form?

In this chapter, I will focus on the distinction between the claim *that* God is triune and the search for models that show us *how* God is triune. The aim is not to reinvigorate a Yale-style approach to metadogmatics, still less to give some account of the grammar and semantics of theology modelled on Wittgenstein's ordinary language philosophy, important though these approaches undoubtedly have been in the history of theology and philosophy, respectively. Rather, my focus will be on defending my own account of Trinitarian minimalism against objections raised in a recent essay by Professor Sameer Yadav. This may seem to be of rather parochial interest, given this preamble. But I hope that by focusing on this discussion, wider issues about the metadogmatic role of the theologian in seeking to understand something of the central mystery of the Christian Faith will come into greater focus. At the very least, what follows should be of interest to those working on the doctrine of the Trinity for whom a mysterian approach holds some attraction.

On Trinitarian minimalism

In *Analyzing Doctrine*, I set out to provide a version of Trinitarian minimalism that I called *chastened Trinitarian mysterianism*.[8] This required two important assumptions, which we have already met in previous chapters. These are a view of what a theological model might be, as well as an idea of what mystery consists in. The thought was that God is a mystery, the complete understanding of which eludes finite human beings, and that one way of trying to get some conceptual grip on things that are too difficult for us to understand is to come up with a model that aids comprehension of the thing in question. I expressed these two assumptions like this:

---

[7] For example, Bas C. van Fraassen, *The Empirical Stance* (New Haven: Yale University Press, 2002).
[8] Crisp, *Analyzing Doctrine*, ch. 4 the dogmatic substance of which was recapitulated in the conclusion. *Caveat lector*: I have made a few minor corrections to some of the constituents of the version of chastened Trinitarian mysterianism given here.

> MODEL: a simplified conceptual framework or description by means of which complex sets of data, systems, and processes may be organised and understood.
> MYSTERY: a truth that is intelligible in principle but which may not be entirely intelligible to human beings in their current state of cognitive development.

Additionally, it seemed important to include among the theological assumptions for thinking about the Trinity a notion of divine transcendence. For this says something important about why God is a mystery. It is because God is above and beyond us that we are unable to comprehend the deity absent divine revelation and accommodation to our human frailty and cognitive limitation. Thus,

> TRANSCENDENCE: God is above and beyond creatures in virtue of being the creator of all things.

To this was added what I took to be the dogmatic framework for the Trinity that was one of the upshots of the early theological controversies in the Catholic Church that yielded the great symbols of the early ecumenical councils. This I set out as follows:

> TRINITY: the conjunction of dogmatic propositions concerning the divine nature, expressing the claim that God is one in essence and subsists in three persons, which are found in the dogmatic deposit of the ecumenical creeds, especially the Nicene-Constantinopolitan symbol that reflect (a particular way of understanding) the teaching of Scripture and the apostolic faith. The dogmatic core of this conjunction of claims is:
> (T1) There is exactly one God;
> (T2) There are exactly three co-eternal divine persons 'in' God: the Father, the Son, and the Holy Spirit;
> (T3) The Father, the Son, and the Holy Spirit are not identical;
> (T4) The Father, the Son and the Holy Spirit are consubstantial.

To these various components was added a chastened mysterian model of the Trinity:

CHASTENED MYSTERIAN MODEL:

1. The triunity of the divine nature is an instance of MYSTERY because God is above and beyond us (as per TRANSCENDENCE).
2. Human beings cannot apprehend the triunity of God absent divine revelation.
3. In revealing Godself to us, God accommodates himself to the epistemic limitations of human beings. (Presumably, this includes allowing for the noetic effects of sin.)
4. TRINITY is a revealed dogma. (That is, a doctrine that has a particular canonical form.)

5. TRINITY provides a dogmatic framework for understanding the divine nature that is theologically minimal.

6. TRINITY does not explain how God is triune; it does not in and of itself offer a particular MODEL of the Godhead; it is metaphysically underdetermined. (For this reason, it is consistent with more than one dogmatic extrapolation, including a range of Trinitarian doctrines and MODELS.)

7. The terms 'person' and 'essence', and their cognates that demarcate the way in which God is three, and the way in which God is one in TRINITY, are referring terms that are placeholders; we do not have a clear conceptual grip on their semantic content. (This is consistent with the claim that we may have a partial, piecemeal, or analogous sense of these terms.)

8. TRINITY is consistent with MYSTERY.

I described TRINITY not as a model of the Trinity but rather as a revealed dogma that provides the believer with the theological basis for thinking about the triunity of God – the conceptual foundation that provides the elements needed to generate a model, if you will. Like other Trinitarian models, the chastened mysterian model of the Trinity takes TRINITY as the foundation on which it builds. It is the dogmatic basis for all the models of the Trinity that are theologically orthodox. Of course, some models of the Trinity build rather elaborate accounts of the triunity of God on the basis of this modest dogmatic foundation. The chastened mysterian model attempts the opposite: to say as little as is needed to generate a theologically adequate model of divine triunity. By 'theologically adequate' I mean a model that can be put to good service in theology in the production of doctrinal statements and arguments, as well as in the life of the Church in its liturgy and community.

What the chastened mysterian model of divine triunity added to the dogmatic framework provided by TRINITY was essentially a claim about theological minimalism. Given that God is a transcendent mystery, we cannot expect to understand the divine nature. Nevertheless, God has revealed Godself as triune according to the dogmatic framework of TRINITY, which is itself a kind of theological condensation of what the early Christian community took to be the right way to read and interpret the biblical texts and apostolic teaching. The Trinity is a revealed dogma. In effect, it provides the grammar for thinking about the divine essence in a Christian manner. But it does not provide us with a complete semantics of the Trinity. As Augustine says at one point in his magisterial work on the Trinity, 'our very thought, when we think of God the Trinity, falls (as we feel) very far short of Him of whom we think, nor comprehends Him as He is'.[9] Having given a brief elaboration of the argument, we can now turn to Yadav's criticism of it.

---

[9] Augustine, *On the Trinity*, Nicene and Post-Nicene Fathers Series 1, Vol. 3, ed. Phillip Schaff (Edinburgh: T&T Clark, 1887), Bk. V. Ch. 1, §1.

Yadav's critique

According to Yadav, the problems with the Trinitarian minimalism of chastened Trinitarian mysterianism turn on the distinction with which we began, namely, that we can know *that* God is triune but not *how* God is triune.[10] Models of the Trinity that move beyond minimalism to provide maximal accounts of the Trinity do so by way of theorising about the metaphysics of the Trinity. For some theologians, God is said to have a trope of divinity shared between three numerically distinct divine individuals; for others, the divine persons are said to be subsistent relations in the one God; for yet others, the divine persons are like Aristotelian forms that organize numerically the same divine nature in three ways; and so on. These different maximal models are all consistent with the dogmatic framework provided by TRINITY. But they are inconsistent with one another. For instance, God cannot be a wholly non-composite entity where the divine persons are subsistent relations within the Godhead *as well as* being three numerically distinct centres of will and consciousness that all share in a common trope of divinity. One or other or neither of these approaches can be true, but not both.

Now, I have not made a judgement about which (if any) of these maximal accounts of the Trinity is coherent. Recall that the sixth sentence in the chastened mysterian model outlined above stated that:

6. TRINITY does not explain how God is triune; it does not in-and-of-itself offer a particular MODEL of the Godhead; it is metaphysically underdetermined. (For this reason, it is consistent with more than one dogmatic extrapolation, including a range of Trinitarian doctrines and MODELs.)

On the face of it, several competing maximal models seem to be plausible ways to construe the dogmatic framework supplied by TRINITY. Is a minimal account consistent with one or more of the maximal accounts? That is, could one hold to TRINITY, chastened Trinitarian mysterianism, and one or other of the maximal accounts of the Trinity one can find in the Christian tradition? I don't see why not. As it stands, the chastened Trinitarian mysterian account I outlined is compossible with several of the extant maximal accounts of the Trinity. It might be thought that the seventh sentence in the chastened Trinitarian mysterian account is a potential problem here, however. For it states:

7. The terms 'person' and 'essence', and their cognates that demarcate the way in which God is three, and the way in which God is one in TRINITY, are referring terms that are placeholders; we do not have a clear conceptual grip on their

---

[10] Thus, 'All maximal models of the Trinity fail for the same reason', he says, 'which is that in trying to move beyond the minimal parameters for saying that God is triune to specify how God is triune, maximal models say too much'. Yadav, 'The Mystery of the Immanent Trinity and the Procession of the Spirit', 82.

semantic content. (This is consistent with the claim that we may have a partial, piecemeal, or analogous sense of these terms.)

But whether this is a problem or not depends on the expansiveness of the semantic shortfall of a given account of divine triunity. For instance, one could say something like this:

> MODERATE MYSTERIANISM: We confess the dogma of the Trinity as expressed in the summary statement given in TRINITY. We understand this in a way that is consistent with chastened Trinitarian mysterianism. That is, we think that the terms 'person' and 'essence' and their cognates are placeholders. The semantic content of these terms is not entirely clear to us; its content outstrips our comprehension. Nevertheless, this way of understanding the triunity of God is consistent with the attempt to provide certain *theologoumena* or theological opinions on how we might make some steps toward filling at least some of that semantic content. For instance, it is consistent with theological speculation that adds to such mysterianism a maximal understanding of the Trinity, such as can be found in historic doctrines such as Latin, social, and constitutional accounts of the Trinity.

Now, in *Analyzing Doctrine* I argued that the problem with maximal models of the Trinity such as the Latin, social and compositional models is that they attempt to say too much.[11] We simply do not have access to the conceptual wherewithal needed to set about constructing these conceptually 'thicker' accounts of the Trinity with any confidence. However, that now seems to me to be mistaken, and Yadav's criticism has helped me to see this. What I should have said was something like MODERATE MYSTERIANISM. This presumes a three-tiered approach to the question of Trinitarian theologising. We may think of it as a kind of pyramid. There is a foundation that is made up of the patristic understanding of the apostolic witness, including Scripture, which is expressed in the symbol of the Nicene-Constantinopolitan creed and summarized in TRINITY. Next, there is a mid-section that rests on this foundation and is metaphysically minimalist. This is expressed by the CHASTENED MYSTERIAN MODEL. This is as far as I was willing to go in *Analyzing Doctrine*. Any further theological construction would be speculation about the divine nature that was unwarranted – or so I thought. But now it seems to me that one could add a third tier to the conceptual pyramid of Trinitarian modelling by allowing that conceptually richer, more developed accounts of the Trinity may be admissible as theological just-so stories. In other words, we can allow that theologians may go beyond the CHASTENED MYSTERIAN MODEL to provide a more complete explanation of the triune life of God, such as we find in traditional Latin, social and now constitutional accounts of the Trinity (among others). But these more elaborate accounts

---

[11] *Analyzing Doctrine*, 82.

Trinitarian Minimalism

are speculative in nature. The theologian drawn to one or other of these views is saying, in effect, 'for all we know, the divine life could be Trinitarian in the following way . . .'.

I am still hesitant about this sort of Trinitarian speculation because it seems to me that there are significant hazards attending such projects. Just think of the way in which the ancients, following Galen, speculated about how human bodies were subject to four humours. This seemed plausible to the educated elites in Western Europe for a very long time until the advent of modern medical science decisively overturned it. What changed was an advance in our knowledge of how human bodies work. This is often how advances in human knowledge go. We theorize about a particular thing, and eventually we come to know more about that thing through investigation and further reflection, as a consequence of which our accounts of the thing in question change – sometimes significantly. In the case of Trinitarian models, the problem is the dearth of information. We simply do not know very much about the divine life, even if we factor in what God has revealed of Godself in Scripture and the tradition. So Trinitarian speculation is hazardous. We may get it wrong. Indeed, we are likely to get it wrong simply because our capacity to theorize accurately has often been shown in history to be very wide of the mark. So, caution is required. That said, there may be good reasons to attempt such Trinitarian speculation. A more developed account of the Trinity could be productive for the generation of doctrinal models that pertain to other areas of Christian theology from creation to eschaton. It may also be of some help in the application of such theological views in liturgy and the life of the Church. Even if that is right, there are risks involved. At the very least, it seems to me that theologians should make it very clear when they are attempting such Trinitarian construction to alert their readers or auditors to the fact that what follows will be theologically speculative – *theologoumena* that may or may not be right, for all we know.

In many other academic disciplines, the generation of new models and new paradigms is usually taken to be a sign of intellectual health. When cultural and literary critics produce new ways of thinking about how to read texts, or the complexities that attend such reading (such as have been entailed by the postmodern turn), we all benefit. Similarly, when scientists develop new paradigms for thinking about aspects of the way the cosmos works, from dark matter to quantum entanglement, we better understand important things about the universe in which we live. It might be thought that the same sort of reasoning applies to new models of the Trinity. This may be true; the ingenuity of human beings should not be discounted. However, without more data, it is difficult to see how real progress can be made by means of Trinitarian theorising. Sometimes new theories about the same data can be illuminating. Often this is because we bring new information from other areas to bear upon the data in question. Consider, for example, the way in which critical race theory, originally developed in the context of jurisprudence, has been applied to a wide range of issues in the humanities. New models of the Trinity do appear from time to time, and the recent interest in constitutional accounts, developed within analytic theology, is a case in point. Nevertheless, it seems to me that such views should be regarded as metaphysical just-so stories that may be true for all we know. Provided we treat them in this manner, they may be of theological use. Problems will arise if they are made the basis of significant theological disagreement. For, lacking further information about the divine life, adjudicating between these different maximal models will be of rather limited theological value.

Yadav also raises a second and more fundamental worry about Trinitarian minimalism. This is that it seems to be incoherent. His concern is that such a view pulls in two different directions and is ultimately unable to hold both in tension.[12] In the first of these directions, Trinitarian minimalism is pulled towards, and ultimately collapses into, maximal Trinitarianism. In the second, the 'minimalism' of Trinitarian minimalism presses its defender towards an unacceptable scepticism regarding the divine nature. Neither of these options is particularly attractive. Both undercut key claims about Trinitarian minimalism and need to be addressed and rebutted for Trinitarian minimalism to be of use.

Let us take the two objections to the coherence of Trinitarian minimalism in order, beginning with the alleged collapse of Trinitarian minimalism into maximalism. Yadav says:

> the full gamut of traditional theorizing in the Nicene tradition is just an attempt to articulate a minimally coherent understanding of God's revealed accommodations to us as a single being who eternally exists as a Father begetting a Son and breathing the Spirit without mutual subordination or collapse of individual identity between the three. Analyzing what the key terms in this understanding ought or ought not ontologically commit us to is inevitably controversial. As such, it predicts genuine metaphysical dispute. The resultant theorizing cannot therefore rightly be regarded as unnecessary, overly speculative, or overweening.[13]

Here, the idea is that all or at least most traditional models of the Trinity are attempting to provide minimally coherent ways of understanding the dogmatic deposit of Nicene Christianity in the Catholic creeds. To say something about the Trinity, one must hazard certain metaphysical notions. In this respect, the minimalist account is no different from any other approach to articulating the dogma of the Trinity.

There are several things to be said by way of response to Yadav at this juncture. First, there is a relevant distinction between substantive and parsimonious claims about a particular thing. Two scientists make substantive claims about how to understand a cluster of data, but one offers a more parsimonious explanation than her colleague. Other things being equal, we should prefer the more parsimonious explanation, and this for several reasons. It is more elegant, and it posits fewer steps in explanation and fewer entities – thus cleaving closer to the blade of Ockham's razor.[14] It is not at all clear to me that extant

---

[12]Yadav, 'The Mystery of the Immanent Trinity and the Procession of the Spirit', 84.
[13]Ibid., 88.
[14]Recall William of Ockham's famous notion that in argument and explanation, 'entities should not be multiplied beyond necessity'.

accounts of the Trinity are always attempting to say in as parsimonious a way as possible something about the substance of God's triunity.[15] But let that pass. The more interesting claim here is that the task of offering some account of the Trinity involves acknowledging that by means of accommodation to our cognitive limitations, God reveals Godself as triune. Our theorising about how to understand that revelation requires that we help ourselves to certain metaphysical notions to do so. As Yadav puts it, '[t]here is no way of articulating a minimalistic Trinitarianism that is not already somehow metaphysically loaded to specify what kind of oneness and threeness is minimally required'.[16] Thus, it is not the case that the minimalist option is somehow better because it is more cautious or metaphysically parsimonious than maximal options. Minimalist Trinitarianism is as metaphysically loaded as its maximalist counterparts.

The point is well taken. Any account of the Trinity will involve making certain metaphysical claims, and Trinitarian minimalism is no different in this respect. But then, I do not think anyone who is party to this debate has claimed otherwise. Theology as such cannot be pursued without metaphysics, so it is no surprise that the same is true of theological attempts to say something about the triunity of God. That said, there is surely a relevant difference between conceding that a particular view is metaphysically motivated, and the question of the amount or number of metaphysical commitments required to motivate it. If two philosophers both set out arguments for a particular conclusion in metaphysics, then presumably they are setting out metaphysically motivated arguments. Yet one may set out a view that requires fewer controversial metaphysical commitments than the other. Yadav thinks that the problem with Trinitarian minimalism is that to get off the ground its defender must assume certain ideas about oneness and threeness as they apply to the divine life just as her maximalist counterparts do. What is more, to avoid traditionally heretical positions like tritheism, modalism, and Arianism, all those who have a stake in the dogma of the Trinity must agree to make substantive claims about divine triunity. For in order to avoid tritheism one would need to stipulate how one's doctrine of the Trinity does not imply that there are three gods; in order to exclude modalism one would need to stipulate how one's doctrine does not imply that there is exactly one god who merely wears different masks in different contexts; and in order to avoid Arianism one would need to stipulate how the divine persons of the Godhead are all co-equal and co-eternal. But once this has been conceded, the minimalist option ceases to be minimalist in any sense that distinguishes its metaphysical minimalism from the more maximalist approaches – or so Yadav claims. Is he right?

Recall, once more, the claims of TRINITY. They were:

---

[15]This claim has been made in the recent literature by Stephen Holmes, who argues that the social Trinitarianism of recent Trinitarian Theology is a departure from the tradition precisely because it assumes a more elaborate way of thinking about the divine nature than other historic views that are unwarranted. See Holmes, *The Quest for The Trinity: The Doctrine of God in Scripture, History, and Modernity* (Downers Grove: IVP Academic, 2012).
[16]Ibid., 85.

(T1) There is exactly one God;

(T2) There are exactly three co-eternal divine persons 'in' God: the Father, the Son, and the Holy Spirit;

(T3) The Father, the Son, and the Holy Spirit are not identical;

(T4) The Father, the Son and the Holy Spirit are consubstantial.

Suppose we add to this the moderate version of Trinitarianism I introduced earlier in this section:

> MODERATE MYSTERIANISM: We confess the dogma of the Trinity as expressed in the summary statement given in TRINITY. We understand this in a way that is consistent with chastened Trinitarian mysterianism. That is, we think that the terms 'person' and 'essence' and their cognates are placeholders. The semantic content of these terms is not entirely clear to us; its content outstrips our comprehension. Nevertheless, this way of understanding the triunity of God is consistent with the attempt to provide certain *theologoumena* or theological opinions on how we might make some steps toward filling at least some of that semantic content. For instance, it is consistent with theological speculation that adds to such mysterianism a maximal understanding of the Trinity, such as can be found in historic doctrines such as Latin, social, and constitutional accounts of the Trinity.

Now, saying something about a thing, call it x, doesn't mean saying everything about x. Saying something about x is consistent with x being mysterious. It may be that our limited epistemic vantage means we can say very little about x. Nevertheless, this is consistent with us being able to say certain things about x that are true. The Trinitarian minimalist can surely say something like the following:

> According to much historic Christian theology, God is incomprehensible, ineffable, and inconceivable. That is, God is literally such that we cannot comprehend the divine nature; God is literally such that we cannot adequately express things about God's nature in words; and God is literally such that we cannot adequately conceive of the divine nature. God is also said to be transcendent. That is, God is above and beyond normal human experience. For these reasons, and given our limited epistemic vantage and finite intelligence, God is said to be mysterious. Now, the claims of TRINITY commit those who endorse it to several key metaphysical notions. These are notions that are agreed upon by all Trinitarians. This includes that God is numerically one, and that there are exactly three divine persons 'in' the Godhead. What is more, these divine persons – the Father, Son, and Spirit – are not identical with each other, and are consubstantial. These are substantive metaphysical claims, and they are plainly inconsistent with historically unorthodox accounts of the divine nature such as Arianism, modalism, and tritheism. Indeed, TRINITY is supposed to express the credal benchmark of

Trinitarianism to which all orthodox Christians adhere. In affirming TRINITY, Christians are in effect denying Arianism, modalism, and tritheism. For, clearly, if one affirms *p* one is denying its contrary, *not-p*. So, God is numerically one, subsisting in three distinct but consubstantial persons that we call the Father, the Son, and the Holy Spirit. Quite how can God be said to be both numerically one in essence and yet consubstantially three persons is the mystery of the Trinity. We cannot penetrate that mystery. The language we use to speak of God's triune nature – language which depends on the formulation culled from the Nicene Fathers and expressed in TRINITY – falls short. The semantic content of 'essence' and 'person' as applied to the triune life of God outstrips our understanding. Yet we may attempt to model the divine life in a more maximal direction, and many historic accounts of the Trinity do just this. Provided we treat such theological constructions as speculations or theologoumena, and provided they comport with TRINITY, they are theologically permissible. Nevertheless, they cannot all be true for a given maximal Trinitarian model is typically inconsistent with other maximal models of the Trinity.

From this, the following three things should be clear. First, that there is a strong theological impetus towards minimalism in much historic Christian theology because we can know so little about the divine nature. Second, that a high tolerance for divine mystery, including notions of incomprehensibility, ineffability and inconceivability, as well as transcendence, is consistent with being able to make certain substantive claims about the divine nature, such as are found in TRINITY. For these claims are traditionally thought to be the deliverances of divine revelation. Third, that there is a relevant difference between Trinitarian minimalism and Trinitarian maximalism. This difference turns not on whether minimalism makes substantive claims about the divine nature, for clearly, commitment to TRINITY implies commitment to substantive metaphysical claims about the Trinity. Rather, the difference turns on the elaboration of these claims. Some Trinitarian models are just more maximal than others and require more metaphysical claims than others. Thus, Yadav is right to say that Trinitarian minimalism is 'metaphysically loaded to specify what kind of oneness and threeness is minimally required'. For its adherents all subscribe to TRINITY as a conceptual benchmark. But Yadav is wrong to think that this means all Trinitarian models are on a conceptual par. Minimalism requires commitment to fewer metaphysically substantive claims than maximalist options precisely because it attempts to endorse TRINITY and MODERATE MYSTERIANISM, or something very like it. And this is clearly more conceptually parsimonious than maximalist alternatives such as the Latin or social accounts of the Trinity.

The second aspect of Yadav's incoherence objection is that the minimalist account yields an unacceptable scepticism regarding the divine nature. The worry is this: Trinitarian minimalism requires that the semantic content of technical language about the Trinity, such as 'person' and 'triunity', outstrips our understanding of these terms. We do not have a clear conceptual grip on their content. But then, says Yadav, we don't have a grip on the semantic content of God's triune life. He writes, 'in the absence of any kind of truth-conditional interpretation of the minimal model, we would have to regard it as literally unintelligible. If it is semantically incomplete, then we literally do not and cannot know what we mean when we say that God is three and God is one'.[17] He goes on to say,

> a semantically incomplete Trinitarianism would also equally well underdetermine an orthodox rejection of tritheism, subordinationism, and modalism, since denying those views would likewise require us to know enough about what our oneness and threeness talk means to rule them out. If God is just somehow one, then we could not say that God is precisely one in such a way as to not multiply beings or entities; if God is just somehow three, then we could not say that God is precisely three in such a way as to admit of intrinsically distinct principles of individuation.[18]

But it should be clear from TRINITY that this is not the view of the Trinitarian minimalist. God is said to be exactly one. There are exactly three co-eternal persons in the Godhead. God is not 'somehow' one. God is numerically one. This is required for monotheism, and Christians are monotheists. There are exactly three co-eternal persons; no more, no less. These divine persons are distinct but consubstantial. All this is clearly stated in TRINITY, which simply sets out some of the main dogmatic claims of the Nicene-Constantinopolitan creed. The problem is not that we can say nothing about the divine nature. That is not what the Trinitarian minimalist claims, and it is not what moderate mysterianism or chastened mysterianism implies either. What motivates Trinitarian minimalism is the idea that we cannot say very much more about the content of God's triunity than what is given in the creed. That does not mean we can say nothing about the divine nature. It just means that what we can say is rather meagre. We can say that God is numerically one because that is a requirement of monotheism. We can say that God subsists in three co-eternal divine persons because that is a deliverance of the creed. But what a divine person is supposed to be is rather more difficult to say – and is the very reason we have a proliferation of more maximal models of the Trinity. The maximalists attempt to supply content to the claim that the one God subsists in three persons. They attempt to give some account of how there may be three persons in the Godhead by providing some explanation of what a divine person is, and how such divine persons may consubstantially subsist within the one Godhead. It is this attempt to specify what is meant by divine persons relative to the divine essence that the minimalist resists. And no wonder: trying to specify what a divine person is, and how the three divine persons do subsist in the one Godhead has proven to be a very significant theological headache. Similarly, it has proven very difficult indeed to give a

---

[17]Yadav, 'The Mystery of the Immanent Trinity and the Procession of the Spirit', 87.
[18]Ibid.

coherent account of the divine nature. Classical theists claim that God is an atemporal, immutable, simple pure act. But explicating this has been difficult to do. Showing how it is consistent with a robust Trinitarianism has been more difficult still. Those who adopt different accounts of the divine nature have similar obstacles to overcome, and there is no prospect of convergence on these contested matters any time soon. Why is this? Surely it is because (a) we have a dearth of data other than what is revealed by Godself in Scripture and tradition, and (b) the semantic content of key Trinitarian terms outstrips our comprehension of those terms.

Does this yield scepticism about the divine nature? Not necessarily (though, as I have mentioned in passing, several key historic theologians seem to think we can know very little about the divine nature, Augustine, Anselm and Aquinas among them). What this does show, I think, is that Trinitarian minimalism has some advantages over views that insist on spelling out what is meant by the divine essence and persons in detail. For inevitably, such accounts will end up in speculation. We are not in an epistemically advantageous position with respect to such questions. Better to admit that and proceed with caution than to presume that we can make grand metaphysical claims about the divine nature and expect to be right.

Does this mean that Trinitarian minimalism corrected to the moderate mysterianism advocated earlier in this chapter is walking a conceptual tightrope between the chasm of theological scepticism to one side and theological maximalism on the other side, and must fall into one or the other of these alternatives? Is it an unstable position that must ultimately give way to scepticism or maximalism? I don't see why it should. We can say enough about the divine nature to avoid heresies like Arianism, modalism, and tritheism. God is numerically one; God subsists in three distinct divine persons; and these divine persons are consubstantial within the one Godhead. This precludes all three heresies and is clearly consistent with monotheism. Are Trinitarian minimalists making substantive metaphysical claims? Yes, they are. Does that mean that the minimalist, like the maximalist, has to say more than their stated minimalism allows? That is, must their position collapse into maximalism? Not necessarily. One can make substantive metaphysical claims that are more parsimonious and require fewer commitments than those presumed by another position. And one can do so for principled reasons. In the case of the triunity of God, the minimalist has a reason for refusing to say as much as the maximalist: God is ineffable, inconceivable, and incomprehensible, as well as transcendent. What we know of the divine nature is communicated to us via divine revelation. And what we have in divine revelation is meagre, conceptually speaking. Perhaps we can fill in the gaps. On the revised moderate mysterianism outlined earlier, one could stop with minimalism or allow some version of maximalism as a kind of project in speculative theology – *theologoumena* about what divine triunity may be like for all we know. But that is not how most maximalists have understood their project. Perhaps if they had, there would have been less grounds for vituperation and more space for principled and collegial disagreement.

Metatheology

Yadav on the *filioque*

An aspect of Yadav's argument that we have not yet touched upon is his claim that Trinitarian minimalism is not able to distinguish between the dual procession of the Son and the Spirit from the Father that is characteristic of Nicene Christianity and the threefold procession of the Son from the Father (eternal generation) and the Spirit from the Father and the Son (spiration), characteristic of the Western Church. He maintains that the controversy over the addition of the *filioque* clause to the Nicene-Constantinopolitan symbol 'may indeed be underdetermined by a minimal Trinitarianism not because the minimal view is semantically incomplete but because its determinate meaning is compatible with both single and joint procession'. This, he thinks, 'would need to be shown by appealing to the metaphysical implications of single versus joint procession interpretations of the minimal model, not by ruling out the legitimacy of interpreting the metaphysics required to understand that model in the first place'.[19]

But it seems to me that this is not quite right. There are good grounds independent of discussion about Trinitarian minimalism for making a judgment about the *filioque* clause. Such reasons have to do with the question of theological authority. As is well known, the Eastern Church has traditionally maintained that the Nicene position sans *filioque* was the position that was agreed by the universal Church. It is the Western Church that has departed from this agreed position in adding the *filioque* to its version of the Nicene-Constantinopolitan symbol. Of course, the Western Church claims otherwise. The traditional Western view has been that the *filioque* is necessary to make clear the different ways in which the Son and Spirit proceed from the Father. It is a matter of underscoring the distinctions that pertain to the persons in the Godhead in their processions.

No doubt one could factor Trinitarian minimalism or Trinitarian maximalism into this historic debate, as Yadav suggests. But I do not see the need to do so. The Eastern Church is surely right to say that the ecumenical form of the creed has no *filioque* clause and is none the worse for that fact. The Western Church is right in saying that its addition underscores the distinction in the procession of the Son and the Spirit, respectively. But it is not an addition that is catholic in the truest sense of that word, for it is not an addition that both Eastern and Western Churches agreed upon in an ecumenical council. Thus, so it seems to me, there is a very good reason to prefer the Eastern to the Western view about the *filioque*, and this reason is independent of the debate about Trinitarian minimalism and Trinitarian maximalism. The Western Church was mistaken in seeking to foist this additional clause upon the Eastern Church. The Eastern Church was right to say that there is no need for such an addition, for the Nicene-Constantinopolitan symbol is sufficiently clear in its demarcation of the divine persons without the addition of the *filioque*. Nevertheless, members of the Western Church may like to think of the

---

[19] Ibid., 86.

filioque as a *theologoumenon* that aids us in distinguishing the processions of the Son and Spirit from the Father. That would be much less controversial, it seems to me. But the *filioque* is now so deeply entrenched in Western Christianity that I imagine this is not likely to happen any time soon. It is deeply regrettable that this has been the source of so much historic unhappiness in ecumenical relations between the different branches of the Christian Church, all of whose members agree upon the fact that their doctrine of God is Trinitarian in nature.

Yadav may well say that this begs the question at issue. For to be able to make the judgement that the *filioque* is an inappropriate addition to the Nicene-Constantinopolitan symbol, one would need to have a clear conceptual picture of the divine processions – which seems like it pushes the Trinitarian theologian in the direction of a maximalist account. But, to repeat, this is to confuse two distinct things. An appeal to authority does not necessarily imply an appeal to additional metaphysical claims that provide some sort of explanatory advantage to one view over another. One could simply say, 'this form of words is what was agreed at the ecumenical council, and it does not include the *filioque*'. The bare appeal to authority may be unpalatable to some, but that is a different question.

Conclusion

In this chapter, I have defended a modified account of the Trinitarian minimalism I set out in *Analyzing Doctrine*. Yadav's careful criticism of that earlier account has helped me see more clearly how the minimalist account might go, and I have tried to set out a revision of this in MODERATE MYSTERIANISM. I have also sought to rebut his criticisms that Trinitarian minimalism is unstable and collapses either into a version of maximalism about the Trinity or into scepticism about the divine life. I do not think the Trinitarian minimalist has to concede either of these points. This represents a step in the dialectic surrounding the expression of one contemporary form of Trinitarian minimalism. I hope it also illuminates some distinctions and challenges facing contemporary constructive Trinitarian theologians that might be of interest to those who do not necessarily have a stake in this debate but who do care deeply about the shape of Trinitarian theology.

CHAPTER 8
GOD'S BODIES

Traditionally, classical theists have claimed that God is essentially incorporeal. That is, God does not have any physical parts; the Deity is without a body, being a spirit (Jn 4:24). I suppose it could be said that, strictly speaking, incorporeality has to do with lacking a physical or material body; it does not entail the lack of any body whatsoever. This is a matter to which we shall return later in the chapter. For now, let us proceed on the assumption that incorporeality is the idea that a thing lacks a material or physical body. I use the terms 'physical' and 'material' interchangeably for the present, though I grant that immaterialists would want to distinguish them, for they think that there is no such thing as matter if we mean by that extended thinking stuff that composes material objects in the world. There are such things as physical bodies on the immaterialist ontology. It is just that these are not bodies composed of matter, but rather, collocated bundles of properties or something of that sort, sustained in being (in the case of theistic immaterialists at least), by divine power.

So, it seems to be a relatively secure theological claim in the mainstream Christian tradition, especially within what we might call creedal Christianity (i.e. Christianity that looks to the great ecumenical creeds of the undivided Church as a source of theological authority) that God is essentially incorporeal. Nevertheless, historic Christianity has consistently maintained that Jesus of Nazareth is God incarnate. Thus, God is essentially incorporeal, yet God has a body. More precisely, in the act of incarnation, the Second Person of the Trinity is personally or hypostatically united with a human nature that includes a human body. What is more, a great many Christians down through the centuries have thought that the blessed elements of the Eucharist are also, in some manner, the body and blood of Christ understood in some corporeal rather than metaphorical or spiritual sense. Here too, then, God is said to be both essentially incorporeal, and yet united in some very strong manner with the matter of the sacramental elements. Recent discussions of panentheism and pantheism have considered the same question about God's relation to matter from a rather different angle. In both cases, God is said to have a 'body' in the sense that God's relation to the created order is analogous to the relation between a soul and its body (in the case of many versions of panentheism), or the relation of an emergent mind to the body (in the case of many versions of pantheism). Similar conclusions have been reached in the recent philosophical literature on divine omnipresence, where some Christian philosophers have argued that God is wholly located at every region of the created order. Thus, we seem to have several different bodies ascribed to God.[1]

---

[1] There are also other minority reports in recent as well as historic Christian thought broadly construed, which imply that God is a material object or is identical with a material object. For instance, Hobbesianism, and at least some of the Cambridge Platonists – especially Henry More.

Metatheology

In this chapter, I shall argue for the apparently paradoxical conclusion that in one sense God does indeed have numerous bodies, and yet this is not inconsistent with the traditional theological claim that God is essentially incorporeal. For none of the various bodies that God has are essential to the divine nature; God is identical with none of the bodies the deity possesses. On the face of it, the idea that God may have one or more bodies and yet be identical with none of them also seems to be a puzzling claim, and one that I will have to explain as we proceed. Although I argue that God does have numerous bodies, this does mean that the way in which much Christian theology views the matter needs some amendment to include this more expansive understanding of divine bodies that I am recommending. However, I do not think this should be particularly troubling. God may be personally related to more than one body, given divine omnipresence and omnipotence. What is more, such relations do not undermine divine immutability or aseity. For, they do not require any relation between God and creation that implies change in God or dependence upon the body in question.[2]

The argument proceeds as follows. In the first place, I offer some terminological clarifications. With these in place, the second section considers the three putative bodies of God just mentioned, discussing each in turn. These are the incarnation, real corporeal accounts of the Eucharist, and the doctrine of divine immensity or omnipresence. In the last section, I offer some theological reflection on these three putative bodies of God and conclude that the incarnation and Eucharist are instances of accidental or contingent divine embodiment and that God does have multiple bodies – yet in such a manner as to preserve the doctrine of God's essential incorporeality.

Terminological clarifications

We begin with some terminological distinctions. I have already introduced one conceptual problem with the notion of incorporeality. I shall assume from here on in that this connotes the lack of a material or physical body. In other words, it is a notion whose semantic content is primarily privative. And, as I indicated at the beginning of this chapter, I say 'material or physical body' advisedly, given that not all parties to the debate hold that there are material objects even if they think there are physical ones (such as is the case with Berkeleyan immaterialists). By contrast, some hold that there are only material objects and no immaterial objects. This would be a rather strong version of materialism. A weaker form might allow that, say, mind is not a purely material object, though it is dependent in some fundamental respect upon material objects. In addition to the strength of materialism envisaged, there is also a distinct question about its scope. There are those who are *global materialists*. They hold that all that exists is material, and that nothing exists that is not material. In the case of global materialists who are

---

[2] I have argued for multiple incarnations elsewhere. See Crisp, *God Incarnate: Explorations in Christology* (London: T&T Clark, 2009).

also theists of some sort, they would be committed to the claim that God is a material object, or is identical with a material object, or composed by a material object. (Recall that I am allowing one to be considered a materialist in the global sense even if God or mind supervenes on matter, being fundamentally dependent upon matter for existence.) However, one may be a materialist about a certain class of objects less than the totality of all objects. For instance, one might claim that all *created* objects are material objects. Clearly, this class of entities excludes God. Thus, *restricted* or *local materialism* about a class of entities is consistent with global dualism. For (so it seems to me), there is nothing incoherent in claiming that an immaterial deity could bring about a material creation.

Next, let us consider the question of the relation of God to putative bodies. We may distinguish between the claim that God is a body, that God has a body, and that the world is God's body.[3] In the case of the claim that God is a body, what is envisaged is a claim about global materialism. On this sort of view, God *is*, that is, *is identical with*, a material object – presumably the universe taken as a whole. Suppose God is identical with the universe, as some versions of pantheism entail.[4] Then, it is not merely the case that God has a body, as you or I have a body. Rather, God is identical with the body in question: God is identical with the world; indeed, God is the world. As Spinoza's memorable aphorism has it: *deus sive natura*. That is, to speak of God is to speak of nature or the universe; and vice versa. This strikes me as a doctrine that will not appeal to many theists, especially classical theists. But it does make clear that if God is identical with the world, then by Leibniz's Law, God *is* the world.

What of the second notion, which was that God has a body? This is much easier to motivate for Christian theists, given the doctrine of the incarnation. For if God is incarnate in Christ, this means that from the first moment of incarnation God the Son has a body, the body of Jesus of Nazareth. This can be extended in the doctrine of the Eucharist so that blessed sacramental elements are said to be the very body and blood of Christ in some literal sense, a view that is held by many Christians both today and in history. But this idea of God having a body is also consistent with versions of panentheism that maintain that God is to the world as the soul is to the body. The world is God's body, but God and the world are not identical and are not completely overlapping entities. Thus, God has a body in this way of thinking too; it is just that God's body for the panentheist is the world. This seems to be the view of Mormon theologians too, who hold that God the Father has a body, as does God the Son, though the Holy Spirit is a rather different case. Joseph Smith writes, 'The Father has a body of flesh and bones as tangible as man's; the Son also; but the Holy Ghost has not a body of flesh and bones, but is a personage

---

[3] I owe these distinctions to William J. Wainwright, 'God's Body', *Journal of the American Academy of Religion* 42, no. 3 (1974): 470–81; 470.

[4] It seems to me that the pantheist need not claim that the world is identical with God. Perhaps some versions of pantheism might be consistent with the weaker claim that God is composed of the world or that God supervenes upon the parts of the world. But here is not the place to explore these suppositions in detail.

of Spirit. Were it not so, the Holy Ghost could not dwell in us'.[5] Nevertheless, for Smith even the Holy Spirit has a body; it is just a body of 'subtle' rather than 'gross' matter. He says, 'There is no such thing as immaterial matter. All spirit is matter, but it is more fine or pure, and can only be discerned by purer eyes; We cannot see it; but when our bodies are purified [or resurrected] we shall see that it is all matter'.[6]

What I have said thus far already addresses the issue of whether the world is God's body. Classical theists will say that God and the world are distinct; panentheists say that the world is somehow contained 'within' God, so that the world is God's body; and pantheists will say that God and the world overlap or are identical with each other.

A final sort of terminological clarification worth noting at this juncture concerns divine presence in the world. Traditionally, this has been understood in terms of divine immensity. Today it is often referred to in terms of the divine attribute of omnipresence. In the recent Anglo-American philosophical literature, the topic of omnipresence has been the subject of some discussion. One key issue is whether divine immensity entails that God is located at every place in the cosmos, and if so, how. An important distinction in this literature, to which we shall return, is between *pertending* and *entending*. This distinction was introduced by Hud Hudson.[7] We may characterize these two notions as follows. To pertend is to be wholly located at a particular region and have parts located at subregions of that region. Most medium-sized objects are like this: they are in a particular region and have parts that are distributed through that region. Thus, Crisp standing in the drawing room is located in a particular region of the drawing room and has parts that are distributed through the subregions of that region, such as his left hand or his right foot. Next, to entend is to be wholly located in a particular region and to be wholly located in every subregion of that region. It is in this sense that God is said to be present in the world. The Deity is not just located but *wholly* located at every point-sized region of the world. This notion of entension is akin to the medieval idea of God's holenmeric immensity. The terminology is different, but (as some recent Christian philosophers have argued) the semantic content of the views is very similar indeed.[8]

---

[5] *Doctrine and Covenants* 130:22. Later in the same passage, Joseph Smith says, 'There is no such thing as immaterial matter. All spirit is matter, but it is more fine or pure, and can only be discerned by purer eyes; We cannot see it; but when our bodies are purified [or resurrected] we shall see that it is all matter'. (*Doctrine and Covenants* 131:7–8.) I owe this reference to the discussion of Stephen H. Webb and Alonzo L. Gaskill, *Catholic and Mormon: A Theological Conversation* (New York: Oxford University Press, 2015), 106.

[6] *Doctrine and Covenants*, 131: 7–8, cited in Webb and Gaskill, *Catholic and Mormon*, 110.

[7] Hud Hudson, 'Omnipresence', in *The Oxford Handbook of Philosophical Theology*, ed. Thomas P. Flint and Michael C. Rea (Oxford: Oxford University Press, 2009).

[8] A point made by Ross Inman. See 'Omnipresence and the Location of the Immaterial', in *Oxford Studies in Philosophy of Religion, vol. 7*, ed. Jonathan L. Kvanvig (Oxford: Oxford University Press, 2017), 168–206.

The bodies of God

With these distinctions in mind, we can turn to the question of the bodies of God. Given that my concern is with Christian theism, I will set aside those views that entail that God is identical with the world. For these are not consistent with Christian theology, which presumes either that God and the world are distinct (as per classical theism) or that the world exists 'in' God, but that God is not identical with the world (panentheism).

As I indicated in the introduction, I will focus on three 'bodies' that God may be said to have simultaneously. I make no claim about this list being exhaustive; there may be more candidates for bodies of God that I will not consider here. Nevertheless, I think the three we will focus on are central in the discussion of God's body in the Christian tradition. They are the incarnation, the Eucharist and the world or cosmos. Let us consider them in that order.

The incarnation

First, the incarnation. Elsewhere, I have defended a version of compositional Christology, according to which Christ is a composite of God the Son and the human nature assumed.[9] Historically, human natures are usually thought to comprise a human body and soul, rightly configured. Thus, in the incarnation we have three 'parts': God the Son; and his human nature, which is typically thought to be the human body and soul of Jesus of Nazareth, rightly configured. These parts are hypostatically united. That is, they are united in the person of God the Son. It is the Son who assumes the human nature of Jesus of Nazareth. In so doing, he comes to have metaphysical ownership of that human nature. Now, for those squeamish about immaterial souls we can make the relevant adjustment to this three-part compositional model of the incarnation so that the incarnation involves the assumption of a human nature by God the Son, where human nature denotes a concrete particular comprising a human body and human *mind*, rightly configured.[10] Since minds are not necessarily souls and may be properties of certain kinds of bodies, this does not necessarily commit the christologist to the existence of human souls, understood as distinct substances that, together with a human body and rightly configured, form a complete human nature.[11] From a certain point of

---

[9] See Crisp, *Divinity and Humanity*.
[10] One could take a slightly different route to a similar conclusion and adopt a Christian hylomorphic account of human nature, along with Thomas Aquinas and his followers. Then, the human soul is located in the body during the life of the body, being distributed throughout the body. It has location and, in some respects, may be considered a material object. For the soul is the form of the body, configuring the matter of the body into a human being. This might be thought of as something akin to a materialist account of human beings. But as Thomas understands matters, the soul may exist without the body after somatic death by means of divine agency. Thus, even if it is a material object during bodily life, the soul is an immaterial residue of human nature upon the death of the body and during the intermediate state. It is a very strange metaphysics that holds a given thing can be a material object at one time and an immaterial object at another time.
[11] I have argued for a materialist Christology in Crisp, *God Incarnate*.

view such a revision to the model would still represent a three-part compositionalism. For there would be God the Son, and the concrete particular the Son assumes, namely, the human body of Jesus of Nazareth, along with the human mind it sustains. For present purposes, I will continue to speak of a three-part compositional account of the incarnation though I concede that if you take the variation that is commensurate with some forms of non-reductive physicalism – that is, human nature as human body plus mind, rather than human body plus soul – you may think it more appropriate to speak of a two-part Christology comprising God the Son and the human body-plus-mind assumed. For present purposes, how we count the 'parts' of Christ does not matter very much. How we think of human nature is the most important thing, and on the compositional view I have in mind (however we construe the question of the existence in humans of immaterial souls), the most important thing to note for our purposes is that human natures are concrete particulars. Thus, in the incarnation we have an immaterial divine person who assumes a concrete particular that has a material part.

So far, so good. But what about the relation between God the Son and the human nature assumed? Some compositionalists seem to think that what happens in the act of assumption is that God the Son 'expands' to include a human nature. However, this seems to jeopardize the incorporeality of God the Son. For 'expanding' to include a human nature that has a material part means the Son comes to have a material part. At the very least, it looks like this view implies that in becoming incarnate God the Son acquires a material part even if he is not transformed into a material object. This would be rather like the war veteran who gains a plastic and metal part when his wounded limb is amputated, and he is given a prosthetic one instead. Perhaps the union between the war veteran and the prosthesis is not sufficiently integrated for it to be considered analogous to the case of the incarnation. In that case, we can tweak the thought experiment. Think instead of the transhumanist idea of metal and plastic implants that act as an interface with organic material in the body so as to enable the human user to connect to certain technologies directly via a neural link – technology that is already being tested by various start-ups in the US today. This seems very much like an 'expansion' of the human person to include a new part that is non-organic in nature. It is surely for this very reason that such technological developments raise important moral questions about the integrity and continuity of human personhood through such change. *Mutatis mutandis*, in the incarnation we have the assumption of a material 'part' by God the Son. On the face of it, this too seems to be a momentous change that involves the acquisition of a new 'part' that raises serious concerns about the integrity and continuity of the divine person who assumes it.

I prefer a rather different approach to the question of the relation between God the Son and the human nature assumed in the incarnation that avoids these complications. Instead of saying that in becoming incarnate the Son 'expands' to include a human nature, including a material body, we could say that in becoming incarnate the Son comes to have metaphysical ownership of the human nature assumed. It becomes the human nature of a divine person. But this does not mean God the Son expands to include a human nature. Rather, it means that God the Son comes to have direct and immediate control over this human nature.

In the recent literature, Tim Mawson has argued that having direct knowledge of a material part of a body, and having direct access by means of acts of will to affect change in the material part of a body, does not necessarily provide an adequate account of the conditions needed for the material part to be owned by the person who has such direct knowledge and access to the material part in question.[12] For suppose your hand was anaesthetized so that you did not directly know it was your hand moving. In such a case, the hand would still be yours, for it is connected to the rest of your body, being a physical part of your body. Or suppose that you were unable to move your hand because of some neurologically degenerative disease. It would still be your hand even if you ceased to have direct control over it. Now, it is possible that on some occasion Jesus of Nazareth did not know he had direct access to some physical part of his body or was unable to directly act upon some part of his body. Perhaps he slept awkwardly one night and woke to find his arm was non-responsive for a few minutes until the blood flow to the limb resumed and sensation was restored. Such occurrences are commonplace. We wake to find we cannot move our arm because it has 'gone to sleep'. Yet after rubbing it for a few minutes, sensation and use return. But for a short period, we have no direct sensation of the limb in question, and no means of directly acting by means of it. If such an occurrence of a limb having 'gone to sleep' happened to Christ, we would not think that it was no longer his limb for the short period in which sensation and use of it was suspended. We should say that the nerves and blood flow needed to be restored to normal working parameters for sensation and use to return. But it is still Christ's limb because it is connected to the rest of his body, as it was before he lost sensation and use.

This is important not just for the trivial case of a limb that has 'gone to sleep' for a few short minutes after an uncomfortable night of sleep. It is also a pressing theological concern when thinking about the relation between God the Son and his human nature on Holy Saturday. We might ask, is God the Son still 'connected' to the dead body of Jesus of Nazareth lying in the tomb? Surely the traditional orthodox answer is in the affirmative. God the Son remains hypostatically united to his human nature throughout his Passion, even during the somatic death between Good Friday afternoon and Easter Sunday morning. Thus, even on a traditional theological accounting, it seems that the relation between God the Son and his human nature is not necessarily dependent on having direct and immediate access to the use of the material parts of his human nature.

Suppose that is right. What does the relation between God the Son and his human nature amount to if it is not necessarily a matter of direct and immediate access to the use of the parts of his human nature? Perhaps we can simply amend our notion of metaphysical ownership with a conditional clause, so that it amounts to the claim that *under normal circumstances*, the relation between any person and their human nature is

---

[12] See T. J. Mawson, 'God's Body', *Heythrop Journal* XLVII (2006): 171–81.

one of direct and immediate access to the use of the parts of that human nature. Where exceptions to this occur, whether temporarily as with anaesthetized limbs or limbs that have 'gone to sleep' or permanently, through neurological disease or severe physical damage to parts of the body, we say that the limb in question is still the limb that under normal circumstances would be directly and immediately accessible to this particular person. Obviously, in the case of damaged or non-responsive limbs, no one has direct and immediate access to their use, which is why the question of metaphysical ownership arises in the first place. But it is still true to say in such circumstances that were the limb operating under normal conditions, it would be directly and immediately accessible by the particular person in question. In this way, it is *her* or *his* limb, not the limb of any other person.

Let us return to the incarnation. On the version of compositionalism I favour, God the Son is related to his human nature in virtue of his metaphysical ownership of that nature. He has direct and immediate access to it, and under normal circumstances he is the only person who does have such direct and immediate access to it. There may be circumstances in which his direct and immediate access is suspended, as with a limb that 'goes to sleep' or during Holy Saturday, when his human body is dead in the tomb. But it is still true to say that in those unusual circumstances, the human nature of Christ, including the parts of his human body, belongs to God the Son alone because normally he and he alone would have direct and immediate access to those parts and that body.[13]

Does this mean that God the Son is really related to his human nature as you and I are really related to the concrete parts of our human nature? At first glance, this might seem to be the case. However, classical theists who want to adopt this sort of view will resist such a conclusion. For they hold that as a perfect being God is essentially incorporeal, metaphysically simple (i.e. without any parts whatsoever), exists *a se* or metaphysically and psychologically independent of all that is not God, is strongly immutable (being incapable of any substantive change whatsoever), and is metaphysically ultimate (i.e. is the *source* of the existence of all that is not God). For these reasons, God cannot be really related to any part of creation, for that would undercut these fundamental metaphysical commitments. Traditionally, the human nature of Christ is said to be contingently related to the Son who assumes it. In principle, the Son may decouple himself from his human nature at any time without loss to his essence, for God is essentially incorporeal. It would be like a hermit crab discarding his shell one day. The shell is important armour for the crab, but it is not essential that he has one. The shell is not part of the essence of the crab.

Yet, even if we agree that human nature is only contingently related to the divine person that assumes it, the relation in question appears to be a real one. The crab is really related to the shell he inhabits. It is his shell, at least until such time as he abandons it for another. And the traditional creedal language used in classical Christology speaks of the hypostatic or personal union of the Son with his human nature. That is a very intimate

---

[13] I have discussed this further in Crisp, 'Christ's Dead Limb', *Scottish Journal of Theology* (2025): 1–12, doi:10.1017/S0036930625000043.

relation indeed, even if (as in the three-part compositional model of the incarnation I have outlined here) the Son is not identical with his human nature and therefore is not identical with Christ.

Perhaps our earlier example of the prosthesis may be of help to the classical theist at this juncture. In one respect, the prosthesis is contingently connected to the body of the veteran so that it becomes his prosthesis. He has direct and immediate access to it. If it is a bionic limb, he can use it to perform tasks like his organic limbs. But he can still disconnect from it. We might say that he is contingently but not *really*, that is, organically, related to it. Perhaps something analogous to this obtains in the case of the incarnation. The Son assumes the human nature of Jesus of Nazareth. In the act of assumption, it becomes his human nature. Under normal circumstances, he has direct and immediate access to it. But the relation he bears to it remains contingent in the sense that it does not become something essential to the divine person assuming it, remaining entirely extrinsic to the Person of the Son.

To sum up: the incarnation is the paradigm case of God's body in Christian thought. I have argued that if we construe the incarnation along the lines of a three-part compositional model, we have an account that does not necessarily jeopardize the relevant aspects of classical theism. For the kind of metaphysical ownership of the human nature of Christ that is envisaged is one that does not require an essential change to the divine nature. Thus, God Incarnate is a divine person truly embodied in a particular human nature. Yet the act of incarnation and its sustenance thereafter does not necessarily imply a substantial change in God. In fact, it may amount to an entirely extrinsic, relational change by analogy with a prosthetic limb.

The Eucharist

Let us turn to our second example of a divine body. This is the Eucharist. More precisely, we are interested in the claim that once blessed, the sacramental elements of the eucharistic meal in some real manner become the body and blood of Christ, which is the majority view in the Christian tradition.[14] Thus, we are interested in what might be called *real corporeal accounts of sacramental presence*. I shall have nothing to say about symbolic and memorialist views of the eucharistic meal, such as those attributed to the Swiss Reformer, Huldrych Zwingli, and his followers, which are a minority report in the tradition, and which can only yield an account of the elements of bread and wine in which Christ's body and blood are present in a figurative or metaphorical sense.[15]

---

[14]This is indisputable both historically and in terms of the number of Christians today who belong to communions whose official position entails a doctrine of real corporeal presence.

[15]For two recent defences of a broadly memorialist account of the Eucharist published the same year by the same publisher, see Steven Nemes, *Eating Christ's Flesh: A Case for Memorialism* (Eugene: Cascade, 2023), and Celine S. Yeung, *Received by Christ: A Biblical Reworking of the Reformed Theology of the Lord's Supper*. Re-Envisioning Reformed Dogmatics (Eugene: Cascade, 2023).

Nor shall I consider those views of the Eucharist that regard Christ's presence in the elements as real but non-corporeal or real but mystical in a manner that precludes corporeal presence in the elements themselves, such as the views usually attributed to John Calvin and his successors or to Thomas Cranmer in Anglicanism. There are various versions of real corporeal presence doctrine in eucharistic theology. These include versions of *transubstantiation* where the substance of the bread and wine, once blessed is transformed into the body and blood of Christ, though its accidental and perceptible properties remain unchanged; *consubstantiation*, where in addition to the elements of bread and wine, the body and blood of Christ come to be corporeally present in, with, and under the elements; and *impanation*, according to which the blessed bread and wine become hypostatically united to God the Son or to Christ, so as to become his bread body and wine body, respectively.[16] In the present discussion, our focus is not upon distinguishing these various doctrines and their metaphysical commitments in detail. Instead, we need to think about the way in which these different doctrines all share the view that (somehow) the consecrated eucharistic elements become the body and blood of Christ in a real, corporeal, and not merely symbolic, metaphorical, spiritual or mystical sense.

I suggest that something like the following principle is true for those eucharistic doctrines that entail Christ is really and corporeally present in the consecrated elements:

> REAL PRESENCE: once blessed, the consecrated elements in the eucharistic meal become really and corporeally united to God the Son either directly, or indirectly via his human nature, so that in some substantive sense the manducated elements are the actual body and blood of Christ.

Now, to understand the import of this principle, we will need to say something about the metaphysics of eucharistic presence. This, in turn, has implications for claims about the consecrated elements being the body and blood of God Incarnate.

First, let us consider the distinction between being *entirely* located at a place and being *wholly* present at a place.[17] A material object is entirely located at a place provided it is in that place and no other. So, if Crisp is standing in the middle of the drawing room, he is entirely located in that place and in no other place distinct from the drawing room. However, a material object may be wholly located in more than one place; that is, it may be located in multiple places simultaneously. REAL PRESENCE implies the corporeal presence of Christ's body in the consecrated eucharistic elements as they are celebrated in multiple locations simultaneously on any given Sunday. Yet this happens in

---

[16]For a taxonomy of these different views of the eucharist, see James M. Arcadi, *An Incarnational Model of the Eucharist*. Current Issues in Theology (Cambridge: Cambridge University Press, 2018), and 'Recent Philosophical Work on the Doctrine of the Eucharist', *Philosophy Compass* 11, no. 7 (2016): 402–12.

[17]A distinction is made in the recent literature on the metaphysics of omnipresence. See, e.g., Inman, 'Omnipresence and the Location of the Immaterial'.

such a way that it does not jeopardize the integrity of the body of Christ that is 'seated' at the right hand of the Father interceding for the saints. How can this be? A second distinction will help us at this juncture. Medieval theologians spoke of the difference between *circumscriptive* and *repletive* presence. A thing is circumscriptively present in a place provided it is located at the place and is spread out in that place. In other words, circumscriptively present things are wholly present in a non-point sized region and have proper parts in subregions of that place. Thus, my body as it stands in the drawing room is circumscriptively in that place because it is wholly present in a Crisp-shaped region of the drawing room and has proper parts in subregions of that region, such as Crisp's hands, feet, trunk and so on. This is what we might think of as a commonsense notion of location. But repletive presence is rather more exotic. For a thing that is repletively present in a place is wholly located in a particular non-point sized region and is also wholly located in each subregion of that region.[18]

Applied to the Eucharist, the idea is that the consecrated elements may really become the actual body (and blood) of Christ in some manner, yet without jeopardizing the integrity of the body of Christ seated at the right hand of the Father in virtue of his repletive presence. That is, Christ is wholly located in or in with and under the consecrated eucharistic elements and is also wholly located in with and under every part of the eucharistic elements. So, the communicant is not eating a part of Christ when they manducate the consecrated bread or wine, such as his spleen or his hand. Nothing so gross is intended. Rather, in consuming the bread and wine they consume the whole corporeal Christ in some manner.[19]

My own view is that this is a rather convoluted way of getting at what most Christians want, namely, the real corporeal presence of Christ in the consecrated elements of the Eucharist. It seems far less complicated and more intuitive to think that once blessed, the eucharistic elements become hypostatically united either to God the Son directly or to Christ (i.e. to God Incarnate). Upon being consecrated in the eucharistic meal, the elements become the 'bread body' and 'wine body' of God the Son or of Christ, as Marilyn Adams memorably put it.[20] The bread and wine are not transformed or changed in the process of their consecration, though they are set apart for this particular purpose and become 'owned' by a divine person.[21] Rather, while retaining their integrity as bread and wine, they become personally united to a divine person or to the human nature of a divine person. It may still be the case that God the Son or Christ is repletively present

---

[18] As Inman points out, the medieval distinction between circumscriptive and repletive presence is very similar to the contemporary distinction between *pertending* and *entending* mentioned earlier.
[19] In fact, defenders of real corporeal presence doctrines of the Eucharist, mindful of the ancient objection that in the eucharistic meal Christians practice cannibalism, normally deny that the physical body of Christ is actually assimilated to the body of the communicant who manducates the elements.
[20] Marilyn Adams, *Christ and Horrors: The Coherence of Christology*. Current Issues in Theology (Cambridge: Cambridge University Press, 2009), ch. 10.
[21] In this way, they are made holy, as James Arcadi argues in *Holiness: Divine and Human* (Minneapolis: Lexington Books/Fortress Academic, 2023).

in the eucharistic elements. But that may be true in virtue of divine omnipresence rather than in virtue of some transformation of the elements if God is repletively present in the whole of creation, as some contemporary defenders of location accounts of omnipresence contend, and as some medieval defenders of holenmeric doctrines of divine immensity maintained.[22]

Let us take stock. According to those doctrines of the Eucharist that imply REAL PRESENCE, the consecrated elements of bread and wine are in some manner the actual body of Christ. Thus, not only is God incarnate in Christ, but God is also 'incarnated' every time the Eucharist is celebrated. However, in the case of transubstantiation and consubstantiation doctrines, this does not mean that God has multiple distinct bodies. Instead, what is meant is that the body of Christ is capable of being wholly corporeally present in more than one location repletively. The case of impanation is rather different because, as we have seen, on that doctrine God does have multiple distinct bodies. He has the body of God Incarnate; and he has the consecrated bread and wine bodies of the eucharistic meals. Thus, one exotic consequence of impanation that is not shared with transubstantiation and consubstantiation is that God does in fact have multiple distinct bodies – very many of them! – even if he is repletively present in the eucharistic elements once consecrated.[23] Finally in this section, I indicated that if divine immensity is regarded holenmerically, as some historic and contemporary philosophical theologians maintain, then the corporeal presence of God in the eucharistic elements does not seem to present quite so peculiar a doctrine as might initially have been thought. For on the holenmeric view, divine immensity entails God's location at every place in the cosmos. Thus, we exchange the oddness of eucharistic presence for a much larger oddness of the same sort, that is, God's present location at every place in creation.

The world

This brings us to our third example of God's body, which is the world or cosmos (I will use the terms interchangeably). Earlier I pointed out that those who are pantheists hold either that God is identical with the world (Spinoza's *deus sive natura*), or that God

---

[22]See the discussion in Inman, 'Omnipresence and the Location of the Immaterial' for details. He cites medievalist Robert Pasau, who writes 'Although it is now commonly supposed that God exists outside of space, this was not the standard conception among earlier theologians. Medieval Christian authors, despite being generally misread on this point, are in complete agreement that God is literally present, spatially, throughout the universe. One simply does not find anyone wanting to remove God from space, all the way through to the end of the seventeenth century. Of course, no one wanted to say that God has spatial, integral parts. So the universally accepted view was that God exists holenmerically throughout space, wholly existing at each place in the universe . . . God can be said to exist everywhere and at every time, and to exist wholly wherever and whenever he exists'. 'On Existing All at Once', in *God, Eternity, and Time*, ed. C. Tapp and E. Runggaldier (Burlington: Ashgate, 2019), 11–29; 19.
[23]Perhaps this is only a consequence of impanation accounts that have God the Son united to the eucharistic elements and not those accounts that have the elements united to the whole Christ. But that is a matter for another occasion.

shares all the same parts as the world. Panentheism is the idea that the world is 'in' God but that God is greater than the world. So, God has parts that the world does not. One standard reference work defines it as the view according to which, '[t]he being of God includes and penetrates the whole universe, so that every part exists in Him, but His Being is more than, and not exhausted by, the universe'.[24] There are difficulties in demarcating panentheism, and the literature on the topic is considerable. But for present purposes, the working definition just given will suffice.[25]

Both pantheists and panentheists can claim that in an important sense, the world is God's body. Discussion of these options is a live debate in contemporary philosophy of religion. So, one way of construing the claim that the world is God's body is to elaborate one or other version of pantheism or panentheism. For the Christian theist, some version of panentheism may be a viable option in thinking about the God-world relation, though it would seem to be contrary to orthodox Christian doctrine to say that God is identical with the world or shares all and only the same parts as the world. There are in fact many Christian panentheists, and various accounts of the way in which God is said to 'contain' the world have been offered, from Jonathan Edwards's immaterialist idealism to Jürgen Moltmann's theology of hope.[26] So, for many Christian theologians, the world is, in some important sense, the body of God or something akin to the body of God. Now, this could be taken one of several ways. It could be thought that this means God has multiple bodies. For there is the body of God Incarnate, to which God the Son is hypostatically united; there is the body of God present in the Eucharist; and there is also the body of the cosmos that is somehow 'contained' within God. Thus, on this way of counting, God has at least three bodies. But this way of counting divine bodies might be rather misleading. For suppose that the world is God's body as (at least some) Christian panentheists appear to think. Then, everything in creation is a 'part' or a 'mode' of God's body. You, me, the tree in the quad, the Grampian mountains, the Milky Way – all these things are 'parts' or 'modes' of the body of God. But then, the bodies of Christ in Jesus of Nazareth and in the eucharistic meal are not in fact distinct, separate bodies of God.

This does not mean that there is no significant metaphysical difference between these 'parts' or 'modes' of divine embodiment, however. It might be that God has a particular metaphysical ownership of the body of Jesus of Nazareth or of the eucharistic elements that does not obtain with respect to your body or mine or a conventional loaf of bread or bottle of wine. The notion of 'metaphysical' ownership would need to be spelled out, of course. Perhaps we could help ourselves to Mawson's notion that God's body must be under his direct and immediate knowledge and access. But if God is omniscient as well

---

[24]F. L. Cross and E. A. Livingstone, eds., *The Oxford Dictionary of the Christian Church*, 3rd ed. (New York: Oxford University Press, 1997), 1213.
[25]I have discussed this in Crisp, 'Against Mereological Panentheism', *European Journal for Philosophy of Religion* 11, no. 2 (2019): 23–41.
[26]For a survey of versions of panentheism in the Christian tradition, see John W. Cooper, *Panentheism: The Other God of the Philosophers. From Plato to the Present* (Grand Rapids: Baker Academic, 2006).

as omnipresent, then it is not clear how we would make such a distinction stable. For surely, if the cosmos is God's body then he has direct and immediate knowledge and access to every part of the cosmos, however small. That includes the incarnation and celebrations of the Eucharist.

I have not tackled location accounts of omnipresence as a distinct way of thinking about the cosmos as God's body in detail in this section. But it is not hard to see how that argument would go. Consider Inman's characterization of entension, which we encountered earlier:

> Roughly, for an object to entend is for all of it (without remainder) to be exclusively located at an extended place, and for all of it (without remainder) to be located at each of the proper subplaces of that place. Entending objects are not 'spread out' or distributed across space such that they are partly located or present at distinct, non-overlapping places; rather, for each of the places where they are located, they are *wholly* located at both the places themselves as well as at each of the proper parts of those places.[27]

Part of the argument offered by Inman involves showing that Divine immensity has been understood in terms very like entension in medieval discussions, where it is characterized as holenmerism. The basic point is the same in both cases, namely, God is present in every place in creation in such a manner that God is wholly present at every place. For if God is metaphysically simple, having no parts whatsoever, as has been traditionally thought to be the case in historic Christianity, then God's presence cannot imply his being partially present in one place and partially in another. It is all or nothing. And since God must be wholly present at all places in creation if he is to be omnipresent (which is usually how divine immensity has been construed in modern discussions of the subject), God must have entension; his presence throughout creation must be holenmeric. This too entails that the world is God's body, and that the incarnation and eucharistic presence of God are something like 'parts' or 'modes' of a more general, all-encompassing doctrine of God's presence.

My concern with such views, whether motivated by panentheism or by location accounts of divine immensity, is that they subsume other, more local senses of divine corporeal presence in the incarnation and Eucharist. As I have intimated, there may be ways around this concern. One might opt for the view that the incarnation and Eucharist represent particular 'modes' of divine presence. But this seems to be a rather ontologically thin way of distinguishing these matters. For my part, I prefer an account of divine immensity that is metaphorical rather than realist: God's presence in creation is a function of divine power and knowledge. God is said to be 'present' at every place in creation because God knows all that happens at each place in an immediate and

---

[27]Inman, 'Omnipresence and the Location of the Immaterial', 10.

complete sense, and God has the power to bring about all logically possible states of affairs in all places in creation in a direct and immediate manner. But this is consistent with God being especially present in some manner in the creation, in the incarnation and Eucharist in particular – as well as in other miraculous actions, like the burning bush or the shekinah cloud. Are these instances of special divine presence indicative of some qualitatively greater presence of God in those places? Surely such a conclusion would undermine attempts to shore up divine immensity. For it would seem to imply that God is more present in the burning bush, shekinah cloud, as well as in the human nature of Christ or the consecrated elements of the Eucharist. If God is omnipresent, he cannot be *more present* here rather than there.

To this worry, I would offer two remarks by way of response. First, if God is omnipresent, then however we understand that doctrine, it must mean God is not more present in one place rather than another. Nevertheless, we might apprehend or perceive God in one place more than in another. Surely that is part of the explanation of the presence of God in the burning bush and the shekinah cloud. It might also be part of the explanation for why it was that not everyone who encountered him perceived that Jesus of Nazareth was God Incarnate; and, of course, there are many who, in eating the bread and wine of the eucharistic meal, call down judgment upon themselves because they eat it without 'discerning the body of Christ', as the Apostle Paul puts it (1 Cor. 11:29). Second, and to repeat what has been said above, God has metaphysical ownership of the human nature of Christ and of the consecrated elements of the Eucharist in a way that is not the case with respect to mundane things that are not hypostatically or otherwise really united with God. (For all we know, God takes temporary metaphysical ownership of the burning bush or the shekinah cloud or the Ark of the Covenant too for particular acts of revelation.) True, God is present everywhere, so that in some manner we may say God is present in my hand or in that stone as well as in God Incarnate or in the consecrated elements. Yet the presence of God in my hand or in the stone is not the same as his presence in Christ or in the Eucharist. We need not collapse all divine presence into one undifferentiated sense of divine immensity. For, as I may be said to be present in the drawing room and yet particularly present in a direct and immediate way in my body standing in the drawing room, so God may be present in the world, and yet present in a direct and immediate way in the incarnation and Eucharist, as well as in the burning bush and the shekinah cloud.

Theological implications

I have argued that there are at least three ways in which God is said to be embodied in Christian theology. The first is the incarnation. The second is in the consecrated eucharistic elements. The third is in the world taken as a whole.

According to the doctrine of the incarnation, God is hypostatically united to the human nature of Jesus of Nazareth. I have suggested that this is understood in terms of a compositional account. This does not mean God is related to the human nature of Christ in such a way that it imperils divine simplicity or aseity. But it does mean that God has particular metaphysical ownership of Christ's human nature, which is his human nature from the first moment of incarnation onward. Indeed, with much of the tradition, I would contend that God the Son is eternally God Incarnate, though his human nature begins to exist at a particular moment in time. Thus, with certain important qualifications, the incarnation is an instance of God having a body.

According to real corporeal doctrines of the Eucharist, God is really and corporeally present in or with and under the consecrated elements. I suggested we think of this in terms of real presence, thus:

> REAL PRESENCE: once blessed, the consecrated elements in the eucharistic meal become really and corporeally united to God the Son either directly, or indirectly via his human nature, so that in some substantive sense the manducated elements are the actual body and blood of Christ.

Different manners of real corporeal presence in the consecrated elements will yield different ways of thinking about REAL PRESENCE. I opted for a version of impanation, according to which God the Son unites himself to the consecrated elements so that they become his 'bread body' and 'wine body', respectively. In one respect, this means that the eucharistic elements are another instance of divine embodiment. For if God the Son is hypostatically united to the eucharistic elements, then they are all his body, even if he is said to be repletively rather than circumscriptively present in each element once consecrated. I accept this as a second sort of divine embodiment closely related to, and dependent upon, the incarnation.

According to the doctrine of divine immensity, God is wholly present in every place in creation. There are different ways in which this can be construed. I considered panentheism and locational accounts of omnipresence. One odd consequence of these views is that they either collapse other instances of divine embodiment into divine immensity, or they so reduce the distinction between divine immensity and special cases of divine embodiment in incarnation and Eucharist, as well as in natural miracles like the burning bush or the shekinah cloud, that they yield rather 'thin' accounts of special divine presence in the world. In place of such views, I suggested one might think of divine immensity metaphorically, as the conjunction of divine omniscience and power. This yields a robust sense in which God is present in every location in creation, yet without the problematic consequence of thinning out or collapsing different instances of divine presence in creation, thereby preserving the several different ways in which, so it seems to me, God is embodied. Yet, as I have tried to argue, none of these senses in which God is embodied, especially in the incarnation or Eucharist, imperils the doctrine of divine incorporeality. God may be essentially incorporeal and yet hypostatically united to the human nature of Christ and to the eucharistic elements. For in each of these two paradigms of divine embodiment, the relation between God and his body, though intimate, is an accidental, not essential one.

CHAPTER 9
CHRIST'S MALENESS

In this chapter, we turn from general considerations about the bodies of God in the plural, to focus on matters of Christology in particular. Of the various problems that theological reflection on the person of Christ has raised, one of the knottiest in the recent literature concerns the maleness of Christ. By 'male' in this context, I mean a human who is biologically male rather than female or intersex. That is, someone whose xy chromosomes are expressed heterogametically as male. This is distinct from 'masculine' or 'masculinity' (and, for that matter, 'feminine' and 'femininity'), which refers to gender rather than biological sex. Fundamentally, the issue with Christ's maleness has to do with how it is that he can be said to represent all of humanity in his particularity. If he is a Semitic human male, then, it is said, he is at best a representative of other humans who are also biologically male. It is less clear how he can be said to represent those who are biologically female. The same is true with respect to those whose genetic make-up does not place them clearly within the binary of biologically male or female because, say, they do not have xy chromosomes expressed heterogametically as male or xx chromosomes expressed homogametically as female.[1] Let us call this *the problem of the maleness of Christ*. It is this concern that I will address in what follows.

I shall do so by way of several steps. The first involves setting out a particular construal of the problem of Christ's maleness. I shall set up the dialectic by outlining one traditional way of understanding the maleness of Christ that does not give it any soteriological privilege. For want of a better label, I shall call this view *the traditional response* to the question of Christ's maleness.[2] This seeks to argue that Christ's humanity is what is important for the purposes of human salvation, not his maleness. Although this sort of view has some merit, it seems to me that more needs to be said to meet the concerns

---

[1] These are not the only relevant factors in human sexual differentiation. The size of gametes is also an important issue (amongst others). But a person's chromosomal makeup is certainly an important factor. For a discussion of this in a theological context, see David Andrew Griffiths, 'Shifting Syndromes: Sex Chromosome Variations and Intersex Classifications', *Social Studies of Science* 48, no. 1 (2018): 125–48. There are also those who claim biological sex is binary or dimorphic. See, e.g., Rashad Rehman '"Intersex" Does Not Violate the Sex Binary', *Linacre Quarterly* 90, no. 2 (2023): 145–54. Even if this is right, it does not affect the central point of the argument to follow, which is that the Second Person of the Trinity, when incarnate can have no biological sex, strictly speaking.

[2] Note that 'traditional' does not entail 'correct' in this context. It is true that the sort of view I label as the 'traditional' response to the question of Christ's maleness is the one that is a kind of default in historic Christianity. However, the default view is not always the right view of the matter. It is worth making this point at the beginning of this chapter so that readers do not think that I am surreptitiously equating the traditional view with the truth of the matter.

Metatheology

posed by *christological symbolism*. This is a term borrowed from the work of post-Christian feminist theologian, Daphne Hampson. She argues that theologians use the symbolism of Christ's male human nature to make unwarranted theological claims about the priority of maleness in representing God in human relationships, even conflating God with maleness. In a second section, by utilizing some well-known metaphysical distinctions, I argue that advocates of the traditional response are right in a limited respect when they say that it cannot be the maleness of Christ that is soteriologically salient. For it is the person of Christ who is said to be the saviour of humanity, and the person 'in' Christ as the agent of salvation is not human but divine. Then, in the third section, I bring these distinctions to bear on the problem of the maleness of Christ, and especially the issue of christological symbolism. In the final section, I deal with two residual questions, having to do with the adoption of classical Christology, and the worry that none of the foregoing gets at the question of why Christ is male rather than female or intersex. I conclude that, armed with the assumptions and metaphysical distinctions marshalled in the previous sections of the chapter, it is possible to meet the very real concerns of feminist thinkers about the maleness of Christ without having to give up traditional ways of conceiving the metaphysics of the incarnation. Nevertheless, this should not leave traditionalists feeling smug. For the soteriologically salient issue is that the Second Person of the Trinity becomes a *human creature*, not that the Second Person of the Trinity becomes male, female, or intersex.[3]

Christological symbolism

It is often argued that given the metaphysical framework of classical Christology, the fact that Jesus of Nazareth was biologically male (if, indeed, Jesus was biologically male[4]) does not pose a christological problem of particularity for soteriology. In other words, it does not necessarily present a problem for the scope of Christ's reconciling work that turns on whether Jesus of Nazareth is able to represent *all* of humanity if he is a male human

---

[3] In this respect, I nod towards the work of the Danish theologian Niels Henrik Gregersen, whose notion of 'deep incarnation' has emphasized, among other things, that what is most fundamental about the incarnation is that God becomes a *creature*, thereby identifying Godself with the things that are created. He writes, 'The Logos of God (the eternal Son) "became flesh" in Jesus, assumed a particular body and mind in him, and hereby also conjoined the material, lived-in, and mental conditions of being a creature in any epoch. God thus became a human being (not only a man), a social being who lived with and for others in a sinful world (not an autistic individual), a living being vulnerable like sparrows and foxes (not just a member of *Homo sapiens*), a material being made out of stardust and earth (not bringing with him a special heavenly flesh), thus susceptible to death and disintegration'. Gregersen, Introduction to *Incarnation: On the Scope and Depth of Christology* (Minneapolis: Fortress Press, 2015), 4.

[4] It may be thought obvious that Christ was male given the way in which he is portrayed in the canonical gospels (a presumption made by christological traditionalists). However, it is not at all obvious, given the paucity of what we know about the historical Jesus of Nazareth, that he was, in fact, biologically male. Nevertheless, for the purposes of this chapter, I shall accept the traditional presumption that Christ was, in fact male and will not keep qualifying references to Christ as male in what follows.

person. After all, Christ had to have some sort of concrete existence as a human being to represent humans in reconciling them to Godself. That means he would normally be expected to be either male or female. But the fact Christ was, in fact, biologically male is not salient as far as the question of human salvation goes. The importance of the incarnation in this soteriological connection is that *God became human*, not that *God became a human male*. It is simply a matter of historical contingency and (presumably) the divine will that Christ was, in fact, male. There may have been good prudential and pragmatic reasons for him to be male in the society in which he lived, where the testimony of women was not regarded as having the same status as that of biological males. Nevertheless, his being male is not what matters for the question of human salvation; it is his being human that matters. I will call this *the traditionalist response* to the problem of Christ's maleness.

This traditionalist response has some merits. For one thing, it helps clarify that what is at stake here as far as traditionalists are concerned is the shape of human salvation. If it is Christ's being human that is salient in this respect, not his being male, then one aspect of the problem of Christ's maleness can be addressed. For, given the traditionalist response, Christ's being male is not what saves human beings. What is more, in the society in which Christ flourished, women were not thought to have the same status as men. This is a matter of sociological fact that is well documented. But it also provides some reason for thinking that an attempt to bring about human salvation in such a society would need to be adapted to the cultural norms and limitations of that society. The thought is that if Christ were a woman in first-century Palestine, it is very unlikely indeed that she would have been heeded, given that the Ancient Near East was steeped in patriarchy.[5]

Nevertheless, it seems to me that the traditionalist response fails to take the problem of Christ's maleness with sufficient seriousness. Yes, in principle, if God becomes human, then that requires God to assume a particular human nature that would normally be biologically male or female – assuming Christ did not have a genetic inheritance that would problematize such easy categorization.[6] However, one worry generated by the problem of the maleness of Christ is that the way in which this has been historically understood in the Christian tradition in some ways identifies maleness with God. It also makes maleness a kind of default that subsumes other human biological distinctions, so that it is as a *male* human that Christ represents the whole of humanity. As Daphne Hampson puts it, it is the symbolism of Christ as male that is the problem. 'Even though it may be said that what is taken on in the incarnation is a humanity in which we all share', she says, echoing the language of the traditionalist response, 'it is still the case that

---

[5] For an interesting recent study of the question of the testimony of women in the ancient Graeco-Roman and Jewish worlds in relation to the Woman at the Well in the Fourth Gospel, see Tommy Wasserman, 'The Woman at the Well as a Witness in John Revisited', *Journal of Theological Studies* 73, no. 2 (2022): 535–88.
[6] There are several such conditions in the medical literature. For instance, de la Chapelle syndrome is a rare congenital condition in which a person has xx chromosomes that would normally be expressed homogametically as a biological female but are, in fact, expressed in such a way that the person concerned, though apparently a genotypical female, is phenotypically male, often having male secondary sexual characteristics.

the form in which this universal nature is said to have been taken on is that of a male human being'.[7] This is *the problem of christological symbolism*.

Hampson's concern is not that Christ is in fact male. For surely, as has just been pointed out, if God becomes incarnate the human nature assumed must have a particular biology – typically, male or female.[8] The worry is not the biology but the symbolism with which the biology is freighted, so to speak. Put differently, the problem is that Christ's human maleness has too often become entangled with his divinity so that maleness gets taken up into our understanding of the divine life and God is, in practice if not in principle, understood to be male not female. To illustrate this concern, consider the 'creation of Adam' fresco on Michelangelo's Sistine Chapel ceiling. In Michelangelo's famous image, which through frequent reproduction and transmission has become a kind of cultural meme, the divine life is depicted in a classical conception of human maleness, complete with flowing white beard.

Such christological symbolism also plays a role in other areas of theology related to Christology. Perhaps the most obvious example of this is the way in which arguments about christological symbolism have been marshalled to defend claims about an exclusively male priesthood.[9] Here the idea is that Christ represents humanity to God, so that any person who acts in a similar priestly role as Christ's vicar must also represent humanity to God as Christ did. Given that Christ was male, this means that to adequately represent Christ to God before the community of the church, the priest must also be male. Such reasoning seems deeply implausible to those outside the Christian faith. However, it is only too familiar to those who have been brought up on sermons that have used the pastoral epistles or the supposed order of creation in the primeval prologue of Genesis as a lens through which to view the priority, if not the supposed superiority, of male humans. Such biblical reasoning is used to undergird their role as ecclesiastical leaders and pastors who model both the order of male headship that is thought to be implied by Scripture as well as the representational component of Christ's redemptive work before God in certain sacramental functions, such as the consecration of eucharistic elements.

Thus, the problem of christological symbolism is that Christ's maleness comes to stand in for the whole of humanity, and even to represent a certain ordering of human beings according to which males have a primacy not accorded those who are biologically female. (Those who are intersex are not usually treated in any detail in these binary discussions.) Not only that: maleness is also in practice predicated of the divine life even when it is conceded that God is without sex. It is no wonder then that traditionalist

---

[7] Daphne Hampson, *Theology and Feminism* (Oxford: Basil Blackwell, 1990), 58.
[8] I will not address the vexed question of gender directly here, though the reasoning offered could be applied to that question, *mutatis mutandis*. In other words, the particularity of Christ's human nature, whether the particularity is biological sex or gender – or race or ethnicity, for that matter – can be addressed by extending the reasoning offered here, though I do not address it directly in what follows.
[9] This is also a matter that vexes Hampson (among other feminist theologians), whose bruising experience in the debates about the ordination of women in the Church of England in the 1970s precipitated her alienation from Christianity, as she explains in *Theology and Feminism*.

attempts to discount the maleness of Christ as soteriologically salient, emphasizing instead his humanity, are regarded by many women (and women theologians) as facile and soteriologically inadequate. Tackling the question of what is biologically necessary for human salvation does not address the issue of the symbolism of maleness with which much traditional christological imagery has been invested.

Some metaphysical distinctions

Deeply felt long-standing disagreements are often difficult to resolve. Typically, in such situations, the arguments have been rehearsed with some frequency and are well-known and understood by both parties. So merely rehearsing standard positions is unlikely to make much headway, dialectically speaking. In the present case, perhaps more progress may be made if instead of attempting to provide more effective rebuttals of one or other objection to a given position in this debate, we step back from the cut-and-thrust of dialectic to think about the metadogmatics of the incarnation. It may be that some metaphysical distinctions will help inform and perhaps address some of the concerns of the different parties. That is what I propose to do in this section.

I shall take as my point of departure classical Christology, according to which Christ is said to be one divine person subsisting in two natures. These comprise his divine nature and his human nature, which he acquires at the first moment of incarnation. This is the two natures doctrine of Chalcedonian Christology – the canonical product of the ecumenical council of the undivided Church at Chalcedon in AD 451 that attempted to give some shape to the claim that Christ is a fully divine being who is also fully human. Here is not the place to rehearse the details of the christological settlement that was passed on to theological posterity or the various political and theological moves that precipitated it. We can simply assume classical Christology as our starting point, since it is a kind of theological foundation on which subsequent christological reasoning was built in the later Christian tradition.[10]

Next, we need to look at the implications of the two natures doctrine in a little more detail. Christ is said to be a divine person who assumes a human nature in the incarnation. Oddly, perhaps, Christ is not a human *person*, strictly speaking. Christ possesses a complete human nature (however we construe that). He is a human being, but he is not also a human person. What is the difference? We might put it like this.

---

[10] This history of early christological debates is well known. Two good reference works in this regard are R. P. C. Hanson's *The Search for the Christian Doctrine of God: The Arian Controversy 318–381* (London: T&T Clark, 1988), and Lewis Ayres, *Nicaea and its Legacy: An Approach to Fourth-Century Trinitarian Theology* (Oxford: Oxford University Press, 2004). J. N. D. Kelly's work, *Early Christian Doctrines*, 5th ed. (London: T&T Clark, 1977), though now somewhat dated, outlines the history up to the Council of Chalcedon in a reliable fashion. Of course, in the modern period, there have been many who have departed from the theological deliverances of classical Christology. But it is still the case that classical Christology informs most ecclesiastical documents, creeds, and confessions and is therefore, in one important sense, theologically normative.

Metatheology

Someone who is a human being instantiates a human nature. They have those qualities necessary and sufficient to be human. They exemplify human nature in the sort of nature that they possess. That human nature is, we might say, particularized and actualized in the given human being in question, thereby making it concrete. So, in addition to those general qualities that everyone with a human nature possesses, such as being a dependent rational animal, there are those qualities that distinguish this human being from that one – things like parentage, place of origin, height, weight and so on. Take the Apostle Paul. He has a particular human nature that is actualized from the moment of his conception. The same is true of Mary Magdalene or any other human being one may want to consider.

Let us adopt the Apostle Paul and Mary Magdalene as placeholders for male and female human beings. In the case of the Apostle, Mary Magdalene and any other mere human being, they not only instantiate a complete human nature so that they are rightly called human beings. They are also human persons. For, in the particularizing of their human natures, they become what the medievals would have called a fundamental substance or *suppositum*. This is a substance independent of other substances. The Roman philosopher Boethius famously remarked that persons are *individual substances of a rational nature*.[11] This is a way of conceiving persons that can include humans, angels and, perhaps, the divine. Those, like the Apostle or Mary Magdalene, who possess a complete human nature, are human beings. But because they are individual substances, that is, fundamental substances independent of other substances, and because they are substances of a rational nature, they are also persons. In fact, they are *human* persons because they are individual substances of a rational nature belonging to a particular natural kind, namely, humanity. However, precisely because they instantiate a particularized human nature, they are both fully and *merely* human.

Christ is like and unlike this. He is like this in that he possesses a particular human nature and so is rightly called a human being. He is *fully* human. That is, he has all those qualities necessary and sufficient to be a human being, exemplified in the particular human nature of Jesus of Nazareth. Yet he is also unlike this. His human nature, though a substance of a rational nature, does not exist as an *individual* substance of a rational nature. That is, his human nature is not a fundamental substance independent of other substances. His human nature belongs to a divine person. From the moment at which it begins to exist it is assumed by a divine person. This act of assumption prevents the human nature in question from being independent of another person, specifically, a divine person, the Second Person of the Trinity, that is, the Word of God. Because Christ's human nature is assumed by a (divine) person from the moment at which it begins to exist and remains in this dependence relation thereafter, it is not a person in this philosophical sense of the term 'person'. For persons cannot have other persons as parts – that is just what it means for a person to be a fundamental substance. Thus, Christ

---

[11] Boethius, 'A Treatise Against Eutyches and Nestorius' in *The Theological Tractates*, trans. H. F. Stewart (London: Heinemann, 1918), 85.

is fully but not *merely* human. Of course, as Thomas Aquinas points out at one point, we may speak colloquially of the person of Jesus of Nazareth or the person of Christ.[12] But this is a loose and non-philosophical way of speaking. If we were being more careful, we would refrain from such language to avoid misunderstanding. For Christ is not a human person strictly speaking, though Christ has a complete human nature. Rather, Christ is a divine person who assumes a complete human nature in the act of incarnation.

A different solution

With these traditional metaphysical distinctions made tolerably clear, we may return to the matter in hand. How might these distinctions help resolve the problems generated by the maleness of Christ and especially the problem of christological symbolism? In the following way.

We have seen that according to classical Christology, Christ is not a human person strictly speaking. This somewhat surprising judgement means that whatever we predicate of Christ, it is not the case that he is a male person. He cannot be a male person in this strict and particular sense because to be a male person he would have to be a person who has a particular biology. And as we saw earlier in the work of Boethius, that means he would have to be 'a fundamental substance of a rational nature' – in this case, a person that is a *human male*. But the person 'in' Christ, so to speak, cannot be a *male person* because the person 'in' Christ is divine, and God (as we saw in the previous chapter) is essentially incorporeal, and therefore lacks human biology. This is simply an entailment of the traditional two natures doctrine, which was propounded largely to keep distinct the two natures Christ possesses from the first moment of incarnation onwards. I take this to mean that although the Word of God 'owns' the human nature assumed from the moment it is generated, this does not mean the Word of God has a particular (male) human biology. For the Word of God does not have proper parts, as creatures do, because God is said to be essentially non-composite.[13] Similarly, in putting on a garment, a person does not gain a proper part. The Second Person of the Trinity cannot be said to be identical with the human nature assumed at the first moment of incarnation precisely because the Word of God is a divine person and (so it has traditionally been thought)

---

[12]He says, 'I answer that . . . the term "Man" placed in the reduplication may refer either to the suppositum or to the nature. Hence when it is said: "Christ as Man is a person," if it is taken as referring to the suppositum, it is clear that Christ as Man is a person, since the suppositum of human nature is nothing else than the Person of the Son of God. But if it is taken as referring to the nature, it may be understood in two ways. First, we may understand it as if it belonged to human nature to be in a person, and in this way it is true, for whatever subsists in human nature is a person. Second, it may be taken that in Christ a proper personality, caused by the principles of human nature, is due to the human nature; and in this way Christ as Man is not a person, since the human nature does not exist of itself apart from the Divine Nature, and yet the notion of person requires this'. Aquinas, *ST* 3. 16. 12, *respondeo*.

[13]This is one aspect of the doctrine of divine simplicity that is firmly rooted in the Christian tradition.

divine persons are immutable in a strong sense, independent of creation (i.e. exist *a se*), and metaphysically simple. On this traditional view, divine persons cannot change, acquiring a new physical part; they cannot begin to have a real relation with a parcel of matter like a human body; and because they are non-composite, they cannot come to have physical or immaterial 'parts'. But of course, if the Word of God is identical with the human nature assumed, then the Word is not immutable. For if the Word is identical with the human nature assumed, then, according to the identity of indiscernibles, the Word shares all its parts and properties with the human nature assumed.[14] But then, on this view, the Word of God would also not be independent of creation, because the Word would be identical with the human nature assumed, which is a part of creation. Nor is the Word metaphysically non-composite because the Word is identical with a human nature that has many different physical parts, such as arms, legs, hands and so on.[15]

So, with the theological traditionalist I say: the Second Person of the Trinity is not identical with the human nature assumed at the first moment of incarnation.[16] For the Word of God is immutable, incorporeal and non-composite. What is more, given the two natures doctrine and the metaphysical distinctions outlined above, the Word is not a human person in the strict and particular sense. Consequently, the Word is not a male person either. So far, so good. Now, let us presume with the Christian traditionalist that Christ does have a male human nature.[17] This sits well with our assumptions about classical Christology, though as I have already indicated, it is a presumption that could be challenged. For now, let us accept it for the sake of argument. Then, we may say that Christ is a whole that includes a divine person who has a human nature that is biologically male; Christ is a composite of the Second Person of the Trinity plus the human nature of Jesus of Nazareth. Does this make the Word of God identical with a male human being? No, it does not. Nevertheless, we may say that Christ names a divine person who possesses a human nature that is biologically male.

---

[14] More precisely, according to the identity of indiscernibles, where W and H represent two objects, for every property x, W has x iff. H has x.

[15] Some medieval thinkers and their contemporary disciples think in the incarnation God the Son expands to include a human nature so that he is in some sense identical with the human nature he assumes. This seems to be the view of Thomas Aquinas. It is not a view I hold, and I leave it to defenders of this Thomist view to provide their own remedy to the problem of Christ's maleness. For a recent account that outlines much of this material, see Timothy Pawl, *The Incarnation*. Cambridge Elements in Philosophy of Religion (Cambridge: Cambridge University Press, 2020).

[16] This is one aspect of a compositional account of the incarnation. A clear example of such a view can be found in Brian Leftow's essay, 'A Timeless God Incarnate', in *The Incarnation*, ed. Steven T. Davis, Gerald O'Collins, and Daniel Kendall (Oxford: Oxford University Press, 2002), 273–302.

[17] As I indicated earlier in this chapter, Christ's biological status as male is not quite as secure as the tradition seems to presume, since we do not know that Christ was male in the sense of having xy chromosomes expressed heterogametically as male. He might have had one of a number of genetically abnormal conditions, such as de la Chapelle syndrome, in which case he could have appeared to be male phenotypically even if he did not have a male genotype. This is a matter that has been raised in the recent literature, though there is not space to pursue it here. For a helpful discussion of some of the issues, see Susannah Cornwall, 'Sex Otherwise: Intersex, Christology, and the Maleness of Jesus', *Journal of Feminist Studies in Religion* 30, no. 2 (2014): 23–39.

This may seem like rather a nice philosophical distinction (in the pejorative sense of 'nice'). To provide some motivation for taking it seriously, consider the following analogy. Suppose an astronaut puts on a spacesuit to do a spacewalk. Further, suppose that the spacesuit must be connected to a wall socket to supply the electricity needed for the suit to function. (This may be thought to be a rather serious defect in a spacesuit, but let us leave that to one side for now.) We do not suppose that in putting on the spacesuit and plugging it into the socket, the astronaut has the electrical cord or the plug in which it terminates attached to her or him. Rather, we think that the spacesuit has such a cord, whereas the astronaut, though inhabiting the spacesuit (so to speak), remains distinct from it. S/he does not necessarily acquire all the qualities of the spacesuit in putting it on. The analogy is admittedly a very partial one. But it serves to make the point that in assuming a particular male human nature, the Word of God does not necessarily thereby assume all the qualities of that human nature. For instance, God is often said to be essentially incorporeal in traditional theology. Yet Christ has a human body. On the face of it, these seem to be puzzling if not paradoxical claims. Contradiction is avoided by simply agreeing that in assuming human nature, the Second Person of the Trinity does not necessarily come to have anything more than an accidental relation to the body assumed.[18] In other words, in becoming incarnate the Word of God does not necessarily become corporeal. Rather, in becoming incarnate the Word acquires a corporeal 'part', so to speak, to which the Word bears a certain accidental relation, making it the Word's human nature. But the same is true of the astronaut. In putting on the spacesuit, the astronaut comes to have a particular relation to the suit, it being her or his suit. But that does not necessarily mean the astronaut, in putting on the suit, comes to acquire the parts of the suit as proper parts. S/he merely has a particular accidental relation to the suit that enables her or him to use it for the purposes of walking in space.[19]

Thus, if Christ is a divine person with a male human nature, it does not follow that the Word – that is, the divine person who assumes this particular human nature, who is the referent here – is a male human. The conventional use of the male pronoun with respect to divine persons as well as God Incarnate is unfortunate because it appears to undercut the point being made. Traditionally, God is referred to in Christian thought using masculine pronouns even though it is normally understood that God is not male, for God has no biological sex, being essentially immaterial. Pronouns are used to predicate a particular gender of a person or (sometimes) a thing, like a ship or vehicle.[20] My concern here is not with whether God has a gender, but with whether the maleness

---

[18] Of course, Thomists will say that God the Son has no real relation to his human nature, though the human nature is dependent on God the Son for its continued existence. We can ignore this complication here, I think.
[19] Lest I be misunderstood and daubed a Nestorian, let me reiterate here that this is an analogy. I do not say that the astronaut example is like the incarnation in every respect. For one thing, the relation between the Second Person of the Trinity and the human nature assumed is, in one important respect, much more intimate than that between the astronaut and her or his space suit. We might say that the relation in question is one of *metaphysical ownership*.
[20] At least, this is the case in the English language. It is not true of all other natural languages, e.g. French.

of Christ is problematic. As the recent literature on gender and biological sex has made abundantly clear, these two things are not to be confused: gender and biological sex are distinct though closely related issues.[21] We may predicate *masculinity* of God with particular pronouns. Traditionalists may claim that this is just a way of speaking – a kind of useful fiction like the convention in the English language of speaking of a ship using feminine pronouns. This, it might be said, is better than having to qualify every reference to the divine in non-gendered language and has the advantage of indicating that God is personal, that is, person-like not merely object-like. Such matters remain the subject of discussion, and we do not have the space to tackle the matter in detail here.[22] Suffice it to say that the use of masculine pronouns in referring to the divine is not a helpful convention and can generate confusion when it comes to thinking about the maleness of Christ. For this reason, I have resisted adopting masculine pronouns in this work when referring to the divine even though such conventions, being deeply rooted in the Christian tradition, are often easier to adopt than challenge.[23] So, to be clear: I presume that God is not gendered, though Christians usually use gendered language when referring to God. God cannot be masculine because God is essentially incorporeal, being a spirit (Jn. 4:24), and it is not clear to me how spirits could be gendered, since gender supervenes on something corporeal – normally a body. Thus, the use of masculine pronouns in referring to God is a way of speaking, nothing more. It is like speaking of a ship or a car by means of feminine pronouns in the English language. When we do such things, we do not really think that the ship or car is *actually* feminine. It is a linguistic convention, a way of speaking; nothing more. However, unlike a ship or car or any other artefact, God is personal. It is just that God is either non-gendered or beyond gender or (perhaps) poly- or omi-gendered.[24]

Let us take stock. Coupled with our starting assumptions of the two natures doctrine of classical Christology, the presumption that Christ had a male human nature, and our distinctions about the metaphysics of the incarnation, we have the following result. Christ is a divine person with a male human nature. This human nature is not identical with the divine nature. Even after the assumption of human nature in the incarnation, Christ's two natures remain distinct. They are united hypostatically, that is, *in* the person of the Word of God. (This is a matter we discussed in the previous chapter in more

---

[21]This is a matter that is helpfully explored in a theological context by Michael C. Rea, 'Gender as a Divine Attribute', *Religious Studies* 52, no. 1 (2016): 97–115.

[22]See, for example, Janet Soskice's recent work *Naming God: Addressing the Divine in Philosophy, Theology and Scripture* (Cambridge: Cambridge University Press, 2023), and (drawing on Soskice and applied to the debate in the Church of England) Nicholas Adams, 'God's Pronouns', *Scottish Journal of Theology* 77, no. 4 (2024): 313–28.

[23]That said, the logic of the traditionalist position about referring to God does mean that the use of exclusively masculine pronouns for the divine is just a convention. To my mind, there is nothing in principle wrong with referring to God using feminine pronouns either, provided they too are understood to be useful fictions. Some theologians have adopted this practice. I prefer to try to refer to the divine without gendered language. But both conventions may be used to make the same theological point.

[24]Rea gestures to these options at the end of his essay, 'Gender as a Divine Attribute'.

detail, and I presume that discussion here). Nevertheless, in being united with the human nature of Jesus of Nazareth, the Word does not become a human *male*, strictly speaking. Nor does the Word become a human *male person*. Rather, the Word remains a divine person united with a particular (male) human nature to which the Word is contingently related via the act of assumption at the first moment of incarnation. The person at the root of Christ, so to speak, is divine. Historically, Christian theologians have held that divine persons are not gendered and are essentially incorporeal because God is a spirit. If that is right, then God cannot be identical with any parcel of matter, including a human nature – or, at least, that part of a human nature that is material, which includes the biological part with which we are concerned here.[25] But if that is correct, then the maleness of Christ is a purely accidental or contingent matter. Although the Second Person of the Trinity chooses to assume a particular human nature, the male human nature of Jesus of Nazareth (presuming his human nature is male), that does not mean God thereby becomes male. That is metaphysically impossible because (as has traditionally been thought) God is essentially a spirit that is immutable, exists *a se*, and is said to be metaphysically simple. So, God has no human biology, can have no human biology, and does not acquire human biology as anything more than a 'part' or 'instrument' to which the Word is contingently related upon assuming the human nature of Jesus of Nazareth.[26] Once this is clear, the problem of Jesus' maleness seems to be much less pressing. For, upon careful consideration, it seems that it does not commit the theologian to a view of the divine whereby Christ's maleness can be assimilated to his divinity. Saying this will not displace the cultural tropes of maleness associated with the Christian God in iconography, paintings and even sometimes in liturgies and Christian practices the world over. But it does give the lie to the claim that because Jesus is a male human being (if he is indeed a male human being), this means God is male. Nor, on this way of thinking, is it theologically feasible to conflate Christ's maleness with the divine.

Two residual questions

This leaves several residual questions, however. First, one or more of the traditionalist assumptions I have made to reach this conclusion might be questioned. Many feminist

---

[25] As the previous chapter indicated, I am aware that recent discussions of divine omnipresence include 'location accounts' that do claim God is located in spacetime. I do not think that spirits can be located, which is one reason why I think God cannot be identical with a given parcel of matter. The reader will recall from the previous chapter that I am attracted to a more metaphorical view according to which omnipresence is a function of omnipotence plus omniscience. A recent monograph that explores the topic of divine location in connection with the views of the Cambridge Platonists that is relevant here is J. D. Lyonhart, *Space God: Rejudging the Debate between More, Newton, and Einstein*. Studies in the Doctrine of God: Exploring Classical and Relational Theism (Eugene: Cascade Books, 2023).

[26] I am using 'part' and 'instrument' in a rather stretched sense here. I am not thereby committed to the view that Christ's human nature is a part of God, even a contingent part. Nor am I committed to the idea that Christ's human nature is literally a divine instrument.

theologians will want to distance themselves from the kind of Chalcedonian Christology that informs the argument I have made. However, there was good reason for going down this path. My concern was to show that even if we make several classical christological assumptions we are not necessarily committed to a view of the maleness of Christ that is theologically problematic. For, it turns out, given these assumptions and the reasoning offered here (none of which is particularly novel), Christ is not a human person strictly speaking, and the Word of God incarnate is not identical with a human male. On the assumption of compositional Christology, Christ is 'composed' of several 'parts': the divine person of the Word of God and the human nature the Word assumes in the incarnation. But in assuming that nature, the Word does not become either male or a human person. Since the Word of God is the only person 'in' Christ, so to speak, it does not make sense to predicate maleness of him. If Christ is a male human being, this provides us with no theological warrant for thinking that God is male or that the Second Person of the Trinity is male whilst incarnate. This undercuts both the problem of the maleness of Christ and the motivation for the problem of christological symbolism that Hampson raises. As I have already said, it will not prevent there from being a problem of christological symbolism. But it should motivate theologians to do their best to dispel this problem when they encounter it as a piece of conceptual confusion that has done much theological damage.

This leaves one further unanswered question: Why does God assume a male human nature in the incarnation? Why not a female human nature? Why not an intersex human nature? To my mind, there may be some merit in the sociological reasons usually adduced for this, which we have already encountered in the traditionalist response in the first section of this essay. These will not cut much ice for many feminist or queer theologians, however. Perhaps the best we can say on the traditionalist view is that this is a matter of contingent fact that is not soteriologically salient, the precise reasons for which are not available to us (Deut. 29:29). That is not an entirely satisfactory response. But I presume that any human nature assumed by God will have a biological sex. It is not the biological sex of Christ that saves us – to that extent, the traditionalists are surely right. But why Christ was male rather than female (or intersex) is a question that remains unanswerable in the absence of further data. Yet it does raise a further issue, one that I have already hinted at in the foregoing that would require a separate discussion. It is this: *was* Christ a male human being? A case could be made for the claim that, for all we know Christ was not biologically male in the sense we understand human biology today. For all we know, Christ was someone who had an unusual genetic makeup that may have been expressed phenotypically in such a way that he presented as a human male (which would have had certain cultural advantages in the time in which he was born), though Christ was not, in fact, biologically a human male.[27] This too is a matter of christological speculation. But it is a speculation that should give hard-nosed traditionalists some pause for thought. For all we know Christ was not, in fact, biologically male even if he appeared to be to those around him.

---

[27]This is an issue that has been made famous in a different but related religious context in Robert Harris's novel, *Conclave* (London: Hutchinson, 2016), and the motion picture of the same name that is based on his work.

CHAPTER 10
REALIZED ESCHATOLOGY

According to traditional Christian theology, this world is a foretaste of another. 'We look forward to the resurrection of the dead and the life of the world to come', as the Nicene Creed puts it.[1] Millions of Christians the world over reaffirm this confession in services of worship every Sunday. Let us call belief in a world to come, and in the expectation of a future resurrected life in a new heavens and earth, *the Christian hope*. I take it that the Christian hope comprises a cluster of beliefs about cosmic and personal eschatology. Cosmic eschatology has to do with the way in which the cosmos features in Christian teaching about the world to come – usually understood in terms of the transformation or annihilation of this world, and the bringing about of a new world, that is, the 'new heavens and earth'. Personal eschatology has to do with the survival of human beings post-mortem. In historic Christian teaching, this is primarily about the resurrection of the dead, although it is often also associated with related doctrines such as belief in an intermediate state and questions of personal identity beyond somatic death, or between somatic death and resurrection.[2]

Perhaps surprisingly, ever since the beginnings of Christianity, there appear to have been those who have denied or revised aspects of the Christian hope. Thus, in one of the earliest epistles in the New Testament, Paul writes in defence of the doctrine of the resurrection as follows:

> Now if Christ is proclaimed as raised from the dead, how can some of you say there is no resurrection of the dead? If there is no resurrection of the dead, then Christ has not been raised; and if Christ has not been raised, then our proclamation has been in vain and your faith has been in vain. We are even found to be misrepresenting God, because we testified of God that he raised Christ – whom he did not raise if it is true that the dead are not raised. For if the dead are not raised, then Christ has not been raised. If Christ has not been raised, your faith is futile and you are still in your sins. Then those also who have died in Christ have perished. If for this life

---

[1] See John H. Leith, *Creeds of the Church: A Reader in Christian Doctrine from the Bible to the Present*, 3rd ed. (Louisville: John Knox Press, 1982 [1963]), 33.
[2] This presumed connection between the intermediate state and the doctrine of the resurrection has been challenged in the recent literature by James T. Turner, Jr.'s monograph, *On the Resurrection of the Dead: A New Metaphysics of Afterlife for Christian Thought*. Routledge New Critical Thinking in Religion, Theology and Biblical Studies (London: Routledge, 2019).

only we have hoped in Christ, we are of all people most to be pitied. (1 Cor. 15: 12–19, NRSV)

In our contemporary world, where we now know that the cosmos is moving towards ever greater entropy, and to an eventual collapse or dissipation, this eschatological worry about whether there is a world to come (a question about cosmic eschatology), let alone the resurrection from the dead (a question of personal eschatology) seems even more pressing. As Kathryn Tanner puts it,

> On the face of it, such end-time scenarios conflict with the future-oriented, this-worldly eschatology of most contemporary Christian theologians. If the scientists are right, the world for which Christians hold out hope ultimately has no future. Hope for an everlasting and consummate fulfilment of this world is futile: destruction is our world's end.[3]

Yet, as Paul exhorts his first-century readers, if for this life only we have hoped in Christ, then we are of all people most to be pitied. Thus, there seems to be a conflict between the cosmic-entropic end for the world envisaged by the natural sciences and the historic theological account of a future-oriented eschatology. What is the contemporary Christian theologian to do? In this chapter, I will address this apparent incommensurability between the sort of naturalistic vision of the end of the world envisaged in contemporary cosmology and the eschatology of the Christian hope. The idea that theologians might address this problem by revising our eschatological orientation from the future to the present, thereby reinterpreting Christian expectation of immortality and a life beyond death so that it corresponds with a naturalistic vision of the eventual destruction of the cosmos is the major concern of this chapter. Let us call this refocusing of eschatology to a this-world frame of reference so as to fit within the sort of naturalistic vision of the end of the world presumed in much contemporary natural science (with a nod in the direction of C. H. Dodd), *fully realised eschatology*.[4] I will focus on one recent attempt to provide metaphysical and theological motivation for a fully realized eschatology provided by the American Episcopal theologian, Kathryn Tanner (tempered with a short foray into Schleiermacher's thought, to which Tanner seems, in some respects, indebted).

---

[3]Kathryn Tanner, 'Eschatology Without a Future?', in *The End of the World and the Ends of God: Science and Theology on Eschatology*, ed. John Polkinghorne and Michael Welker (Harrisburg, PA: Trinity Press, International, 2000), 222–37; 222. This paper is reproduced, with some minor modifications, as the final chapter of Tanner, *Jesus, Humanity and the Trinity: A Brief Systematic Theology* (Minneapolis: Fortress Press, 2001).

[4]C. H. Dodd was a well-known British biblical scholar of the first half of the twentieth century who argued, amongst other things, that the Jesus of the canonical gospels thought that the eschaton was realized in his own teaching. The Kingdom of God is not merely some future hope but breaks into history through Jesus' teaching. I am borrowing this notion and pushing it in a more radical direction, as will become clear. For Dodd's position, see his *Parables of the Kingdom* (London: Fount, 1988 [1935]).

Although she presents a rich and suggestive version of fully realized eschatology in the form of an extended thought experiment, in the final analysis, it is, I think, incomplete, insufficiently motivated, and consequently is not preferable to traditional accounts of the Christian hope.

We proceed as follows. In the first section, I shall set out some terminological distinctions that will be important for clarifying what is at stake. Then, in the second section, I outline and discuss Tanner's version of fully realized eschatology. In the third section, I raise some objections to her argument. Finally, in a concluding section, I consider the theological upshot of this discussion.

Eschatological terminology

To begin with, it will be helpful to clarify some of the terms of art that inform the discussion that follows. I have already given a rough-and-ready definition of *the Christian hope* in passing, comprised of two components. These were, first, belief in a world to come (cosmic eschatology); and second, belief in a resurrected life in a new heavens and earth (personal eschatology). I take it that both components of the Christian hope are theologically realist in nature. That is, both presume that there is a mind-independent world to come in which the cosmos is renewed, and human beings exist as embodied entities in intimate communion with God. Some theologians have entertained the idea that traditional theological language of the world to come could be transmuted into language of the continued remembrance of each individual human life history by God, or even of some way in which the 'information-bearing pattern of souls' (as John Polkinghorne puts it) could be held in the mind of God.[5] But it would seem that such speculations are not (or not necessarily) theologically realist in the sense I am after, because they do not necessarily presume that the world to come is mind-independent. It may be that the world to come is, in fact, a purely mental world of minds and their ideas. But that is not the prospect we shall be focused on here, and it is not (I submit) the prospect that seems to have informed the historic Christian account of the world to come, including a corporeal resurrection.[6] As I shall understand it here, the Christian

---

[5] This from theoretical physicist and theologian John Polkinghorne. See Polkinghorne, *The God of Hope and the End of the World* (London: SPCK, 2002), 121. Note, however, that this is only a speculative aspect of Polkinghorne's account, and it is not clear from the context the extent to which he is committed to it.

[6] This is true even given the qualification of Paul's discussion in 1 Corinthians 15 about the *soma pneumatikon*, or spiritual body that will be the lot of the resurrected. Whatever he meant by a 'spiritual body', it seems clear to me that he did not think of such a 'body' as a purely mental item. However, for those enamoured of Berkeleyan idealism, where there are only minds and their ideas, a different metaphysical backstory would be needed that construes language of bodies as percepts and property bundles without some material substrate, understood in terms of unthinking extended 'stuff'. There is not space to address these concerns here, fascinating though they are. Interested readers might consult Marc A. Hight and Joshua Bohannon, 'The Son More Visible: Immaterialism and the Incarnation', *Modern Theology* 26, no. 1 (2010): 120–48, for a recent attempt to motivate such Berkeleyan-style arguments in the case of the incarnation.

hope as it has been traditionally understood is a theologically realist hope about the world to come and about the resurrection from the dead.[7]

Next, something more should be said about what I mean by fully realized eschatology. This in turn requires some conceptual context. Eschatology is traditionally that theological locus that deals with the four last things: death, judgement, heaven, and hell. However, in modern theology, the content of eschatology has broadened out considerably to include the idea, found particularly in the four canonical gospels, of God's reign or kingdom breaking into this world in the life and ministry of Christ. This broadening of eschatology to include the way in which God's reign – often thought to be God's future reign – breaks into the present, or is revealed in the present, has profoundly shaped contemporary theological discussion of the topic. It has also led to a refocusing of eschatology. Rather than being the discussion of the four last things at the end of a systematic theology, eschatological language is now often thought to imbue the whole of the Christian message. For much of the twentieth century, it was widely thought to have been an important constituent of the teaching of Christ. Although some biblical scholars have begun to move away from this claim with respect to the Jesus of the gospels, there is a cohort of Pauline scholars that have made the case that the Apostle's doctrine was thoroughly 'apocalyptic'.[8] And, in systematic theology, the reevaluation of eschatology from biblical studies has led to a reassessment of its place among other doctrines in systematic theology.[9] One of the important changes in the discussion of Christian doctrine since the 1960s has been the realization that eschatology imbues theology as a whole, not just in part. Thus, Jürgen Moltmann, in setting out his programmatic theology of hope, writes 'From first to last, and not merely in the epilogue, Christianity is eschatology'. What is more, eschatology is not merely one element of Christianity, he avers, but 'is the medium of Christian faith as such, the key in which everything is set, the glow that suffuses everything here in the dawn of an expected new day'.[10]

---

[7]This could be amply demonstrated from the tradition. For a good overview of the development of theological accounts of the Christian hope, see the gobbets collected together in Peter Hodgson and Robert King, eds, *Readings in Christian Theology* (London: SPCK, 1985), Part XII, especially the excerpted pieces from Irenaeus, Origen, and Augustine.

[8]See, for example, Beverly Gaventa's comment that 'Paul's apocalyptic theology has to do with the conviction that in the death and resurrection of Jesus Christ, God has invaded the world as it is, thereby revealing the world's utter distortion and foolishness, reclaiming the world, and inaugurating a battle that will doubtless culminate in the triumph of God over all God's enemies (including the captors Sin and Death). This means that the Gospel is first, last, and always about God's powerful and gracious initiative'. *Our Mother Saint Paul* (Louisville: Westminster John Knox, 2007), 81. For useful discussion of this, see Samuel V. Adams, *The Reality of God and Historical Method: Apocalyptic Theology in Conversation with N. T. Wright* (Downers Grove: IVP Academic, 2015). An important recent dogmatic appropriation of biblical notions of apocalyptic theology can be found in Philip G. Ziegler, *Militant Grace: The Apocalyptic Turn and the Future of Christian Theology* (Grand Rapids: Baker Academic, 2018).

[9]For a very helpful account of the theological context of such modern revisionist understandings of eschatology, see Kärkkäinen, *Hope and Community*.

[10]Moltmann, *Theology of Hope* (London: SCM Press, 1967), 16.

Realized Eschatology

In a very helpful overview of the modern revolution in theological reflection on eschatology, Richard Bauckham speaks of the twentieth century recovery of an eschatological focus for the teaching of the Jesus of the canonical gospels, and the refocusing of theology in an eschatological key in German theology from the 1960s onwards as two 'turning points'. The theological turning point of 1960s Teutonic theology put the future – the parousia, the eschaton – on the theological map. As Bauckham puts it, for German theologians who came to prominence in this period, like Moltmann, Wolfhart Pannenberg, and others, 'It is God who will finally establish his rule over the world. But, because that rule of God is the final future of the world, promises and anticipations of it occur already in history, and the church's mission in the world has this future of the world in view'. He adds, 'This retrieval of a properly future eschatology has enabled systematic theology to reckon with both the "already" and the "not yet" of New Testament eschatology and to relate history and eschatology without collapsing eschatology into history'.[11]

So, eschatology has been regarded for some time as much more than the discussion of arcane matters like death, judgement, heaven, and hell, which are usually pushed to the back of textbooks of systematic theology. Eschatology is now an important theological topic that frames a range of literatures in biblical studies and systematic theology.

How then should we understand the notion of fully realized eschatology? Here a brief taxonomy will help situate our discussion. *Consistent or thoroughgoing eschatology* treats language about the breaking in of God's kingdom in the canonical gospels as entirely future-oriented – the expectation of an imminent end to this world order and the establishment of the reign of God. This is a view often associated with the work of New Testament scholar, physician, and organist, Albert Schweitzer. A *realised eschatology* translates language about the future eschaton and God's coming kingdom into language about the ministry and work of Christ – as per the work of the Cambridge biblical scholar, C. H. Dodd. *Inaugurated eschatology* is often regarded as a kind of *via media* developed out of these two approaches, where language about the eschaton in the canonical gospels is thought to be indicative of a kind of prolepsis: the kingdom of God is inaugurated via the ministry of Christ, but is not fully realized or made manifest until the end of the age.[12] On my way of thinking, a *fully realised eschatology* denies that language about the eschaton refers to a coming or future kingdom of God at all. Instead, all apocalyptic language is thought to be about the establishment of the reign of God *in this life*. In effect, a fully realized eschatology presumes that the Christian hope is not about a world to come, but about how to live this life in a manner that reflects the purposes and character of God. It responds to the challenge posed by entropic scientific accounts of the future of the cosmos by conceding that there is no future to the world and recalibrating expectations about eschatology accordingly. We might say that a fully

---

[11]Richard Bauckham, 'Eschatology', in *The Oxford Handbook of Systematic Theology*, ed. John Webster, Kathryn Tanner, and Iain Torrance (Oxford: Oxford University Press, 2007), 306–22; 308.
[12]Bauckham, 'Eschatology', 307.

realized eschatology demythologizes the doctrine, making it a topic concerned solely with the present in-breaking of God's reign in the world.

As Tanner (and others) point out, an important motivation for fully realized eschatology is the popular scientific idea that the world is moving inexorably towards eventual destruction in a heat death or entropic dissipation and chaos. Let us call this claim *cosmic death*. Suppose that cosmic death is indeed the received view of most of the scientific community. Even if that were the case, it would be insufficient to motivate a fully realized eschatology because, without further explanation, it lacks a salient metaphysical reason for thinking that the Christian hope is incommensurate with the eventual destruction of the cosmos. One would need to add to the claim about entropy and the ultimate destruction of the cosmos a claim that there is no reason for thinking that there is any life beyond this one, or any agency that might change this outcome. For, on the face of it, it looks like the combination of the claim about cosmic death and the claim about the Christian hope is perfectly commensurate. That is, it is perfectly possible that both cosmic death and the Christian hope are true with respect to one and the same state of affairs. This world may be destroyed by heat death; and there may be a world to come that succeeds this world, and that includes human bodily resurrection. There is nothing incoherent about the conjunction of both claims.

As I have already intimated, the obvious (though, perhaps, not the only) candidate view that could be inserted as motivation for a fully realized eschatology is some version of naturalism. Unfortunately, the word 'naturalism' is a somewhat slippery term that means rather different things in different contexts. At first glance, it might appear that what is needed in this instance is a version of naturalism understood as a metaphysical thesis, but further reflection suggests that cannot be right. Here is why. According to the metaphysical naturalist, all that exists is the physical world. Once one has given some explanation of the content of the physical world, one has exhausted what there is to explain; there are no additional supernatural agents.

Apply this way of thinking about metaphysical naturalism to our claim that the world is moving inexorably towards eventual destruction in a heat death or entropic dissipation and chaos (which we are calling cosmic death). Taken together, these do indeed seem to yield a problem for the defender of the Christian hope. But the problem generated is not the problem we are concerned with because it excludes at the outset the possibility of supernatural entities. Introducing metaphysical naturalism is a cure that kills the patient by excising the supernaturalism of Christian theology, so that any question about the motivation for the Christian hope is beside the point. For metaphysical naturalism excludes the conditions necessary for the Christian hope, namely, the existence of God.

So, we need something other than metaphysical naturalism to motivate a fully realized eschatology. Specifically, if we are using some version of naturalism to motivate fully realized eschatology, we need a way of thinking that does not preclude supernatural agency. As we shall see, the two theologians we will consider in this connection do not really make explicit appeal to naturalist assumptions to motivate their arguments. But perhaps we can supply this deficit. One option would be a weaker metaphysical claim to the effect that all that exists are objects within space and time, so that all things, including all mental things (and I presume God is a mental subject), become subject in principle to scientific inquiry. On this way of thinking, as Wilfred Sellars puts it, 'science is the measure of all things: of what is that it is and of what is not that it is not'.[13] The natural sciences are often thought to be the best, most successful means of providing us with an explanation of what exists within space and time. If all that requires explanation are the entities that exist within space and time, and the natural sciences are the best and most successful way of providing explanations of things that exist in space and time, then science really does become the measure of all things as Sellars says. We might call this *scientific naturalism*. But it also seems too strong. Although it may not be a cure that kills the patient like metaphysical naturalism, it does require a significant revision to how we think about God. For God now falls within the scope of scientific inquiry as an entity that exists within space and time. Although some theologians may be willing to countenance such momentous changes to their Theology Proper, having such a significant conceptual cost front-loaded in the argument, so to speak, is a significant drawback, and falls prey to God-of-the-gaps worries. (For suppose God falls under the description of all that exists in space and time. Then, divine agency may be inferred where we don't currently have an adequate scientific explanation, but such gaps will close as scientific knowledge increases until, at last, God is squeezed out or becomes explanatorily otiose.)

There are other candidate versions of naturalism to which the advocate of fully realized eschatology may turn. For instance, *methodological naturalism*. Suppose with Andrew Torrance, we think of methodological naturalism as the claim 'that the reality of the universe, as it can be accessed by empirical enquiry, is to be explained solely with recourse to natural phenomena'.[14] This does not preclude the existence of supernatural agents. But it doesn't provide a sufficient motivation for fully realized eschatology either. Saying that for the purposes of a particular scholarly enquiry we shall restrict the scope of our investigation to exclude supernatural agency from the sources of explanation does not exclude the possibility that such supernatural agency may provide some further level of explanation not countenanced within the scope of the enquiry. But if that much is conceded, then we are back to the conjunction of cosmic death and the Christian hope. There is no motivation for denying that cosmic death plus the Christian hope turn out to be partial, incomplete, and compossible explanations of the future.

Michael Rea has suggested that we think about naturalism as a research programme rather than a doctrine or thesis. In his way of thinking, a research programme 'is a set of methodological dispositions – dispositions to trust particular cognitive faculties as sources of evidence and to treat particular kinds of experiences and arguments as evidence. Naturalism . . . is a research program that treats the methods of science, and those methods alone, as basic sources of evidence (where a putative source of that

---

[13]Wilfred Sellars, 'Empiricism and the Philosophy of Mind', in *Science, Perception, and Reality* (London: Routledge & Kegan Paul, 1963), 127–96; 173.
[14]Andrew Torrance, 'Should a Christian Adopt Methodological Naturalism?', *Zygon* 52, no. 3 (2017) 691–725; 692.

Metatheology

evidence is treated as basic just in case it is trusted in the absence of evidence in favor of its reliability)'.[15] This is more promising for our purposes. For it pinpoints the fact that the sort of naturalism in view is one that privileges the methods of science in providing *sources of evidence* for explanatory hypotheses. But it too raises significant problems for the defender of fully realized eschatology. For it requires the theologian to concede that the methods of science, and those methods alone, provide basic sources of evidence when it comes to thinking about cosmic death in relation to the Christian hope. Farewell, divine revelation.

The difficulty with finding an appropriate motivation for fully realized eschatology is, it seems to me, a significant problem for the doctrine, to which we shall return later in the chapter when assessing its merits. For now, what we need to see is that fully realized eschatology requires *some* motivation, and that an appropriate candidate for such motivation, in the form of some version of naturalism, is difficult to come by without requiring important theological concessions at the outset.

Fully realized eschatology

Hints of something like a fully realized eschatology can be found in theology influenced by German idealism of the nineteenth century. A good example of this is the work of Friedrich Schleiermacher. In *The Christian Faith*, he distances himself from theologically realist eschatology. He writes, 'Strictly speaking, therefore, from our point of view we can have no doctrine of the consummation of the Church, for our Christian consciousness has absolutely nothing to say regarding a condition so entirely outside our ken'.[16] One might read Schleiermacher's attitude towards eschatological doctrine not so much as a denial of theological realism as a scepticism about any claims regarding the world to come because such claims are by definition beyond the scope of present Christian consciousness as he understands that term. In which case, Schleiermacher's position is not an example of fully realized eschatology, but rather of a kind of theological scepticism towards the conceptual content of eschatology as Christian doctrine. It would be like saying, 'we cannot really have any definite view on this matter because it is so far beyond our ken that anything we say would be merely figurative or speculative'. But even if that is the case, the theological upshot of Schleiermacher's position is still a significant step away from the teaching of the apostle Paul in 1 Cor. 15, and the tradition of historic Christian teaching about the Christian hope that has followed on its heels.

A more recent treatment of eschatology that is fully realized, and which is indebted to Schleiermacher, though it takes a rather different line, is that of Kathryn Tanner. In

---

[15]Michael Rea, 'Naturalism and Moral Realism', in *Knowledge and Reality: Essays in Honor of Alvin Plantinga*. Philosophical Studies Series, ed. Thomas Crisp, David VanderLaan, and Matthew Davidson (Dordrecht: Kluwer Academic Publishers, 2006), 215–42; 217.
[16]Schleiermacher, *The Christian Faith*, II. iii. §157, 697.

an extended thought experiment, she sets out a kind of hypothetical scenario which expounds the consequences of the conditional: *if the scientific view of cosmic death is correct could the Christian theologian opt for an account of eschatology that was fully realised?*[17]

What Tanner is after is 'an account of a salvific relation to God that undercuts the religious importance of the question whether the world will end'. In more general terms, she wants 'an account of the world's relation to God as Redeemer that lessens the religious interest in what the world is like considered independently of that relation'.[18] In some important respects, this is very much like Schleiermacher. The strategy is a sophisticated one. Rather than simply rejecting the biblical and traditional orthodox theological claims about the Christian hope, Tanner, like Schleiermacher, proposes to reinterpret these claims in such a way that a future orientation for eschatology, including the expectation of a future consummation of creation along with the parousia and resurrection, drops out of the theologian's purview. Now, of course, one might attempt such redescription in a crass way, rather like the way the pigs revised the new political order in George Orwell's fable, *Animal Farm*. Recall that the original socialist revolution on the farm that precipitates the main action of the novel leads to the public proclamation of the principle, 'All animals are equal' daubed on the barn door. To this, the pigs in their new role as leaders of the revolution add, 'But some animals are more equal than others'.[19] Tanner's thought experiment is not like this. It is sophisticated precisely because it draws upon resources within the tradition to call into question fundamental aspects of that tradition.

This would be much more difficult to entertain for an Orthodox or Roman Catholic theologian because, in both cases particular creedal, conciliar and ecclesiastical decisions have canonical status that make the kind of revisionism she has in mind a non-starter. This is an assuredly Protestant enterprise. Unsurprisingly, then, one of the main ways in which she provides theological grounds for fully realized eschatology involves appeal to Scripture. More accurately, she sets out a twofold hermeneutical strategy for dealing with biblical material that bears on this topic.

First, instead of interpreting the earlier Old Testament passages that imply death is the end of human existence in light of later Old Testament ideas of Sheol and New Testament teaching on the eschaton, she privileges the earlier Old Testament passages over the New Testament ones, reading the later in light of the earlier textual material.[20]

---

[17] I am putting the words of this conditional in Tanner's mouth, but I think it represents the substance of what she says. Interestingly, the conditional language of the thought-experiment is clearly stated in the version of the essay that appears in 'Eschatology Without a Future'? but is much more muted in the version that appears as the final chapter in *Jesus, Humanity and the Trinity*.
[18] Tanner, 'Eschatology Without a Future?', 226.
[19] George Orwell, *Animal Farm: A Fairy Story* (London: Penguin Classics, 2000 [1945]), 90.
[20] She writes, 'I suggest . . . modifying the usual New Testament understanding of eternal life to bring it into conformity with an Old Testament recognition of death as the end – not just for individual persons, but for humanity and the cosmos'. Tanner, 'Eschatology Without a Future', 231.

Thus, choosing life (Deut 30:19–20) is reinterpreted in these worldly terms, and poetic language about God as the psalmist's portion and cup (Ps 16:5) or his steadfast love that is better than life (Ps 63:3) is understood as referring to cleaving to God in this life, despite its many pitfalls.[21] Then, second, she reads the significance of human life in light of the incarnation so that Christ is the paradigm of human faithfulness, and our lives in this life are brought into conformity with Christ's incarnate life.[22] Drawing on passages like Rom 8:38, Tanner writes that 'There is a life in God (in Christ) that we possess now and after death. Ante- and post-mortem do not, then, mark any crucial difference with respect to it. Death makes no difference to that life in God in the sense that, despite our deaths, God maintains a relationship with us that continues to be the source of all benefit'.[23] Later, she says that eternal life is not conditional upon anything other than the steadfast faithfulness of God. So not even death can interrupt it.[24] In fact, eternal life 'infiltrates . . . the present world' in order 'to bring life, understood as a new pattern or structure of relationships marked by life-giving vitality and renewed purpose'.[25] She is clear that 'After the world's death, when we no longer exist as independent beings apart from God, there must be some different and greater manifestation of such goods in the life we continue to live in God'.[26] (However, it is not entirely clear how we may continue to live in God under such circumstances, and she does not really spell out clearly how such a state of affairs might obtain.) In a passage that is crucial to her way of thinking about the shape of this version of fully realized eschatology, Tanner writes:

> The key to intelligibility here is not to think of our mortality being overcome independently of our life in God. One does do this – one does think of the overcoming of the creature's mortality independently of life in God – when one focuses, as most contemporary eschatology does, on the character of the creature in itself pre- and post-mortem and on the overcoming of mortality as a change in its intrinsic constitution with the transition between the two. This makes eternal life the return of creatures, after the hiatus of death, to something like the existences they had before, but now in a form no longer susceptible to death. Although creatures in such a contemporary eschatology might be said to be living in God, independently of that relation they seem to have become immortal themselves.[27]

---

[21] See Tanner, *Jesus, Humanity and the Trinity*, 105.
[22] 'A hope, then, to counter despair in the present comes not from the idea that God Himself is the coming future; but from the fact that despite appearances to the contrary in a world of sin, God has in fact already assumed our lives in Godself'. Ibid., 235.
[23] Tanner, 'Eschatology Without a Future', 228.
[24] Ibid., 229.
[25] Ibid., 231.
[26] Ibid.
[27] Ibid., 232–3.

Immortality, she contends, is not some new principle of everlasting life granted to humanity post-mortem. Rather, it is God's 'animating eternity' shining through humans whose continued (post-mortem?) existence is held in God.[28]

Assessing fully realized eschatology

Whilst Schleiermacher's position might be charitably read as one step removed from a *fully* realized eschatology, Tanner's essay represents a rich and nuanced account of fully realized eschatology. Nevertheless, as I have already intimated, as it stands Tanner's thought experiment is incomplete – more suggestive than explanatory. Perhaps that is inevitable when tackling a topic as sublime and arcane (and removed from human experience) as eschatology. Be that as it may, there are significant conceptual lacunae in the account she provides. These include how the defender of fully realized eschatology should treat those biblical passages, like Matt 24–25, or 1 Cor 15, that seem to teach personal survival after somatic death, as well as what she means by the claim that the cessation of human somatic life in a world of cosmic death need not separate human beings from God. What is more, as we saw when discussing terminological questions at the beginning of our enquiry, she doesn't spell out the metaphysical motivation for adopting the claim of cosmic death that appears to be requisite for a fully realized eschatology. Finally, it would seem that in order to make good on her claims about the theological benefits of fully realized eschatology she needs to make significant revisions to the traditional understanding of the Christian hope, perhaps to the point of conceding theological realism.[29] These are not insignificant problems. Let us examine them in turn.

Consider, first, the textual-hermeneutical problems Tanner faces. Theologians who read the Bible chronologically, as it were, rather than 'backwards' as she suggests in the case of eschatology, tend to privilege later biblical material over earlier, perhaps incomplete or partial material. To do this, Old Testament passages that seem to suggest there is no life after death must be read in light of later passages that suggest there is such life. The Tanner aficionado may claim that it is those earlier passages that should be privileged over later biblical material in the case of eschatology so that Pauline utterances about the resurrection turn out to be rather overdrawn and need to be scaled back in favour of the

---

[28]Ibid., 233. Tanner does seem to think that much traditional eschatology cedes too much ontological independence to creatures in the world to come. They bear immortality and are said to live everlastingly. But much traditional theology couches such language in terms of participation in the divine life. Indeed, for many classical theologians, all creaturely life involves participation in the divine life, without which no creature can exist. Her criticism of traditional eschatology in this regard seems impoverished in important respects.

[29]This point has not escaped other theologians commenting on Tanner's essay. For instance, Kärkkäinen writes, 'With all its brilliance and freshness, Tanner's proposal suffers from serious problems, the most important of which is this: . . . the Christian vision is historical and thus futurist, as it is based on divine promises to be fulfilled. It is impossible to even begin to imagine the redeeming of the promise of the "new creation" if entropy is not reversed and all that eschatology has to offer is a temporary improvement of a life otherwise necessarily on the way to nothingness'. *Hope and Community*, 90.

more austere no-survival passages of the early Hebrew Bible. The problem is it is difficult to see how that can be done with any hermeneutical plausibility. The results inevitably look forced, and the method contrived. For surely the Christian theologian wants to privilege the later voices of the New Testament on matters of eschatology precisely because the thought is that Christ's advent has brought about the fulfilment of messianic expectation and the inauguration of a new age in which salvation is offered to all. In that respect, divine revelation unfolds over time so that God's purposes in creation and consummation are understood more fully at the close of the New Testament than they were at the beginning of Genesis.

Second, there is the problem of spelling out the relationship between cosmic death and some metaphysical motivation for fully realized eschatology. Earlier I suggested that the most plausible candidates for such motivation are to be found in the family of views that goes by the moniker 'naturalism'. The problem is it is difficult to find a version of naturalism that fits the bill. Metaphysical naturalism is too strong; scientific naturalism requires significant theological concessions to the doctrine of God; and methodological naturalism is too weak. One might adopt Rea's idea that naturalism is not a doctrine or thesis as such, but a research programme that privileges scientific data as basic sources for explanation. Yet, when applied to the matter in hand, it too requires significant concessions on the part of the theologian, who must effectively give up on theological authorities as basic sources of evidence. Although I have not shown that there are no candidate versions of naturalism that might motivate fully realized eschatology (that would require a different sort of argument), what I think does emerge from the foregoing is the fact that *some* motivation for fully realized eschatology is required, and that finding an appropriate candidate for such motivation is a difficult task – and most probably will come at significant theological cost.

Third, there is the matter of theological revisionism. Here the worry is that fully realized eschatology eviscerates traditional teaching on eschatology by demythologizing it. To see this, let us consider a parallel scenario. Imagine a situation in which members of a religious sect awaiting a new world order that is to be brought about by an invading alien race are told by their leadership that, in fact, they have received a new communication from their alien superiors who have told them that there will be no extra-terrestrial led revolution. Instead, the language of an actual alien planetary takeover should be understood as metaphorical, rather than literal. The right way to think about the previous teaching is as a way of speaking about a change within society that the members of the religious sect are themselves to bring about through carefully planned social action and political agitation. It is the political agenda of the alien masters that they are to realize through such action in the world, thereby bringing about the sort of society that their alien leaders would want – a more just, egalitarian, and fair society in which all humans and non-human creatures are treated with respect.

Now, of course, this way of thinking is strictly speaking consistent with the postponement of an actual alien invasion. Who is to say whether this will, in fact, happen? After all, such an event is outside our present experience. Some of the members of the religious sect may well think that their alien overlords will appear at some later date, just not as quickly as expected – in a kind of delayed parousia. Nevertheless, demythologizing the expected invasion in this way, and reconceiving it as motivation for this-worldly political and social action for the betterment of human society today does make a significant change to the conceptual content of the sect's teaching about the expected alien invasion. It requires a new hermeneutical framework to be applied to the teaching, one that, on its face, seems inconsistent with the actual historic teaching of the sect, and which can only be made consistent with that historic teaching by means of some quite sophisticated reinterpretation.

It seems to me that this is just what Schleiermacher's teaching on eschatology amounts to, as well as Tanner's extended thought experiment. Although, as I understand him, Schleiermacher's position does not amount to a denial of historic teaching on the Christian hope, it invites a wholesale re-conception of that doctrine in this-worldly terms with little or no remainder. That is revisionism of a certain sort. Similar things could be said *mutatis mutandis* with respect to Tanner's proposed account. Now, revisionism is not necessarily a bad thing, and almost all theologians are involved in some sort of revision at some point in their theologizing. (Consider revisions that contemporary theologians have made to, say, traditional accounts of the inspiration and authority of Scripture; to notions of a historic fall; to attributes like divine wrath or of the divine nature more generally; to our understanding of the nature of the atonement; or to the incarnation. The list could go on.) If that is right, then it would be odd if the very idea of revisionism in theology turns out to be the problem to which we object. For many theologians are engaged in that sort of project. Nevertheless, some reason must be given for revisionism in theology, given the fact that the Christian theologian is engaged with a tradition. My worry is that the sort of revisionism envisaged by defenders of fully realized eschatology comes at too great a cost and seems, on balance, to be a significant departure from the tradition that is not sufficiently motivated.

To sum up: I have said that the Christian hope as it has been traditionally understood is a theologically realist hope about the world to come and about the resurrection from the dead. It seems to me that the adoption of fully realized eschatology does involve redrawing the lines of theological realism to exclude much that has traditionally been thought about the Christian hope. Thus, on balance, it seems to me that Tanner does not provide sufficient motivation for her extended thought experiment about fully realized eschatology.

But this raises a final concern: Tanner's account is a thought experiment. It is not a position she endorses. Thought experiments are ways of testing out how things might have been. 'Suppose there was no Christian hope as traditionally conceived', we might ask. 'What would the Christian gospel look like under such conditions? Could it survive such a loss'? Asking such a question is not the same as endorsing the state of affairs to which it refers. Granted; nevertheless, even if Tanner does not endorse the fully realized eschatological scenario she sets out, she is placing it before us for our theological consideration. There is surely a place for such things, and when presented with theological thought experiments of this sort, it is surely appropriate to ask pressing questions of them. Here is a possible scenario, we might say, one in which a fully realized eschatology obtains. Such a state of affairs has significant theological drawbacks. Perhaps that is why it is merely a possible state of affairs and not, in fact, the actual state of affairs.

The upshot for Christian theology

It is now commonly thought that eschatology is no longer one doctrine among others in systematic theology but rather is a way of conceiving the whole of Christian doctrine (however that is construed). This is certainly true of much modern theology, which has been deeply imprinted by various ways of thinking about theology in an eschatological key, from the realized and inaugurated eschatological discussions of early twentieth-century biblical studies, through the theology of hope in German-speaking 1960s theology, to the Pauline apocalypticism of the early twenty-first century.

Juxtaposed with this modern theological emphasis on the significance, even the centrality, of eschatology in Christian doctrine, is the scientific claim about cosmic death. Does cosmic death pose a theological problem for the traditional, future-oriented eschatology of the Christian hope? I have argued that in order to generate a genuine quandary for the theologian in this matter, some sort of metaphysical motivation is required. Tanner has attempted to provide such an account, which draws in some respects upon the kind of sensibility found in earlier classical liberalism like that of Schleiermacher. Her argument is an ingenious piece of systematic theology cast in the form of a thought experiment. Nevertheless, it seems to me that the scenario she conjures is incomplete, insufficiently motivated, and consequently is not preferable to traditional accounts of the Christian hope that presume an actual – not merely, possible – inaugurated or even consistent eschatology.

CHAPTER 11
CREATION FULFILLED

This final chapter offers a kind of interim report on a larger project in constructive dogmatics which I am currently engaged in writing. It builds in important respects on work I have undertaken over the course of almost two decades and in several different monographs.[1] Usually, in an academic discussion of this sort one presents an argument and defends it against objections. This chapter departs from that format. Rather than offering an argument for certain theological conclusions that would be too time consuming to argue for in detail here (and for which I have offered detailed argument in previous publications), in this chapter I will give an overview of one important facet of the larger work. Whereas many academic arguments present the reader with a detailed conceptual picture of a particular view that represents a small corner of a bigger landscape, in this final chapter I will attempt to zoom out and give a bird's-eye view of a larger tract of conceptual topography. Thus, this chapter is both a summary statement of a dogmatic work-in-progress, as well as being a kind of reflection on the work and the process itself – making this a fitting conclusion to this volume on metatheology.

There are good reasons for wanting to attempt this sort of summation. It is a useful scholarly exercise to take stock of where we have come from on the way to a destination that is still before us, so to speak. And it is useful to summarize or report on the content of previous work in the hope and expectation that there may be the time and space to provide a more complete and detailed account of things at some later date. That is what I want to do here. It is helpful to hang my thoughts on the topic of Christ as the fulfilment of creation. For, in important respects, my own work in systematic theology is centrally concerned with Christology as a lens through which to view the whole shape of Christian doctrine. In this respect (though not in others) my work is closer to that of, say, Karl Barth than it is to Katherine Sonderegger's more recent constructive project. I take Sonderegger to be engaged in a correction of the modern western theological tradition, bringing it back to the centrality of the unity of God. As she says numerous times in the first volume of her systematic theology, 'not all is Christology'.[2] While I find

---

[1] See especially Crisp, *Divinity and Humanity*; *God Incarnate: Explorations in Christology* (London: T&T Clark, 2009); *The Word Enfleshed*; *Deviant Calvinism: Broadening Reformed Theology* (Minneapolis: Fortress Press, 2014); *Analyzing Doctrine*; and *Participation and Atonement: An Analytic and Constructive Account* (Grand Rapids: Baker Academic, 2022).

[2] This is a view shared by others. Take, for example, Ian McFarland's judicious review of Volume 2 Sonderegger's *Systematic Theology*: 'Rejecting recent theological objections to 'mere monotheism', Sonderegger continues in this volume her turn away from the programmatic christocentrism that has dominated Western Christian

much of value in Sonderegger's project, my own sensibilities are firmly among those for whom christological considerations shape the whole of dogmatics. It may be that not all is Christology. But – so it seems to me – Christology is at the heart of the dogmatic project and is a lens through which to view God's end or goal in creation.

In what follows, I shall argue that Christ is conditionally necessary for God's purposes in the fulfilment of creation, which is the reconciliation of all things to Godself and participation in the divine life in keeping with New Testament passages like Col 1:20. I shall get to this conclusion by means of an argument that makes the goal of the reconciliation of all things to Godself a matter of the ordering of creation according to God's good pleasure and will (Eph 1:5). Thus, eschatology is the outworking of protology.

Four fundamental assumptions about creation

There are four fundamental assumptions concerning the nature of creation that underpin the project. Let us consider them in turn. It is a principle of Catholic theology that 'the external works of the Trinity are indivisible, the distinction and order of the persons being preserved' (*opera trinitatis ad extra sunt indivisa servato discrimine et ordine personarum*). Let us call this *the Trinitarian Appropriation Principle* (TAP). According to this principle, all the external works of God in creation are works of the whole Trinity. Works may be associated with particular divine persons. Such works may be said to 'terminate' upon a particular member of the Trinity, as with the incarnation. Nevertheless, all created works are triune. The incarnation is ordained by the Father, executed by the Son, and brought about by the Holy Spirit. It is the Son that becomes incarnate. Yet this is still a triune work, thereby preserving the distinction and order of the divine persons. So, the first of our assumptions is an assumption about the triune shape of all of God's action in creation.[3]

A second fundamental assumption of this project is it is not feasible that the purpose of God in creation is frustrated, which is a claim about the scope of divine power. A person may intend to bring about some action but be frustrated in its execution by all manner of things that obstruct it. For instance, a tree falling may prevent passage to a desired destination. But the obstacle placed in the way of the successful execution of an

---

reflection on God since Schleiermacher. As a result, her argument takes the form of a firm (if always respectful) rejection of the modern tendency to ground the Trinity in the economy in favour of a counter-proposal according to which the doctrine is understood and developed in terms of divine immanence – and thus in sharp distinction from proposals that view Trinitarian thinking as augmenting (let alone correcting) the doctrine of God found in the Old Testament'. Ian A. McFarland, Review of Katherine Sonderegger, *The Doctrine of the Holy Trinity: Processions and Persons*, volume 2 of *Systematic Theology* (Minneapolis: Fortress Press, 2020), in *Scottish Journal of Theology* 76, no. 1 (2023): 71–6; 71. McFarland quotes Sonderegger's claim that not all is Christology on p. 71. It is taken from Volume 1 of her *Systematic Theology*.

[3] I have dealt with this topic previously, in *The Word Enfleshed*. A recent book-length treatment of the topic is Adonis Vidu, *The Same God Who Works All Things: Inseparable Operations in Trinitarian Theology* (Grand Rapids: Eerdmans, 2021).

action need not be external to a person. To take just one example, a medical condition may imprison a person within their bodies making them incapable of bringing about most bodily action such as happens with motor neuron disease. However, there are no *in principle* external constraints on God's action in creation, for God exists *a se* and is the source of all that is created. In this way, God has a kind of ultimacy that no creature possesses.

We might think that God's character or moral nature constrains the sort of action God can bring about, so that there is the power of God absolutely considered, and the power of God ordained to a particular end. This would be a kind of internal constraint upon divine action. It is indeed true that things act according to their nature, so that, say, apes act according to their simian natures in a simian fashion and not according to an angelic nature in an angelic fashion. God may not act against God's nature, so to speak, any more than an ape can act against its nature. But that is no real constraint on God, any more than it is a constraint on the ape. God cannot act in a way that is evil, but, like Anselm, I do not think this is a real constraint on the divine nature any more than in discussions of divine power it is any limitation on God that the Deity is incapable of creating a stone too heavy for the power of God to lift. Such things are pseudo-problems, not real ones. For, either the 'problem' in question is no real problem but a kind of conceptual mirage; or possession of such a 'power' would be a deficit, not a perfection.

We say that God is omnipotent. Divine power is maximal: in principle, God may bring about any logically possible state of affairs. Yet God ordains to bring about the particular world God does bring about, which is this world. In doing so, God in some sense 'chooses' to bring about one world rather than a myriad number of other worlds. But this is no in-principle constraint on God, though it is a constraint in fact – that is, a constraint in the Pickwickian sense that once God has ordained to bring about the particular world God does, that world must obtain. So, divine power is maximal; God ordains to bring about a particular world, namely, this world; and it is infeasible that the purpose of God in creating this world is frustrated. What God ordains will come to pass. Some theologians distinguish between God's *antecedent* and *consequent* will, according to which God may will the salvation of all humanity logically antecedent to the bringing about of human beings and the fall. But consequent upon this act, God may will the damnation of some of fallen humanity according to divine justice. Thus, it is said, God may will the salvation of all according to the divine antecedent will, though only some of humanity are redeemed according to God's consequent will. As Aquinas puts it, 'whatever God simply wills takes place; although what He wills antecedently may not take place' (ST 1a. 19.6. ad. 1.).

We shall return to this distinction at the end of the chapter. For now, let me say that God ordains the creation of this particular world inclusive of the number of human beings that are the object of divine grace in salvation brought about via Christ's atonement. There is no human action that can frustrate the divine will, for the divine will is effectual (Deut 29:29; Prov 16:33; Rom 8:28–30; Eph 1). God's will in creation is not contingent on any human act of will. Rather, God wills the whole state of affairs that is this world as well as each and every event that obtains in the world, including the particular agency of individual humans and the circumstances in which they act as agents. In which case, the distinction between antecedent/consequent will applied to the scope of salvation in this world seems redundant. For God's inexorable will creates not just the world but the states of affairs and agents that exist in that world.[4] Alternatively, we could reframe the distinction christologically (which is how I shall proceed in the sequel). On this way of thinking about God's will in human salvation, one might say that the antecedent divine will is the salvation of all humanity. The consequent divine will is the atoning work of Christ that is both a supreme act of grace as well as the demonstration of divine justice. In other words, on this christologically framed understanding of divine power, God's antecedent will is not frustrated but actualized by means of Christ's saving work consequent upon the creation of a world of fallen human creatures. Call this idea that God's maximal power in creation cannot be frustrated *the Power Principle* (PP).

A third fundamental assumption is that God's purpose in creation is unitive. That is, God ordains to bring about a world of creatures that may participate in the divine nature, thereby uniting creatures with Godself according to their natures. Adapting a Thomistic theme in the work of Eleonore Stump, we may say that God's action in creation is fundamentally an act of love: God desires to be united with creatures (according to their natures), and God desires the flourishing of creatures (according to their natures).[5] This brings glory to God, but (*pace* Jonathan Edwards), God's end in creation is not bare self-glorification, but rather loving union with that which God creates.[6] Call this *the Unitive Principle* (UP).

To the objection that God cannot love creatures until they are created, so that God's motivation in creation cannot be one of love (for one cannot love that which only exists as an idea or possibility, rather than concretely), we may make two responses. The first is that this is anthropomorphic. If God is atemporal and creates the world with time, as Augustine suggests in the *Confessions*,[7] then there is no time at which God exists without

---

[4] Objection: God could will the creation of the world as a whole without directly willing the actualization of every part or every event in the world. Thus, God could antecedently will the salvation of all humanity taken as a whole without necessarily willing the salvation of every individual human. (Compare willing the salvation of everyone in the burning building without willing the salvation of every individual thereof.) Consequent upon human sin, God could then will the damnation of some according to his justice. Since God has not willed the salvation of every individual according to his simple or undivided will, but only the salvation of humanity as a whole, this seems consistent. Nevertheless, if it is feasible for God to will the salvation of every individual, and if it is objectively morally better for God to do so (because, say, the outcome is the salvation of *all* humanity), then it is difficult to see why God would not bring this state of affairs about if God is able to do so. For God is surely motivated to do so given the divine antecedent will that all should be saved.

[5] This is a notion Stump has developed over time in several different places in her work. But see, for example, Eleonore Stump, 'Dante's Hell, Aquinas's Moral Theory, and the Love of God', *Canadian Journal of Philosophy* 16 (1986): 181–98.

[6] This is the view Edwards develops in his dissertation, *Concerning the End for which God Created the World* in *The Works of Jonathan Edwards Volume 8: Ethical Writings*, ed. Paul Ramsey (New Haven: Yale University Press, 1989).

[7] Augustine, *Confessions*, Book XI.

creatures. There is still a logical distinction between God's intention and the execution of that intention in creation. But it is not a chronological distinction.

Second, we can also say that God's idea of creatures as exemplars in the divine mind lacks only concrete existence as instantiated entities. One can love the perfect representation of a thing as the perfect representation of the object of one's desire. Since there is no temporal succession in the divine life, there is no time at which God contemplates the exemplar of humanity that is succeeded by a later time at which God brings about humanity as the object of God's desire. There is the exemplar; and there is its exemplification in creation. But these are conceptual, not chronological 'moments' in the divine life. God loves the object of God's desire, the creature. And God loves the perfect representation of that object of desire in the exemplar of the creature. God may love the exemplar and the thing exemplified. God may also love the exemplar as an exemplar of the thing exemplified. But God's love of the exemplar is, in some manner, *directed* at the exemplification of the thing in question. Analogously, Michelangelo loves the idea of the statue he 'sees' in the block of marble before he chisels it out of the block. But this love is directed towards the object that is exemplified once his work is done and the statue stands before us fully formed. In a similar manner, God's love is directed at the instantiation of the divine exemplar. We might say that God's love of the creature is teleological, yet without making the creature something merely instrumental – as if creatures are merely the means to some greater end. Put differently, God's love is timelessly *directed* at the end for which God creates, which is union with the creature according to its nature and the flourishing of the creature according to its nature in union with Godself. Thus, God's love of the creature is not of some bare idea. Rather, it is directed at the unitive goal of creation that includes the creature as a subordinate end in that larger work.

So, all God's works in creation are triune works (the TAP); it is not feasible that the purpose of God in creation is frustrated (the PP); and God's purpose in creation is unitive (the UP). To these three assumptions, we may add a fourth. Elsewhere, I have called this the *intention-application principle* (IAP).[8] According to this principle, that which is first in God's intention in creation is last in execution in the actualizing or application of that intention in the created order. In this way, protology drives eschatology. Just as the information contained in the fertilized egg will in time bring about a fully formed entity, so the end of creation is 'contained', as it were, in the divine fiat that brings about this world rather than some other one according to the divine idea of the world.

What God intends in creation is the unitive goal of love: the participation by creatures in the divine life according to their natures. This is the 'end of creation', to borrow Jonathan Edwards's memorable phrase. It is God's intention in creation and is therefore logically 'first' in the order in which God decrees what God does with respect to the

---

[8] See Crisp, *The Word Enfleshed*.

creation of this world. But it is brought about last, once the creation is 'fulfilled' or has reached this goal, participating in the divine life as God intended.

Now, God could have refrained from creating a world; and God could have refrained from creating this world. Thus, God's intention in creating this world as a world in which the end of creatures is their participation in the divine life according to their natures is only hypothetically necessary. That is, it is conditional upon God ordaining to bring about a world, and in particular this world. But once God ordains the bringing about of a world, and this world in particular, God's intention in bringing about this world comes into play, so to speak. God's unitive intention in creation is conditionally necessary – the condition being the intention of God in bringing about a world and this world in particular. Thus, God is free to create a world, and this particular world. There is no external constraint on God's action in this respect. Creation itself is an act of divine grace, for by definition grace cannot be constrained. And the creation of this particular world is an act of divine grace, for myriad other worlds were consistent with the goodness and power of God, though God did not, we presume, bring them about instead of this world.[9]

Two Christological conditioning principles

Next: to these four general assumptions about the nature of God's relation to creation needs to be added two christological conditioning principles. These provide the dogmatic lens through which to view the end for which God creates the world. These two principles are a *christological union account of the incarnation*, and a *christological account of the divine image in human beings*, respectively.

As to the first of these, given our four fundamental assumptions about the nature of creation, it is important not to overstate the way Christ functions as a dogmatic lens. It is not that God *had* to create a world in which Christ obtained. Rather, the incarnation is a *fitting* means by which God can provide an interface between divinity and humanity so that human beings may participate in the divine life. There is something eminently condign about such an arrangement. For consider: if God creates a world of creatures with whom the Deity seeks union according to their natures, that is, in a manner appropriate to the nature of the thing in question, then God must provide some means by which such union may be brought about. It is appropriate that this be by means of a divine incarnation. For, in becoming incarnate, the divine person of God the Son is united with a human nature, interfacing with it in the act of assumption. The incarnation provides a hub between divinity and humanity, a means by which humanity may be taken up into divinity (as Athanasius has it), and a means by which divinity may be conveyed to humanity (by means of union with Christ by the power of the Holy Spirit). It is like the

---

[9] Whether God brings about other worlds in addition to this one is a matter of speculation, it seems to me. We have no data on the basis of which to form a view. Arguments in support of such modal realism can be found in the work of the late Princeton philosopher, David Lewis.

interface between the world wide web and your computer provided by the radio signals generated and received by a wireless router that is hardwired to the internet. Christ is the router or hub between divinity and humanity.

Now, it seems to me that some kind of interface between divinity and humanity would be needed for human creatures to participate in the divine life. If union with God is a goal of creation, God must provide the means by which this is achieved. For no mere creature can do so. We cannot bootstrap ourselves into communion with God. This is true irrespective of human sin, just in virtue of the massive ontological gulf that exists between God and creation. Without an interface between divinity and humanity, we would not be able to be united with God just as, in the case of the wireless internet connection, without a router of some description we would not be able to wirelessly connect to the world wide web. Thus, some sort of interface between divinity and humanity is requisite for participation in the divine life independent of human sin, and the incarnation is a fitting means by which God provides for this outcome.

The second christological conditioning principle is closely related to the first. It has to do with the divine image in humanity. There are many different accounts of the image of God in theology. Some are substantive; some are functional. Substantive accounts tend to tie the image of God to something substantial in human beings, whether it is reason, the bearing of a rational soul, or whatever. Functional accounts tie the divine image to some function that human beings perform, such as being the vicegerent of God on earth. But there are also those who tie the divine image specifically to Christ based on those New Testament passages that gloss the divine image christologically, e.g. Col. 1:15 which says that Christ is the 'image of the invisible God'. It is this sort of view to which I am appealing here. According to this christological account of the image of God, Christ is the prototypical image of the invisible God after whose image the rest of humanity is fashioned. Put slightly differently (as I have expressed it elsewhere),

> his human nature is the archetype of human nature. Human beings are ectypal images of God, made after the image of Christ, the archetypal image of God. Mere human beings bear the divine image in virtue of the fact that human nature is in principle created with the capacities and powers necessary and sufficient to be in hypostatic union with a divine person. Because of these capacities and powers human beings are in principle capable of union with God by means of Christ, the image of God.[10]

The goal of participation

We are now in possession of four fundamental assumptions about the nature of creation and two christological conditioning principles that provide a kind of dogmatic lens

---

[10] Crisp, *Participation and Atonement*, 233.

for understanding the way in which the end of creation has to do with the unitive and participative intention of God. The goal of creation is participation in the divine life. As Robert Jenson says (taking a cue from Jonathan Edwards), 'the end is music'.[11]

But what does this account of participation amount to? At the end of his short but dense dissertation on God's end in creation, Jonathan Edwards says this:

> The creature is no further happy with this happiness which God makes his ultimate end than he becomes one with God. The more happiness [enjoyed by two entities] the greater union: when the happiness is perfect, the union is perfect. And as the happiness [shared between the elect and God] will be increasing to eternity, the union will become more and more strict and perfect; nearer and more like to that between God the Father and the Son; who are so united, that their interest is perfectly one. If the happiness of the creature be considered as it will be, in the whole of the creature's eternal duration, with all the infinity of its progress, and infinite increase of nearness and union to God; in this view, the creature must be looked upon as united to God in an infinite strictness.[12]

Those united to God in Christ by the power of the Holy Spirit become partakers of the divine nature (2 Pt 1:4). But this is not an end that has a terminus; it is an infinite progression in which the creature is united ever more closely with the divine nature, yet without merging with the divine or being lost in an ocean of divinity. Edwards's vision of an everlasting divinization is like a mathematical asymptote: as the curve approaches the line, it draws ever closer yet never intersects. It is a trajectory that yields ever closer union yet without finally merging. Edwards's position is noteworthy in several respects, and especially in this notion that participation in the divine life is an everlasting trajectory into God, so to speak. It seems to me that Edwards is onto something important. Participation is an everlasting relation of ever greater union with God. We might express it in terms of *theosis*. Taken together with our christological conditioning principles, this gives us the following:

> THEOSIS: The doctrine according to which redeemed human beings are conformed to the image of Christ in his human nature. By being united to Christ by the power of the Holy Spirit, redeemed human beings begin to exemplify the qualities of the human nature of Christ, and grow in their likeness to Christ (in exemplifying the requisite qualities Christ's human nature instantiates). This process of transformation and participation goes on forevermore. It is akin to a mathematical asymptote.[13]

---

[11] Robert W. Jenson, *Systematic Theology Vol 1: The Triune God* (Oxford: Oxford University Press, 1997), 369.
[12] Edwards, *Concerning the End for which God Created the World* II.VII, 533–534. I have discussed Edwards's doctrine of theosis in detail in Crisp, *Jonathan Edwards on God and Creation* (New York: Oxford University Press, 2012).
[13] Crisp, *Analyzing Doctrine*, 247.

Theosis as participation in the divine life is the end or fulfilment of creation, which, in the divine purpose, is ordered by means of the person and work of Christ. Given that in the world God creates, human beings have sinned, achieving theosis requires something more than the conjunction of the two christological conditioning principles. It requires an act of atonement. Fallen humans first need to be reconciled to Godself in order to be made suitable subjects of theosis. There are different accounts of atonement, and more than one of the historic models of atonement would be consistent with the goal of theosis expressed above. Nevertheless, it seems to me that the atonement is an act of *vicarious, reparative, penitential representation*. Christ is accountable but not responsible for human sin, and he performs an act of vicarious penitence on behalf of fallen humanity that begins with his incarnation and culminates in his death and resurrection. This way of thinking about the atonement includes elements of something like an Athanasian as well as an Anselmian way of thinking, and aspects of something akin to the nineteenth-century Scottish Reformed theologian John McLeod Campbell's vicarious penitence view too. It is a kind of mash-up account of atonement, as I like to call such views.[14] I have dubbed it *the representational union account*. We can express it in a kind of theological just-so story or narrative about atonement, which goes like this:

> Taken together, Adam (from the fall onwards) and all post-fall humanity barring Christ constitute a distinct group,[15] that is, 'fallen humanity' (Rom. 5:12–19). Fallen humanity exists across time in a way analogous to the different stages of the life of an organism, like a tree, from its beginning as an acorn to its maturity as an oak. Members of fallen humanity possess the moral corruption of original sin as a consequence of Adam's primal sin. It is passed from Adam to the later members of the group because he is the first human in covenant relationship with his maker. As such, his primal sin violates the conditions of the covenant with God and incurs the penalty of original sin, which is then passed down the generations to subsequent members of fallen humanity. In a similar manner, a chronic disease introduced to an acorn affects all the later phases of the life of the oak tree in a way that a disease introduced at some later moment developmentally downstream of the acorn would not.
>
> Christ is the second Adam. He is the first member of a new humanity, one that is cleansed from sin and reconciled to God. Christ and those he comes to save form, together, a second group: 'redeemed humanity'. Christ is the interface between God and humanity and a fitting means by which humans may be reconciled to God. As the God-human, Christ can act on behalf of both God and humanity, communicating between them and acting as a conduit of divine grace to humanity, as a representative of humanity. Christ has a kind of priority or

---

[14] I set out what a mash-up account of atonement amounts to in Crisp, *Approaching the Atonement: The Reconciling Work of Christ* (Downers Grove: IVP Academic, 2020).

[15] Roman Catholic and Eastern Orthodox readers may like to make the mental adjustment, 'barring Christ and his Mother, Mary *Theotokos*'.

privilege over other 'parts' of redeemed humanity, although he exists later in time than some of them, because he is the first of a new, resurrected humanity that is ordered eschatologically rather than (as with the first Adam) protologically. Thus, although he lives later than, say, Abraham, his work as the second Adam reconciles Abraham to God (Heb. 11:8–16; 39–40). In the purposes of God, those living prior to Christ can be proleptically incorporated into Christ's work as the second Adam. Christ is not guilty of sin; yet he acts vicariously on behalf of the other members of redeemed humanity that bear original sin and stand in need of reconciliation as members of fallen humanity. Christ's reconciling work (comprising his incarnation, death and resurrection) removes the obstacle of sin and defeats death. He represents humanity before God and, as the impeccable God-human, is held accountable for the sin of other, fallen human beings. He atones for human sin through a performative act of vicarious penitence that culminates in his death and resurrection, which satisfy the demands of God's moral law and the penalty incurred by the primeval fall and curse. Through union with Christ by the power of the Holy Spirit, in regeneration, members of fallen humanity begin a process of transformation into the likeness of God as members of redeemed humanity, becoming partakers of the divine nature. This process of transformation goes on forevermore. It is like a mathematical asymptote in that the human members of redeemed humanity draw ever closer to God in this process, yet without ever becoming God, or losing themselves in God.[16]

This view is consistent with much in the tradition of atonement theology, but (I hope) avoids some of the problems besetting ways of thinking about atonement that depend on notions of Christ either literally taking on human sin and thereby becoming sinful, or literally taking on human guilt and thereby becoming guilty as a penal substitute. For if Christ is God incarnate, then it is not possible for him to become sinful or culpable for sin, for he is without sin and culpability is not, I think, a transferable quality.

Regeneration and union with Christ

The means by which atonement is appropriated is normally the regenerative action of the Holy Spirit, infusing a new supernatural disposition or habit into the fallen human being, thereby providing a new 'spiritual sense', as Edwards puts it.[17] This divine work brings about union with Christ, that is, the uplink to Christ as the hub between divinity and humanity. This uplink, which has been interrupted by human sin, must be restored in fallen humanity for fallen human beings to be able to participate in the divine life

---

[16] Crisp, *Participation and Atonement*, 202–4, with minor changes.
[17] See Edwards, *Religious Affections, The Works of Jonathan Edwards Vol. 2* ed. John E. Smith (New Haven: Yale University Press, 1959).

once more. Union with Christ is a two-place or binary relation between the believer and Christ brought about by the agency of the Holy Spirit that unites the believer with Christ so that she may grow in grace and participate in the divine life as God intended.[18] Thus, as I see it, the work of salvation is truly a triune work for the Holy Spirit is integral to the application and appropriation of Christ's work by the believer.

In sum, if God's first intention is to be united with creatures according to their natures, its application, being the last thing brought about by God in creation, is eschatological. But, as we have seen, the conditions for this eschatological goal depend upon protological considerations. And these protological concerns are dogmatically shaped and framed by way of christological conditions. With this final piece concerning regeneration and union with Christ in place, we can turn next to the question of the *scope* of God's participative intention in creation.

The reconciliation of all things to Godself

I began by outlining four fundamental theological principles about the nature of God's action in creation. These included the claim, deeply rooted in the Reformed tradition, that it is not feasible that the purpose of God in creation is frustrated – the Power Principle. To this, I added the Unitive Principle to express the first intention of God in creation, which is last in application. Thus, the Power Principle and the Unitive Principle are conjoined with the Intention-Application Principle. These three principles were wrapped up in the Trinitarian Appropriation Principle, according to which all the works of God in creation are triune works, the distinction and order of the persons being preserved.

Now, these four fundamental principles about the nature of God's act in creation are distinct from the two christological conditioning principles. They are more general claims about the divine nature in respect of creation. We might put it like this. God's nature is such that God's action *ad extra* in creation is triune and reflects the Power Principle, the Unitive Principle and the Intention-Application Principle. If God creates a world of creatures like us, then (we presume) in that world something like the christological Conditioning Principles will apply. For in such a world, where the Unitive Principle motivates God's action, God will want to unite human creatures to Godself by means of an interface with divinity. Such an interface is fittingly provided for by means of the incarnation. What is more, the human nature of God incarnate will be the protological human made in God's image, suitable for union with God. Because in the world God creates, humans fall into sin, Christ's work is more than merely unitive. That is, it entails more than providing the means by which human beings may become partakers of the divine nature – the interface between God and human beings. Christ's work must make the very action of becoming partakers in the divine life feasible. For sin has ruptured

---

[18] Crisp, *Participation and Atonement*, 240.

the connection between divinity and humanity that Christ makes possible in principle. Thus, given the fall of humanity, Christ's work in the world must first be redemptive and regenerative for it to be unitive.

But what is the scope of this work? If the Power Principle is right, and the Unitive Principle expresses the heart of God's first intention in creation according to the Intention-Application Principle, then there is nothing to prevent God from bringing about the reconciliation of all things with Godself as per Col 1:20. This goal of creation is fulfilled through Christ, who is conditionally necessary for the outcome of theosis, and whose atoning work makes feasible regeneration and union with God. So, there is no impediment to the achieving of God's end in creation because God has ensured that the divine purpose will be fulfilled by the instrument of Christ. We thus have a christologically conditioned reason for thinking that God desires the reconciliation of all things to Godself, and in Christ has not only made that possible, but brought it about. Here is one way of expressing this:

> TAP: the external works of the Trinity are indivisible, the distinction and order of the persons being preserved.
> PP: it is not feasible that the purpose of God in creation is frustrated.
> UP: God ordains to bring about a world of creatures that may participate in the divine nature, thereby uniting creatures with Godself according to their natures.
> IAP: that which is first in God's intention in creation is last in execution in the actualizing or application of that intention in the created order.

Assume UP expresses God's first intention in creation. To this, we add:

> *Christological Union Account of Incarnation*: The incarnation is a fitting means by which God is able to provide an interface between divinity and humanity so that human beings may participate in the divine life. This state of affairs would have obtained independent of human sin.[19]

> *Christological Account of the Image of God*: Christ is the image of the invisible God. His human nature is the archetype of human nature. Human beings are ectypal images of God, made after the image of Christ, the archetypal image of God. Mere human beings bear the divine image in virtue of the fact that human nature is in principle created with the capacities and powers necessary and sufficient to be in hypostatic union with a divine person. Because of these capacities and powers human beings are in principle capable of union with God by means of Christ, the image of God.[20]

---

[19] *Participation and Atonement*, 233.
[20] Ibid.

Now, to this point the expression of God's first intention in creation (in UP) is consistent with the reconciliation of some but not all creatures, including some but not all fallen human beings. It might be that God intends to bring about a world of creatures that may participate in the divine nature, thereby uniting creatures with Godself according to their natures. But this is commensurate with the notion that not all creatures will participate in the divine nature.[21] It may be that some creatures are never reconciled to Godself. This is consistent with PP as stated above because PP only stipulates that it is not feasible that the purpose of God in creation is frustrated. It does not give content to that purpose. (For instance, it might be that God's purpose in creation is the salvation of some number of humanity less than the total number of humanity, thereby displaying his justice and mercy in creation, a view that can be found in the work of a number of historic theologians; or it may be that some version of the antecedent–consequent will of God is in play that has the same outcome – that is, the final reconciliation of some number of humanity less than the total number.)

Elsewhere, I have wrestled with the scope of human salvation.[22] For it seems to me that Scripture is clear that God does not desire the death of the wicked (Ez 18:33, 23:11) and that God desires that all human beings be saved (1 Tim. 2:4). Scripture also states that in Christ God reconciles to Godself all things (Col. 1:14; compare 1 Cor 5:19 and Jn 3:16). Now, of course, there are traditional ways of interpreting such passages that are consistent with the claim that in the final analysis not all fallen humanity is, in fact, reconciled to Godself. I am fully aware of such interpretations. In the Reformed tradition, these arguments have historically turned on the distinction between what God *may do* and what God *must do*. God may save all human beings, but God may not. For salvation is an act of grace and grace cannot be coerced. God may be gracious to all; but God may be gracious only to some in order that divine justice be seen in the punishment of those whom God passes over in preterition.[23] Given such a particularist view of the scope of salvation, it may still be that God saves the vast majority of fallen humanity – perhaps all but a handful who are the objects of God's judgement instead.[24] Nevertheless, such a view, even if it is optimistic about the number of those finally reconciled to Godself, still falls short of the idea that God reconciles all of humanity to Godself, let alone all of creation.

Now, it could be argued that God's justice must be served. God cannot set aside divine justice any more than God can set aside divine goodness. God is essentially just. So, sin must be punished; it cannot be merely winked at or forgiven without cost. Here, there is a moral intuition at work about the heinousness of human sin that requires some suitable

---

[21] I have argued this point elsewhere. See Crisp, 'Divine Retribution: A Defence', *Sophia* 42 (2003): 35–52.
[22] In various places, in fact. But see Crisp, *Deviant Calvinism* in particular.
[23] See Crisp, 'Divine Retribution: A Defence' for more on this point. Also pertinent is Jonathan L. Kvanvig, *The Problem of Hell* (New York: Oxford University Press, 1993), ch. 1.
[24] Several notable nineteenth-century Reformed theologians held this optimistic version of the particular number of those saved, less than the total number of humanity. These included William G. T. Shedd and Benjamin Warfield. It is a view that I defended in *Deviant Calvinism*.

act of atonement – an intuition deeply rooted in Western Christian theology, going back at least to Anselm's argument for satisfaction in *Cur Deus Homo*. (There is a biblical basis for this claim, of course, in passages like Rom 6: 23, according to which the wages of sin being death and the gift of God is eternal life through Christ.) Let us grant this intuition for the sake of argument. The problem is that the incarnation and reconciling work of Christ provide all that is needed to motivate an argument for the reconciliation of all human beings to Godself, including all fallen human beings – and perhaps all of creation as well (though I shall not address the cosmic scope of salvation here). For if Christ is the hub between divinity and humanity, making union with God possible, and if Christ's atonement makes Christ accountable for the sin of all humanity, then divine justice is satisfied *in Christ*, and the avenue by which humans can be united with God is provided for by means of the incarnation. The Holy Spirit may then unite humans to Christ. And this provides all that is needed for a version of dogmatic universalism. For, crucially, this reasoning provides a way in which God's justice can be met in the saving work of Christ as the God-human acting vicariously on behalf of all humanity, representing them and being held accountable for their sin. Since, according to Scripture, God does not desire the death of the wicked but desires the salvation of all, and since there is nothing to frustrate the will of God in creation according to the Power Principle, the Union Principle may be extended to all of humanity via the saving work of Christ. Thus, all are saved. And, crucially for the purposes of this chapter, all are saved by means of the incarnation and atonement. Christ is, indeed, the fulfilment of creation, for it is by means of Christ and his saving work that God's intention in creation is marvellously fulfilled in the reconciliation of all of humanity to Godself.[25]

Coda

There is much more to be said about these matters than I have been able to say here. In addition to questions about various steps in the argument I have offered, some will wonder about various lacunae that remain. One obvious concern springs to mind. It may be worthwhile to say something in anticipation of it being raised. This is that if Christ does indeed reconcile all fallen humans to Godself, this suggests that regeneration is not a condition of human salvation. For it appears that many, many human beings go to their graves without any apparent saving relation to Christ. What are we to make of this hoary old soteriological problem?

There are several possible responses that might be offered to it, which are familiar to those who have perused the relevant literatures in theology and philosophy. One is to concede that the exercise of faith is not always a necessary condition for human salvation. This is the view that I favour. Normally, salvation is brought about by regeneration and

---

[25] My debt to Karl Barth on this point should be obvious, though I grant that Barth was not a dogmatic universalist. This too is a matter I discussed previously in *Deviant Calvinism*.

union with Christ. However, there are classes of humans who are incapable of such faith, including those who are severely mentally impaired and those who die before they are capable of exercising faith. With the nineteenth-century Reformed theologian William Shedd, I am minded to say that God elects such individuals to salvation by means of the work of Christ independent of the exercise of faith.[26] It may be that such reasoning can be extended to include all manner of individuals who either are not in a position to exercise faith due to their epistemic limitations (through no fault of their own), or who die in ignorance of the gospel. But what of those recalcitrant individuals who are fully cognisant of the gospel and yet appear to deny their salvation to the very end? Some, like Eleonore Stump, maintain that it would be inappropriate for God to interfere with such individuals, 'reprogramming' them in some fashion so as to be susceptible to the suasions of the Holy Spirit. I am less convinced by this reasoning (and the language of reprogramming, which is question-begging). God ordains all that comes to pass. Who is to say that God has not made provision for this outcome such that, in the final analysis and in the world to come, eventually all of humanity *will freely* turn to Godself and be saved by means of Christ's incarnation and atonement? This does not appear to me to be beyond the bounds of possibility if God's call is, in some important sense, finally irresistible and his purposes irrevocable (Rom 11:29).

But this is to start another discussion, one that has to do with what is meant by God's ordination and the relationship between God's power and human free will. For now, let me end by saying that I am fully aware that the overview I have offered here is only a partial account of a much larger and more complex picture. Such a picture needs to be filled out and qualified in important respects – including the matter of divine power and human freedom. But for now, at least, I hope it is clear that in my view Christ is indeed the fulfilment of creation in an important sense, one that is conditional upon God's free decision to create a world like this one. For in this world (and worlds like it), without the incarnation there would be no interface between divinity and humanity for human participation in the divine life to take place. And, without the atonement, there would be no means by which human sin could be blotted out so that humans could be reconciled to Godself in order that they might be able to participate in the divine life through Christ. For if God's final end or goal in creation is participation of creatures in the divine life according to their particular natures, then given the world God has made, that goal requires Christ in order to be fulfilled.

---

[26] See William G. T. Shedd, *Dogmatic Theology*, 3rd ed., ed. Alan W. Gomes (Phillipsburgh: Presbyterian and Reformed, 2003 [1888]). I have discussed this at greater length in Oliver D. Crisp, *An American Augustinian: Sin and Salvation in the Dogmatic Theology of William G. T. Shedd* (Milton Keynes: Paternoster, and Eugene: Cascade, 2007).

BIBLIOGRAPHY

Abraham, William J. *Canon and Criterion in Christian Theology. From the Fathers to Feminism.* Oxford: Oxford University Press, 1998.

Abraham, William J. *The Divine Inspiration of Holy Scripture.* Oxford: Oxford University Press, 1981.

Adams, Marilyn McCord. *Christ and Horrors: The Coherence of Christology.* Current Issues in Theology. Cambridge: Cambridge University Press, 2009.

Adams, Nicholas. 'God's Pronouns'. *Scottish Journal of Theology* 77, no. 4 (2024): 313–28.

Adams, Samuel V. *The Reality of God and Historical Method: Apocalyptic Theology in Conversation with N. T. Wright.* Downers Grove: IVP Academic, 2015.

Anselm of Canterbury. *Anselm: Basic Writings*, translated by Thomas Williams. Indianapolis: Hackett, 2007.

Anselm of Canterbury. *The Complete Treatises*, translated by Thomas Williams. Indianapolis: Hackett, 2022.

Anselm of Canterbury. *S. Anselmi cantuariensis archiepiscopi opera omnia, volumen primum*, edited by Francis. S. Schmitt. Edinburgh: Thomas Nelson & Sons, 1946 [1938].

Aquinas, Thomas. *Summa Theologica*, 5 vols, translated by Brothers of the English Dominican Province. New York: Benziger Brothers, 1911.

Arcadi, James M. *An Incarnational Model of the Eucharist.* Current Issues in Theology. Cambridge: Cambridge University Press, 2018.

Arcadi, James M. *Holiness: Divine and Human.* Minneapolis: Lexington Books/Fortress Academic, 2023.

Arcadi, James M. 'Recent Developments in Analytic Christology'. *Philosophy Compass* 13, no. 4 (2018): e12480.

Augustine, Aurelius. *Confessions*, translated by R. S. Pine-Coffin. Harmondsworth: Penguin Classics, 1961.

Augustine, Aurelius. *Eighty-Three Different Questions. Fathers of the Church Patristics Series*, translated by David L. Mosher. Washington, DC: Catholic University of America Press, 1982.

Augustine, Aurelius. *On The Trinity*, Nicene and Post-Nicene Fathers Series 1, vol. 3, edited by Phillip Schaff. Edinburgh: T&T Clark, 1887.

Ayres, Lewis. *Nicaea and its Legacy: An Approach to Fourth-Century Trinitarian Theology.* Oxford: Oxford University Press, 2004.

Barbour, Ian G. *Religion and Science: Historical and Contemporary Issues.* San Francisco: HarperCollins, 1997.

Barr, James. *Holy Scripture: Canon, Authority, Criticism.* Oxford: Oxford University Press, 1983.

Barth, Karl. *Church Dogmatics 1/I*, 2nd ed., translated by G. W. Bromiley, edited by G. W. Bromiley and T. F. Torrance. Edinburgh: T&T Clark, 1975.

Barth, Karl. *The Epistle to the Romans*, 6th ed., translated by Edwyn C. Hoskins. Oxford: Oxford University Press, 1968 [1933].

Barton, John. *Reading the Old Testament, Revised and Expanded: Method in Biblical Study.* Philadelphia: Westminster John Knox, 1997.

Bauckham, Richard. 'Eschatology'. In *The Oxford Handbook of Systematic Theology*, edited by John Webster, Kathryn Tanner, and Iain Torrance, 306–22. Oxford: Oxford University Press, 2007.

Bibliography

The Belgic Confession (1561), the website of the *United Reformed Churches in North America*, located at: https://www.urcna.org/threeforms (last accessed October 10, 2023).

Berkouwer, G. C. *Holy Scripture. Studies in Dogmatics*, translated by Jack B. Rogers. Grand Rapids: Eerdmans, 1975.

Boethius. *The Theological Tractates*, translated by H. F. Stewart. London: Heinemann, 1918.

Bøhn, Einar Duengar. *God and Abstract Objects*. Cambridge Elements in Philosophy of Religion, edited by Yujin Nagasawa. Cambridge: Cambridge University Press, 2019.

Boland, Vivian. *Ideas in God According to Saint Thomas Aquinas: Sources and Synthesis*. Studies in the History of Christian Thought. Leiden: Brill, 1996.

The Book of Concord website, located at: https://bookofconcord.org/epitome/#ep-rule-and-norm-0007 (last accessed October 8. 2023).

Brennan, Andrew. 'Necessary and Sufficient Conditions'. T*he Stanford Encyclopedia of Philosophy* (Fall 2022 Edition), eds. Edward N. Zalta & Uri Nodelman, URL = <https://plato.stanford.edu/archives/fall2022/entries/necessary-sufficient/>.

Calvin, John. *Institutes of the Christian Religion*, 2 vols, edited by John T. McNeill, translated by Ford Lewis Battles. Philadelphia: Westminster Press, 1960 [1559].

Cooper, John W. *Panentheism: The Other God of the Philosophers. From Plato to the Present*. Grand Rapids: Baker Academic, 2006.

Cornwall, Susannah. 'Sex Otherwise: Intersex, Christology, and the Maleness of Jesus'. *Journal of Feminist Studies in Religion* 30, no. 2 (2014): 23–39.

Craig, William Lane. *God and Abstract Objects: The Coherence of Theism: Aseity*. Cham, Switzerland: Springer, 2016.

Craig, William Lane. *God Over All: Divine Aseity and the Challenge of Platonism*. Oxford: Oxford University Press, 2016.

Crisp, Oliver D. 'Against Mereological Panentheism'. *European Journal for Philosophy of Religion* 11, no. 2 (2019): 23–41.

Crisp, Oliver D. 'Analytic Theology as Systematic Theology'. *Open Theology* 3 (2017): 156–66.

Crisp, Oliver D. *Analyzing Doctrine: Toward a Systematic Theology*. Waco: Baylor University Press, 2019.

Crisp, Oliver D. *An American Augustinian: Sin and Salvation in the Dogmatic Theology of William G. T. Shedd*. Milton Keynes: Paternoster, and Eugene: Cascade, 2007.

Crisp, Oliver D. *Approaching the Atonement: The Reconciling Work of Christ*. Downers Grove: IVP Academic, 2020.

Crisp, Oliver D. 'Christ's Dead Limb'. *Scottish Journal of Theology* (2025): 1–12, doi:10.1017/S0036930625000043.

Crisp, Oliver D. *Deviant Calvinism: Broadening Reformed Theology*. Minneapolis: Fortress Press, 2014.

Crisp, Oliver D. *Divinity and Humanity: The Incarnation Reconsidered*. Cambridge: Cambridge University Press, 2007.

Crisp, Oliver D. 'Divine Retribution: A Defence'. *Sophia* 42 (2003): 35–52.

Crisp, Oliver D. *God Incarnate: Explorations in Christology*. London: T&T Clark, 2009.

Crisp, Oliver D. *Jonathan Edwards on God and Creation*. New York: Oxford University Press, 2012.

Crisp, Oliver D. *Participation and Atonement: An Analytic and Constructive Account*. Grand Rapids: Baker Academic, 2022.

Crisp, Oliver D. *The Word Enfleshed: Exploring the Person and Work of Christ*. Grand Rapids: Baker Academic, 2016.

Crisp, Oliver D., James Arcadi, and Jordan Wessling. *The Nature and Promise of Analytic Theology*. Brill Research Perspectives in Humanities and the Social Sciences. Leiden: E. J. Brill, 2019.

Bibliography

Crisp, Oliver D. and Michael C. Rea, eds. *Analytic Theology: New Essays in the Philosophy of Theology*. Oxford: Oxford University Press, 2009.

Crisp, Thomas M. 'On Believing that the Scriptures are Divinely Inspired'. In *Analytic Theology: New Essays in the Philosophy of Theology*, edited by Michael C. Rea and Oliver D. Crisp, 187–213. Oxford: Oxford University Press, 2009.

Cross, F. L. and E. A. Livingstone, eds. *The Oxford Dictionary of the Christian Church*, 3rd ed. New York: Oxford University Press, 1997.

DeHart, Paul J. *The Trial of the Witnesses: The Rise and Decline of Postliberal Theology*. Oxford: Blackwell, 2006.

Deterding, Sebastian and José Zagal, eds. *Role-Playing Game Studies: Transmedia Foundations*. London: Routledge, 2018.

Dodd, C. H. *Parables of the Kingdom*. London: Fount, 1988 [1935].

Doolan, Gregory T. *Aquinas on the Divine Ideas as Exemplar Causes*. Washington, DC: Catholic University of America Press, 2008.

Edwards, Jonathan. *Concerning the End for which God Created the World* in *The Works of Jonathan Edwards Volume 8: Ethical Writings*, edited by Paul Ramsey. New Haven: Yale University Press, 1989.

Edwards, Jonathan. *Religious Affections, The Works of Jonathan Edwards Vol. 2*, edited by John E. Smith. New Haven: Yale University Press, 1959.

Faith and Order Commission of the Church of England. *God's Unfailing Word: Jewish-Christian Relations*. London: Church House Publishing, 2019.

Gaventa, Beverley. *Our Mother Saint Paul*. Louisville: Westminster John Knox, 2007.

Geach, Peter. *Reference and Generality*, 3rd ed. Ithaca: Cornell University Press, 1980.

Gentile, Jesse. *Bridge Building in Theological Method: Critical Realism and Analytic Theology in Conversation*. unpublished PhD thesis, Fuller Theological Seminary, 2023.

Gould, Paul M., ed. *Beyond the Control of God?: Six Views on the Problem of God and Abstract Objects*. Bloomsbury Studies in Philosophy of Religion. London: Bloomsbury, 2014.

Gregersen, Niels Henrik. *Incarnation: On the Scope and Depth of Christology*. Minneapolis: Fortress Press, 2015.

Griffiths, David Andrew. 'Shifting Syndromes: Sex Chromosome Variations and Intersex Classifications'. *Social Studies of Science* 48, no. 1 (2018): 125–48.

Hampson, Daphne. *Theology and Feminism*. Oxford: Basil Blackwell, 1990.

Hanson, R. P. C. *The Search for the Christian Doctrine of God: The Arian Controversy 318-381*. London: T&T Clark, 1988.

Harris, Robert. *Conclave*. London: Hutchinson, 2016.

Hartmann Stephan. 'Models in Science'. *Stanford Encyclopedia of Philosophy*, located at: https://plato.stanford.edu/entries/models-science/ (last accessed May 13, 2020).

Hasker, William. *Metaphysics and the Tripersonal God*. Oxford Studies in Analytic Theology. Oxford: Oxford University Press, 2013.

Helm, Paul. *The Divine Revelation*. London: Marshall, Morgan & Scott, 1982.

Helm, Paul. *Faith and Understanding*. Edinburgh: Edinburgh University Press, 1997.

Heppe, Heinrich. *Reformed Dogmatics*, edited by Ernst Bizer, translated by G. T. Thomson. London: Collins, 1950.

Hewitt, Simon. *Negative Theology and Philosophical Analysis: Only the Splendour of Light*. Palgrave Frontiers in Philosophy of Religion. Cham: Palgrave Macmillan, 2020.

Hight, Marc A. and Joshua Bohannon. 'The Son More Visible: Immaterialism and the Incarnation'. *Modern Theology* 26, no. 1 (2010): 120–48.

Hodgson, Peter and Robert King, eds. *Readings in Christian Theology*. London: SPCK, 1985.

Holmes, Stephen R. *The Quest for The Trinity: The Doctrine of God in Scripture, History, and Modernity*. Downers Grove: IVP Academic, 2012.

Bibliography

Hudson, Hud. 'Omnipresence'. In *The Oxford Handbook of Philosophical Theology*, edited by Thomas P. Flint and Michael C. Rea. Oxford: Oxford University Press, 2009.

Inman, Ross. 'Omnipresence and the Location of the Immaterial'. In *Oxford Studies in Philosophy of Religion, Vol. 7*, edited by Jonathan L. Kvanvig. Oxford: Oxford University Press, 2021.

Insole, Christopher J. *The Realist Hope: A Critique of Anti-Realist Approaches in Contemporary Philosophical Theology*. Heythrop Studies in Contemporary, Philosophy, Religion and Theology. Aldershot: Ashgate, 2006.

Jacobs, Jonathan D. 'The Ineffable, Inconceivable, and Incomprehensible God: Fundamentality and Apophatic Theology'. In *Oxford Studies in Philosophy of Religion 6*, edited by Jonathan L. Kvanvig, 158–76. Oxford: Oxford University Press, 2015.

Jenson, Robert W. *Systematic Theology Vol 1: The Triune God*. Oxford: Oxford University Press, 1997.

Kärkkäinen, Veli-Matti. *Hope and Community. A Constructive Christian Theology for the Pluralist World*, vol. 5. Grand Rapids: Eerdmans, 2016.

Kaufman, Gordon D. *In the Face of Mystery: A Constructive Theology*. Cambridge, MA: Harvard University Press, 1993.

Keller John A. 'Theological Anti-Realism'. *Journal of Analytic Theology* 2 (2014): 13–42.

Kelly, J. N. D. *Early Christian Doctrines*, 4th ed. London: T&T Clark, 1977.

Kilby, Karen. *God, Evil and the Limits of Theology*. London: T&T Clark, 2020.

Kuhn, Thomas. *The Structure of Scientific Revolutions*. Chicago: University of Chicago Press, 1962.

Kvanvig, Jonathan L. *Depicting Deity: A Metatheological Approach*. Oxford: Oxford University Press, 2021.

Kvanvig, Jonathan L. *The Problem of Hell*. New York: Oxford University Press, 1993.

Leftow, Brian. 'A Timeless God Incarnate'. In *The Incarnation*, edited by Stephen T. Davis, Daniel Kendall SJ, and Gerald O'Collins, 273–302. Oxford: Oxford University Press, 2002.

Legge, Dominic. *The Trinitarian Christology of St Thomas Aquinas*. Oxford: Oxford University Press, 2017.

Leith, John H. *Creeds of the Church: A Reader in Christian Doctrine from the Bible to the Present*, 3rd ed. Louisville: John Knox Press, 1982 [1963].

Le Poidevin, Robin. *Religious Fictionalism*. Cambridge Elements in Philosophy of Religion, edited by Yujin Nagasawa. Cambridge: Cambridge University Press, 2019.

Lindbeck, George. *The Nature of Doctrine: Religion and Theology in a Postliberal Age*. Louisville: Westminster John Knox, 1984.

Loke, Andrew Tern. *The Origin of Divine Christology*. Society for New Testament Studies Monograph Series 169. Cambridge: Cambridge University Press, 2017.

Lyonhart, J. D. *Space God: Rejudging the Debate between More, Newton, and Einstein*. Studies in the Doctrine of God: Exploring Classical and Relational Theism. Eugene: Cascade Books, 2023.

Mackie, J. L. 'Causes and Conditions'. *American Philosophical Quarterly* 12 (1965): 245–65.

Matava, Robert J. *Divine Causality and Human Free Choice: Domingo Báñez, Physical Premotion and the Controversy de Auxiliis Revisited*. Brill's Studies in Intellectual History, vol. 252. Leiden: Brill, 2016.

Mawson, T. J. 'God's Body'. *Heythrop Journal* XLVII (2006): 171–81.

McCall, Thomas H. *Which Trinity? Whose Monotheism? Philosophical and Systematic Theologians on the Metaphysics of Trinitarian Theology*. Grand Rapids: Eerdmans, 2010.

McCall, Thomas H. and Michael C. Rea, eds. *Philosophical and Theological Essays on the Trinity*. Oxford: Oxford University Press, 2009.

McFague, Sally. *Metaphorical Theology: Models of God in Religious Language*. Minneapolis: Fortress Press, 1982.

Bibliography

McFarland, Ian A. *From Nothing: A Theology of Creation*. Louisville: Westminster John Knox, 2014.

McFarland, Ian A. 'Review of Katherine Sonderegger, *The Doctrine of the Holy Trinity: Processions and Persons, volume 2 of Systematic Theology* (Minneapolis: Fortress Press, 2020)'. *Scottish Journal of Theology* 76, no. 1 (2023): 71–6; 71.

Moltmann, Jürgen. *Theology of Hope*. London: SCM Press, 1967.

Morris, Thomas V. and Christopher Menzel. 'Absolute Creation'. *American Philosophical Quarterly* 23, no. 4 (1986): 353–62.

Murphy, Nancey. *Theology in the Age of Scientific Reasoning*. Cornell Studies in Philosophy of Religion. Ithaca: Cornell University Press, 1990.

Nemes, Steven. *Eating Christ's Flesh: A Case for Memorialism*. Eugene: Cascade, 2023.

Nemes, Steven. *Orthodoxy and Heresy*. Cambridge Elements on the Problems of God. Cambridge: Cambridge University Press, 2022.

Ortlund, Gavin. *Anselm's Pursuit of Joy: A Commentary on the* Prosologion. Washington, DC: Catholic University of America Press, 2020.

Orwell, George. *Animal Farm: A Fairy Story*. London: Penguin Classics, 2000 [1945].

Ott, Ludwig. *Fundamentals of Catholic Dogma*. Rockport: Tan Books, 1950.

Panchuk, Michelle. 'Created and Uncreated Things: A Neo-Augustinian Solution to the Bootstrapping Problem'. *International Philosophical Quarterly* 56, no. 1 (2016): 99–112.

Pasnau, Robert. 'On Existing All at Once'. In *God, Eternity, and Time*, edited by C. Tapp and E. Runggaldier, 11–29. Burlington: Ashgate, 2019.

Pawl, Timothy. *The Incarnation*. Cambridge Elements in Philosophy of Religion. Cambridge: Cambridge University Press, 2020.

Plantinga, Alvin. 'How to Be an Anti-realist' (Presidential Address). *Proceedings of the American Philosophical Association* 80 (1983): 47–70.

Plantinga, Alvin. *Warranted Christian Belief*. Oxford: Oxford University Press, 2000.

Plato. *Euthyphro* in *The Last Days of Socrates. Penguin Classics*, translated by Christopher Rowe. Harmondsworth: Penguin, 2010.

Plato. *Phaedrus* in Plato, *Lysis, Symposium, Phaedrus*. Loeb Classical Library, edited and translated by Chris Emlyn-Jones and William Preddy. Cambridge: Harvard University Press, 2022.

Polkinghorne, John. *The God of Hope and the End of the World*. London: SPCK, 2002.

Pseudo-Dionysius. *Pseudo-Dionysius: The Complete Works*, translated by Colm Subhead. Mahwah: Paulist Press, 1987.

Rea, Michael C. *Essays in Analytic Theology*, vol. 1. Oxford Studies in Analytic Theology. Oxford: Oxford University Press, 2020.

Rea, Michael C. 'Gender as a Divine Attribute'. *Religious Studies* 52, no. 1 (2016): 97–115.

Rea, Michael C. 'Naturalism and Moral Realism'. In *Knowledge and Reality: Essays in Honor of Alvin Plantinga*. Philosophical Studies Series, edited by Thomas Crisp, David VanderLaan, and Matthew Davidson, 215–42. Dordrecht: Kluwer Academic Publishers, 2006.

Rea, Michael C., ed. *Oxford Readings in Philosophical Theology: Volume 1: Trinity, Incarnation, and Atonement*. Oxford: Oxford University Press, 2009.

Rea, Michael C. 'Realism in Theology and Metaphysics'. In *Belief and Metaphysics*, edited by Conor Cunningham and Peter Candler, 323–44. London: SCM Press, 2007.

Rea, Michael C. and Jeffrey Brower. 'Material Constitution and the Trinity'. *Faith and Philosophy* 22, no. 1 (2005): 57–76.

Rehman, Rashad. '"Intersex" Does Not Violate the Sex Binary'. *Linacre Quarterly* 90, no. 2 (2023): 145–54.

Root, Michael. 'What is Postliberal Theology? Was there a Yale School? Why Care?'. *Pro Ecclesia* XXVII, no. 4 (2018): 399–411.

Bibliography

Salis, Fiora. 'The New Fiction View of Models'. *British Journal for the Philosophy of Science* 72, no. 3 (2020): 1–28.

Sanders, Fred. *The Triune God*. New Studies in Dogmatics. Grand Rapids: Zondervan Academic, 2017.

Schleiermacher, Friedrich. *The Christian Faith*, translated by H. R. MacIntosh and J. S. Stewart. Edinburgh: T&T Clark, 1999 [1830].

Sellars, Wilfred. 'Empiricism and the Philosophy of Mind'. In *Science, Perception, and Reality*, 127–96. London: Routledge & Kegan Paul, 1963.

Shedd, William G. T. *Dogmatic Theology*, 3rd ed., edited by Alan W. Gomes. Phillipsburgh: Presbyterian and Reformed, 2003 [1888].

Sonderegger, Katherine. *The Doctrine of the Holy Trinity: Processions and Persons*, volume 2 of *Systematic Theology*. Minneapolis: Fortress Press, 2020.

Soskice, Janet. *Naming God: Addressing the Divine in Philosophy, Theology and Scripture*. Cambridge: Cambridge University Press, 2023.

Stump, Eleonore. *Aquinas*. New York: Routledge, 2003.

Stump, Eleonore. 'Dante's Hell, Aquinas's Moral Theory, and the Love of God'. *Canadian Journal of Philosophy* 16 (1986): 181–98.

Sweeney, Eileen. *Anselm of Canterbury and the Desire for the Word*. Washington, DC: Catholic University of America Press, 2012.

Swinburne, Richard. *The Christian God*. Oxford: Oxford University Press, 1994.

Swinburne, Richard. *The Coherence of Theism*, 2nd ed. Oxford: Oxford University Press, 1993 [1977].

Swinburne, Richard. *Revelation: From Metaphor to Analogy*. Oxford: Oxford University Press, 1992.

Tanner, Kathryn. 'Eschatology Without a Future?'. In *The End of the World and the Ends of God: Science and Theology on Eschatology*, edited by John Polkinghorne and Michael Welker, 222–37. Harrisburg, PA: Trinity Press, International, 2000.

Tanner, Kathryn. *Jesus, Humanity and the Trinity: A Brief Systematic Theology*. Minneapolis: Fortress Press, 2001.

Ticciati, Susannah. *A New Apophaticism: Augustine and the Redemption of Signs*. Brill Studies in Systematic Theology, vol. 14. Leiden: Brill, 2013.

Torrance, Andrew. 'Should a Christian Adopt Methodological Naturalism?'. *Zygon* 52, no. 3 (2017): 691–725.

Torrance, Thomas Forsyth. *Theological Science*. Edinburgh: T&T Clark, 1969.

Turner, Jr., J. T. *On the Resurrection of the Dead: A New Metaphysics of Afterlife for Christian Thought*. Routledge New Critical Thinking in Religion, Theology and Biblical Studies. London: Routledge, 2019.

van Fraassen, Bas C. *The Empirical Stance*. New Haven: Yale University Press, 2002.

van Fraassen, Bas C. *The Scientific Image*. Oxford: Oxford University Press, 1980.

Vanhoozer, Kevin J. *Biblical Authority After Babel: Retrieving the* Solas *in the Spirit of Mere Protestant Christianity*. Grand Rapids: Brazos, 2016.

van Inwagen, Peter. 'And Yet They Are Not Three Gods But One God'. In *Philosophy and the Christian Faith*, edited by Thomas V. Morris, 241–78. Notre Dame: University of Notre Dame Press, 1981.

van Inwagen, Peter. 'God and Other Uncreated Things'. In *Metaphysics and God: Essays in Honor of Eleonore Stump*, edited by Kevin Timpe, 3–20. New York: Routledge, 2009.

Vidu, Adonis. *The Same God Who Works All Things: Inseparable Operations in Trinitarian Theology*. Grand Rapids: Eerdmans, 2021.

Visser, Sandra and Thomas Williams. *Anselm*. Great Medieval Thinkers. Oxford: Oxford University Press, 2009.

Wainwright, William J. 'God's Body'. *Journal of the American Academy of Religion* 42, no. 3 (1974): 470–81.

Ward, Timothy. *Word and Supplement: Speech Acts, Biblical Texts, and the Sufficiency of Scripture*. Oxford: Oxford University Press, 2002.

Warfield, Benjamin B. *Revelation and Inspiration. The Works of Benjamin B. Warfield*, vol. I. New York: Oxford University Press, 1927.

Wasserman, Tommy. 'The Woman at the Well as a Witness in John Revisited'. *Journal of Theological Studies* 73, no. 2 (2022): 535–88.

Webb, Stephen H. and Alonzo L. Gaskill. *Catholic and Mormon: A Theological Conversation*. New York: Oxford University Press, 2015.

Webster, John B. *God Without Measure: Working Papers in Christian Doctrine Vol. 1: God and the Works of God*. London: T&T Clark, 2016.

Weisberg, Michael. *Simulation and Similarity: Using Models to Explain the World*. Oxford: Oxford University Press, 2013.

Wittgenstein, Ludwig. *Philosophical Investigations*, 2nd ed., translated by G. E. M. Anscombe. Oxford: Basil Blackwell, 1958 [1953].

Wolfe, Judith. 'Christian Theology'. *Saint Andrews Encyclopaedia of Theology* (2021), located at: https://www.saet.ac.uk/article/christian-theology.

Wolterstorff, Nicholas. *Divine Discourse: Philosophical Reflections on the Claim that God Speaks*. Cambridge: Cambridge University Press, 1995.

Wolterstorff, Nicholas. *On Universals: An Essay in Ontology*. Chicago: University of Chicago Press, 1970.

Wood, William. *Analytic Theology and the Academic Study of Religion*. Oxford Studies in Analytic Theology. Oxford: Oxford University Press, 2020.

Wood, William. 'Modeling Mystery'. *Scientia et Fides* 4, no. 1 (2016): 39–59.

Yadav, Sameer. 'Biblical Revelation and Biblical Inspiration'. In *The Oxford Handbook of Revelation*, edited by Mezei M. Balázs, Francesca Aran Murphy, and Kenneth Oakes, 25–49. Oxford: Oxford University Press, 2021.

Yadav, Sameer. 'The Mystery of the Immanent Trinity and the Procession of the Spirit'. In *The Third Person of the Trinity: Explorations in Constructive Dogmatics*, edited by Oliver D. Crisp and Fred Sanders, 55–67. Grand Rapids: Zondervan Academic, 2020.

Yadav, Sameer. 'Mystical Experience and the Apophatic Attitude'. *The Journal of Analytic Theology* 4 (2016): 17–43.

Yeung, Celine S. *Received by Christ: A Biblical Reworking of the Reformed Theology of the Lord's Supper*. Re-Envisioning Reformed Dogmatics Series. Eugene: Cascade, 2023.

Ziegler, Philip G. *Militant Grace: The Apocalyptic Turn and the Future of Christian Theology*. Grand Rapids: Baker Academic, 2018.

INDEX

Note: Page numbers followed by 'n' indicate note number(s).

Abraham, William   102, 105
Adams, Marilyn   135
Adams, Nicholas   150 n.22
Adams, Samuel V.   156 n.8
Anselm   4, 48, 49, 54, 55 n.6, 56 n.8, 57, 61–71, 108 n.3, 121, 169, 175, 180
anti-realism   27, 30–2, 34–6, 40–3, 49, 56 n.7
apophaticism   29, 33, 37 n.26, 42–3, 90 n.1, 91–2, 107–8
Aquinas, Thomas   1–2, 12 n.2, 21–6, 52, 54, 56 n.8, 57, 65, 67–70, 107–8, 121, 129 n.10, 147, 148 n.15, 169
    divine ideas   58–61
    sacred doctrine   13–20, 22, 24, 25
Arcadi, James   21 n.11, 34 n.19, 134 n.16, 135 n.21
Arianism   96, 117–19, 121
Aristotle   13, 16 n.7, 56 n.7
Articles of Religion   76, 77, 79, 85, 100
Athanasius   172, 175
atonement   5, 81 n.20, 82, 84, 86–8, 96–7, 100, 165, 169, 175–6, 179–81
Augsburg Confession   79 n.14
Augustine   54, 56 n.8, 57–8, 62, 64, 65, 70, 112, 121, 156 n.7, 170

baptism   92, 94–5
Barbour, Ian   27, 32 n.15
Barth, Karl   7, 29, 70, 82 n.23, 167, 180 n.25
Bauckham, Richard   93 n.3, 157
Berkouwer, G. C.   73 n.3
Boethius   146–7
Bohannon, Joshua   155 n.6
Bøhn, Einar Duengar   56 n.8
Boland, Vivian   54 n.4
Book of Concord   77, 79
Brennan, Andrew   73 n.1
Brower, Jeff   25, 35

Calvin, John   79, 134
Campbell, John McLeod   175
Causation   73 n.2
chastened theological realism   39–40, 44–6, 49–52, 101
Christology   8, 96, 129, 141–52, 167–8, 172–3, 177
    christological account of the image of God   172–3, 178
    christological union account of incarnation   172–3, 178
    feminist criticism of   8, 142 (*see also* Daphne Hampson)
    hypostatic union   36, 44, 54, 67–8, 125, 129–35, 137, 139–40, 150
    symbolism   142–5, 152
Classical Christology   7, 36, 96, 132–3, 142, 145–8, 150–1
classical theism   34 n.18, 65, 121, 125, 127–9, 132, 143
Cooper, John W.   137 n.26
Cornwall, Susannah   148 n.17
cosmic death   158–61, 163–4, 175
Council of Chalcedon   36, 96, 145, 145 n.10
Council of Nicaea, First   96
Craig, William Lane   35 n.22, 54 n.4, 56 n.7, 56 n.8, 64 n.28
Cranmer, Thomas   134
creation   4, 7–9, 55–9, 62–7, 69–70, 83 n.24, 92–4, 126, 167–81
    artistic analogy   55–6, 59, 64
    ex nihilo   58, 64, 67
    God's presence in   132–42
    intention-application principle   171, 178
    unitive goal of   9, 170–2, 177–80
creeds   98, 101, 104, 153
Crisp, Oliver D.   1 n.2, 21 n.11, 21 n.12, 23 n.16, 28 n.3, 36 n.24, 46 n.15, 49 n.19, 69 n.34, 75 n.6, 110 n.8, 126 n.2, 137 n.25, 167 n.1, 175 n.14, 179 n.31, 179 n.32, 179 n.33, 181 n.36
Crisp, Thomas M.   78 n.13
critical realism   31 n.12
Cromwell, Oliver   45

death   8, 101, 129 n.10, 131, 142 n.3, 153–6, 156 n.8, 157, 161–4, 166, 175–6, 179–80; *see also* cosmic death
DeHart, Paul J.   108 n.4
demythologization   9, 158, 164–5
Deterding, Sebastian   40 n.4
divine aseity   4, 53, 63–4, 67, 126, 140

Index

divine ideas 4, 53–71
  exemplar 4, 54, 59–61, 61 n.21, 63, 66–70, 171
  logocentric account of 68–70
divine image 172–3, 178
divine ineffability 41–4, 90, 101, 118–19, 121; *see also* apophaticism
divine life 69–70, 93–4, 115–17, 119, 144, 163 n.28, 171–8, 181
divine locution 64–6
divine mind 4, 54–5, 56 n.7, 58–61, 64, 71, 171
divine nature 4, 6–7, 29, 33, 34 n.18, 35–6, 41–6, 48–52, 61, 64–7, 83–4 n.24, 93, 96, 101, 103–4, 107–8, 111–21, 177–9; *see also* chastened theological realism
  as mysterious 89–92
divine simplicity 34 n.18, 36, 65, 67, 107, 140, 147 n.13
divine transcendence 41–2, 91–2, 101, 110–12, 118–19, 121
doctrine of God 7, 89, 101, 104–5; *see also* classical theism; divine life; divine simplicity; divine transcendence; omnipotence; omnipresence
  Power Principle 169–71
Dodd, C.H. 154, 157
dogma 2, 26, 68–70, 74–5, 77, 79, 85–6
  of the Trinity 5–7, 25, 43, 49–52, 89–106, 111–14, 118
dogmatic theology 2, 20, 167–8; *see also* metadogmatics
Doolan, Gregory T. 54 n.4, 59, 59 n.17
Dunn, James 93 n.3

Edwards, Jonathan 137, 170–1, 174, 176
eschatology 8–9, 153–66, 177
  cosmic 153, 155
  distinctions of 157–8
  fully realized 160–6
  personal 153–5
  reconciliation 9, 168, 176–80
eucharist 7, 80, 125–7, 129, 133–6, 136 n.23, 137–40
  real presence 133 n.14, 134–6, 140

Feuerbach, Ludwig 104
Fictionalism 30 n.7, 32, 36–7
filioque 109, 122–3
First Council of Constantinople 95–6
First Council of Nicaea 95–6

van Fraassen, Bas C. 23 n.14, 40 n.2, 110 n.7
Frei, Hans 108
Frigg, Roman 28 n.4, 29 n.6

Gaventa, Beverly 156 n.8
Geach, Peter 35
Gentile, Jesse 32 n.12
gospel 6, 79 n.14, 94–5, 142 n.4, 154 n.4, 156–7, 181
Gould, Paul 54 n.4, 56 n.8
Gregersen, Niels Henrik 142 n.3
Griffiths, David Andrew 141 n.1
Guin, Ursula K. Le 44

Hampson, Daphne 142–4, 152
Hartmann, Stephan 28 n.4, 29 n.6
Hasker, William 33 n.17, 35 n.22
Helm, Paul 58
hermeneutics 5, 28–9, 74, 80–1, 83 n.24, 97–8, 101–3, 105, 161–4
Hewitt, Simon 42 n.9
Hight, Marc A. 155 n.6
Hill, Jonathan 36 n.25
Holmes, Stephen 117 n.15
hope 9, 137, 153–66
Hudson, Hud 128
Hughes, Christopher 35 n.22
human freedom 83–4, 90, 181
human nature 129–32, 146, 173
human nature of Christ 8, 36, 96, 129–34, 139–52, 172–4, 178
  as male 141–5, 147–51
  metaphysical ownership 129–33, 139–40, 149 n.19
Hurtado, Larry 93 n.3

incarnation 5–8, 27, 33, 69–70, 82, 84, 86–8, 92, 94, 97, 100, 125–52, 162, 168, 172–8, 180; *see also* christological union account of incarnation
  as hub between divinity and humanity 69–70, 172–3, 176, 182
  two natures doctrine 36, 45, 96, 139–40, 145, 147–8, 150–1
Inman, Ross 128 n.8, 134 n.17, 135 n.18, 136 n.22, 138
Insole, Christopher 9
instrumentalism 27, 30, 33–6, 40–1
Inwagen, Peter van 35, 53
Irenaeus 156 n.7

Jacobs, Jonathan 35 n.23, 41 n.7, 43–4, 51, 90 n.1
James, William 30
Jenson, Robert W. 70, 174
John Chrysostom, St 41 n.7
justice 169–70, 179–80

Kärkkäinen, Veli-Matti 9 n.12, 156 n.9, 163 n.29
Kaufman, Goron 31

Index

Keller, John A.   31 n.8
Kelly, J. N. D.   145 n.10
Kelsey, David   108
Kilby, Karen   90 n.1
Kuhn, Thomas   23 n.14
Kvanvig, Jonathan L.   2 n.3, 179 n.23

Leftow, Brian   35 n.22, 36 n.24, 148 n.16
Legge, Dominic   60 n.20
Leith, John H.   153 n.1
Lindbeck, George   108
Lodenstein, Jocodus   80 n.17
Lyonhart, J. D.   151 n.25

McCall, Thomas H.   33 n.17, 34 n.20
McFague, Sallie   27, 31
McFarland, Ian   55 n.6, 167 n.2
McIntosh, Mark A.   54 n.4
Mackie, J. L.   73 n.2
Magisterial Reformation   73–6, 76 n.7, 79–82, 87–8
Matava, Robert J.   84 n.25
Menzel, Christopher   57 n.9
metaphor   7, 31, 31 n.9, 31 n.10, 84, 96, 125, 133–4, 138, 140, 151 n.25, 164
metaphysics   7–8, 11–15, 43, 68–9, 75, 112, 115–23, 134 n.17, 145–8; see also Kathryn Tanner
    of theism   13–14, 20
metatheology   2, 11–26
    criticism of   12–13, 16–17
    definition of   11, 21
    metadogmatics   2, 5, 7–9, 107, 108, 110, 145
mind-independence   3, 31 n.12, 32–4, 34 n.18, 39–50, 55, 101, 155
modalism   117–21
models   3, 7–8, 27–40
    antirealist view of   31–2
    arealist view of   33
    definition of   28
    instrumentalist view of   30–1
    realist view of   32–3
    theological   29–33, 46–52, 100–6, 110–16, 119–20
Moltmann, Jürgen   137, 156–7
Mormonism   127–8
Morris, Thomas V.   57 n.9
Murphy, Nancey   23 n.14, 40 n.3
naturalism   158–60, 164
Nemes, Steven   133 n.15
Nicene-Constantinopolitan symbol   5, 50, 101, 105, 111, 122–3
nominalism   54 n.2, 56 n.7, 56 n.8

omnipotence   151 n.25, 168–70
omnipresence   7, 125–6, 128, 134 n.17, 136–40, 136 n.22, 151 n.25

ontology   30–3, 56 n.7, 108 n.3
Origen   156 n.7
Ortlund, Gavin   108 n.3
Orwell, George   161
Ott, Ludwig   65

Panchuk, Michelle   56
panentheism   125, 127–9, 137–8
Pannenberg, Wolfhart   157
pantheism   125, 127, 127 n.4, 128, 136–7
participation   163 n.28, 168, 171–9, 181; see also divine life
Pawl, Timothy   148 n.15
Perrier, Emmanuel   61 n.21
Plantinga, Alvin   31 n.8
Plato   4, 40, 49, 53, 55, 58
Poidevin, Robin Le   30 n.7, 32, 41 n.5
Polkinghorne, John   155
post-liberalism   29, 108–9
Pseudo-Dionysius the Areopagite   42–3, 48–9, 51, 58, 90 n.1, 110

Rea, Michael C.   21 n.10, 31 n.8, 34 n.20, 35, 41 n.6, 150 n.21, 159, 164
regeneration   5, 74, 79, 176–8, 180–1
Rehman, Rashad   141 n.1
resurrection   128, 153–6, 158, 161, 165, 175–6
    of Christ   5, 156 n.8
revelation   13–16, 24–6, 45, 51–2, 65–6, 65 n.31, 74 n.4, 81 n.19, 85, 91–2, 101, 111, 117, 119, 121, 164
    Scripture as witness to   97–8, 100
Root, Michael   108 n.4

Salis, Fiora   32 n.13
salvation   73, 77–9, 82–8, 141–5, 152, 161, 169–70, 170 n.4, 179–81; see also regeneration
    as triune work   177
Sanders, Fred   5 n.8, 86 n.29, 92 n.2
Schleiermacher, Friedrich   2, 96, 154, 160–1, 163, 165–6, 168 n.2
Schweitzer, Albert   157
Scripture   3, 5–6, 47, 50, 82–3, 82 n.23, 87, 89, 92–100, 114, 161–3
    authority of   61, 65, 88, 98–9, 101
    as divine revelation   14–16, 24, 39
    as insufficient   75, 82–9
    as metaphysically underdetermined   82–100
    as necessary   76, 77, 79, 82–8, 82 n.22
    as normative   8, 74, 77, 80, 87–8, 99–100
    sufficiency of   73–88
Sellars, Wilfred   159
semantics   51–2, 107–14, 118–21
Senor, Thomas   36 n.25
Shedd, William G. T.   179 n.24, 181

Index

sin 6, 70, 74, 170 n.4, 173, 175–6, 179–80
Smith, Joseph 127–8
Sonderegger, Katherine 167, 167 n.2
Soskice, Janet Martin 31 n.10, 150 n.22
soteriology 141–5, 152, 180–1; *see also* salvation
speech-act 63, 67, 81
Spinoza, Baruch 127, 136
Stump, Eleonore 34 n.18, 170, 181
Sweeney, Eileen 62 n.26
Swinburne, Richard 33 n.17, 34 n.18, 81 n.19, 85 n.26

Tanner, Kathryn 9, 154–5, 160–3, 165–6
theistic activism 56–7, 70
theistic conceptualism 56–7, 70
theological teleology 3, 39; *see also* chastened theological realism
theology 20, 39–52, 100–2, 107–10, 114–15, 155–7, 160, 164, 166
  analytic 11, 21–2, 26, 33–8
  divinity, discipline of 17–26
  expansive sensibility 12–13, 16–18, 21
  fallibilism 45–6
  limitations of 40–6
  nonrealism 42–5, 51
  philosophical 14–15, 20–5
  progress 22–5
  realism 31, 34, 39–51, 101, 160, 163, 165
  recalcitrant expansive sensibility 16–18
  revealed 13–18, 20, 25
  systematic 17, 20, 22, 156–7, 166, 167
  as world-building 32, 47
theosis 174–5, 178
Thomism 16–17, 34 n.18, 148 n.15, 149 n.18, 170
Ticciati, Susannah 42 n.9
Torrance, Andrew 159
Torrance, T.F. 6
tradition 3, 7, 16 n.7, 89, 97–102, 105
  as authoritative source for confessional theology 17, 20, 22, 24–6
  dogmatic constraint 98–9
Trinity 6, 6 n.9, 34–5, 40, 43–4, 46, 49–52, 68, 82, 84, 86, 88–106, 111–12, 117–18, 168, 168 n.2

constitutional account of 7, 34 n.19, 35, 37, 114, 115, 118
  Latin view 7, 114, 118, 119
  models of 33–5, 50–2, 100–4, 111–21
  social Trinitarianism 7, 30, 100, 114, 117 n.15, 118–19
Trinitarian Appropriation Principle 168, 171, 178
Trinitarian maximalism 113–23
Trinitarian minimalism 6, 107–23
Trinitarian mysterianism 6–7, 51, 107, 110–14, 118–21, 123
Trinitarianism 5, 89–106
Tritheism 117–21
Turner, James T. 153 n.2
Vanhoozer, Kevin 80 n.16
Vidu, Adonis 168 n.3
Visser, Sandra 54 n.3, 62

Wainwright, William J. 127 n.3
Ward, Thomas M. 54 n.4
Ward, Timothy 74 n.3, 81, 82
Warfield, Benjamin 179 n.24
Wasserman, Tommy 143 n.5
Webster, John 13, 21
Weisberg, Michael 28 n.5, 30
Welty, Greg 54 n.4
Wessling, Jordan 21 n.11
Westminster Confession 77, 77 n.11, 79, 85, 100
Williams, George Hunston 76 n.7
Williams, Thomas 54 n.3, 62
Wittgenstein, Ludwig 100–10
Wolfe, Judith 12 n.2, 13
Wolterstorff, Nicholas 53
Wood, William 27 n.1, 34 n.19, 37 n.26
Wright, N. T. 93 n.3

Yadav, Sameer 6, 6 n.10, 33 n.16, 37 n.26, 107 n.1, 110, 113–23
Yandell, Keith 53
Yeung, Celine S. 133 n.15

Zagal, José 40 n.4
Ziegler, Philip G. 156 n.8
Zwingli, Huldrych 133